ALLEGORIES OF NEOLIBERALISM

Simultaneously a critique of Foucauldian governmentalist interpretations of neoliberalism and a historical materialist reading of contemporary South Asian fictions, *Allegories of Neoliberalism* is a probing analysis of literary representations of capitalism's "forms of appearance."

This book offers critical discussions on the important works of Akhtaruzzaman Elias, Amitav Ghosh, Aravind Adiga, Arundhati Roy, H. M. Naqvi, Mohsin Hamid, Nasreen Jahan, Samrat Upadhyay, and other writers from South Asia and South Asian diaspora.

It also advances a re-reading of Karl Marx's *Capital* through the themes and tropes of literature—one that looks into literary representations of commoditization, monetization, class exploitation, uneven spatial relationship, financialization, and ecological devastation through the lens of the German revolutionary's critique of capitalism.

Sarker Hasan Al Zayed is Associate Professor of English and Modern Languages at the Independent University, Bangladesh (IUB).

ALLEGORIES OF NEOLIBERALISM

Contemporary South Asian Fictions, Capital, and Utopia

Sarker Hasan Al Zayed

NEW YORK AND LONDON

Designed cover image: © Shutterstock Images

First published 2023
by Routledge
605 Third Avenue, New York, NY 10158

and by Routledge
4 Park Square, Milton Park, Abingdon, Oxon, OX14 4RN

Routledge is an imprint of the Taylor & Francis Group, an informa business

© 2023 Sarker Hasan Al Zayed

The right of Sarker Hasan Al Zayed to be identified as author of this work has been asserted in accordance with sections 77 and 78 of the Copyright, Designs and Patents Act 1988.

All rights reserved. No part of this book may be reprinted or reproduced or utilised in any form or by any electronic, mechanical, or other means, now known or hereafter invented, including photocopying and recording, or in any information storage or retrieval system, without permission in writing from the publishers.

Trademark notice: Product or corporate names may be trademarks or registered trademarks, and are used only for identification and explanation without intent to infringe.

British Library Cataloguing-in-Publication Data
A catalogue record for this book is available from the British Library

Library of Congress Cataloging-in-Publication Data
Names: Zayed, Sarker Hasan Al, author.
Title: Allegories of neoliberalism : contemporary South Asian fictions, capital, and utopia / Sarker Hasan Al Zayed.
Description: New York, NY : Routledge, 2024. | Includes bibliographical references and index.
Identifiers: LCCN 2023004733 (print) | LCCN 2023004734 (ebook) | ISBN 9781032349862 (hardback) | ISBN 9781032349848 (paperback) | ISBN 9781003324768 (ebook)
Subjects: LCSH: Capitalism in literature. | Neoliberalism in literature. | Utopias in literature. | South Asian fiction--History and criticism. | English fiction--South Asian authors--History and criticism. | LCGFT: Literary criticism.
Classification: LCC PN51 .Z36 2024 (print) | LCC PN51 (ebook) | DDC 809/.933553--dc23/eng/20230505
LC record available at https://lccn.loc.gov/2023004733
LC ebook record available at https://lccn.loc.gov/2023004734

ISBN: 978-1-032-34986-2 (hbk)
ISBN: 978-1-032-34984-8 (pbk)
ISBN: 978-1-003-32476-8 (ebk)

DOI: 10.4324/9781003324768

Typeset in Bembo
by MPS Limited, Dehradun

My parents—

A.K.M. Alauddin Sarker

Rahima Sarker

CONTENTS

Acknowledgments		*viii*
1	Introduction: Allegorizing Neoliberalism	1
2	"Kanna" and the Monetization of Affect	32
3	*The White Tiger* and the Subsumption of the Rural	55
4	*Home Boy, The Reluctant Fundamentalist,* and "the Reserve Army of Capital"	75
5	Conclusion: In the Ruins of Neoliberalism	100
Works Cited		*122*
Index		*131*

ACKNOWLEDGMENTS

Any book is a fruit of collective labor—present and past. That I have been able to bring this long stretch to an end has been made possible by the generous support and encouragement of my teachers and family members, most notably by Dr. Bret Benjamin, who has been a mentor and a guide, and Liza Reshmin, my wife, who has devoted all her energies to make sure that my work does not get disrupted. Dr. Benjamin has been as much responsible for this work as I have been. It is his encouragement and inspiring comments that have made me bring this project to a conclusion. Dr. Paul Stasi's thoughtful comments and editorial suggestions have been immensely helpful as well. Aside from being an amazing teacher and committee member, he has been a wonderful mentor as well, one whose generosity has helped me steer this work forward. I am also equally indebted to Professor Glyne Griffith. A man of refined critical sensibility, he has been a guide and an ardent supporter. Professor Mahmud Hasan Khan, my colleague and friend, has quietly shielded me from all kinds of storms. I'm equally grateful to his wife and my ex-colleague Nadia Rahman for her kindness. I have seldom come across more generous human beings than the two of them.

My teachers, Professor Fakrul Alam and Professor Azfar Hussain, have assisted me on different occasions with their encouragements, editorial comments, and ideas. Professor Alam's lifelong mentoring and suggestions have helped me become a better writer than I was. If it was not for him, I would not have pursued an academic career. Professor Hussain's camaraderie and constant encouragement have helped me overcome the challenges I faced on different occasions, especially during my doctoral years. He introduced me to Marx a long time ago when I was in my sophomore year—an introduction that has turned into a lifelong pursuit. I am immensely grateful to him for what he has taught me.

Professor Kaiser Haq's deeply insightful comments about Bangladeshi history have helped me get my first chapter in shape. A compassionate guardian and wonderful mentor, he has helped this project in many capacities. I am deeply grateful for his generous but quiet support.

I met Bill Pederson in 2006 at a conference in India. Since then he has become one of my ardent supporters and closest friends. LSU's International Lincoln Center—Bill's child and constant preoccupation—has been extremely generous on many occasions, hosting my research and helping me shape my ideas. Bill's generosity as a friend has made it possible for me to get my hands on the books and materials I would not have been able to have at my disposal. I am also in debt to Professor PC Kar, whose Center for Contemporary Theory offered me a fellowship in 2006, paving the way for my intellectual development.

I am thankful to Raihan Rahman and Nasir Uz Zaman for their camaraderie and probing questions. These two have been my close associates since 2016, introducing me to new ideas and forcing me to read the books I would not have. Mufle and Jahanara, my students from IUB, likewise, have assisted me every time I needed them to. I am thankful to these two and the rest of their cohorts who were wonderful students and interlocutors. Teaching them and others has been a humbling and enriching experience.

My cohorts and teachers at UAlbany have left a deeper impression on me than they are aware of. Dr. Jonah Richards has done what only a brother can do, and my numerous conversations with him have helped me organize my ideas better. I am also equally grateful to Jessy, Jessica, and Eunai for sharing their ideas with me and to Dr. Helene Scheck, Professor Mike Hill, Dr. Derik Smith, and Dr. Patricia Chu for teaching me things I had no idea about.

My comrades Zaeed Aziz, Faruk Wasif, Firoz Ahmed, and Arup Rahi have taught me more than they know. I have a much deeper bond with them than they know of. I'm also thankful to Zonayed Saki—Saki Bhai—for his spirited discussions on local history and politics. They have opened new windows, to say the least. In 2008, Professor Anu Muhammad initiated a lecture series on Marx's *Capital I*. My first introduction to the Grand Old Revolutionary's political economic analyses, his lectures have opened new vistas, luring me into reading the mammoth book firsthand. I take this opportunity to express my deep gratitude to him.

My institution, Independent University, Bangladesh, has been remarkably generous in terms of lending their support to bring this work to a completion. Professor Tanweer Hasan, the Vice Chancellor of the University; Professor Bokhtiar Ahmed, the Dean of SLASS; and Dr. Naureen Rahnuma, the Chair of my Department, have been wonderfully supportive. I am also thankful to my colleague and friend Dr. Shaiful Islam for his constant encouragement and my ex-colleague and friend Dr. Manzur Alam for his camaraderie.

Dean Birkenkamp and his team have provided me with all kinds of support. I am deeply grateful to Dean for his generous assistance and timely intervention.

x Acknowledgments

That this work is finally making it to the world owes a lot to his team's prompt assistance and efficiency.

My father passed away when I began drafting this book. A man of rare moral courage and unmatched compassion, he unknowingly passed on to me some of his virtues. Without me being conscious of it, his views have shaped my thought and my work in significant ways. This book is dedicated to him and my mother, both champions of integrity, empathy, and generosity. Amaranth Zayed, my daughter, and Liza, my wife, have been the inspirations behind this work. The hours that I have stolen from them and the love I have received from them have made this book possible. I am equally grateful to my extended family—Abba, Amma, Bhaiya, Lubna Apa, Vashkar, Suzanna, Faruk, Munni, Dhipti, and Himu Bhaiya—for their kindness and love. That I am surrounded by so many loving people makes life worthwhile.

A part of my introduction was published earlier as "Allegorizing Neoliberalism: Contemporary South Asian Fictions and the Critique of Capitalism" in a Bangladeshi journal titled *Crossings* ("Special Volume on Marx," 2020, pp. 117–136). The current chapter is very different from the draft that was published in the journal.

My third chapter stands on the foundation of an essay I published in 2016 in a volume titled *South Asian Racialization and Belonging after 9/11*. This chapter makes significant departure from that early essay and retains very little of what was published in that volume.

1
INTRODUCTION
Allegorizing Neoliberalism

Introduction

In Akhtaruzzaman Elias' short story "Kanna," Afaz Ali, who loses his elder son to a common, treatable intestinal disease, struggles to express his grief because his debt to a fellow villager persistently disrupts the process of mourning, silencing him and hurtling him back into the hapless situation he desperately wants to escape. Money, literally and figuratively, torments him, piercing and singeing his skin, and leaving him numb. Unable to pull himself out of the quagmire of his material struggles, he eventually lets his emotion loose while praying for the dead son of a wealthy expatriate, crying profusely and complaining about his misery to Allah, his creator. Ali, whose struggles propel him to find comfort in vicarious mourning, strikes as markedly different from Balram Halwai, the garrulous and commanding narrator of Aravind Adiga's Booker winning novel *The White Tiger,* who rises to prominence by murdering his employer, Ashok. Balram, who is in hiding for the murder, is surely more comfortable in his skin—the kind of confidence that convinces him to leave behind epistolary evidence of his meteoric rise—than Ali is. Unlike the latter, whose morose and defeatist attitude throttles his articulatory capacity, Balram is feisty and darkly comical, unafraid to communicate his absurd thoughts and feelings. Although they come from similar social circumstances—both hail from struggling rural communities—their pursuits and struggles are different. What troubles the former is his debt, while what traumatizes the latter is the prison house of caste and class. Balram is so resentful of the cultural practices of his birthplace that he quips at one point that Buddha, who was born nearby, must have run through his village and "never looked back," instead of merely walking through it (*The White Tiger* 15). Two contemporary Pakistani novels in English figure the structural

DOI: 10.4324/9781003324768-1

2 Introduction

constraints determining the life choices of South Asian immigrants. Changez, the young protagonist of Mohsin Hamid's *The Reluctant Fundamentalist*, and Shehzad, the youthful narrator of H.M. Naqvi's *Home Boy*, return to their country of birth after experiencing racial and religious antipathy in New York City, the global finance capital and the place they call home. Changez and Shehzad are part of their nation's educated middle class, and their anguished returns, marked by anxiety and ambivalence, symptomatically capture the trauma experienced by Muslim communities in the wake of September 11, implying in the process that return to the place of origin is perhaps the only palatable option left to them, whatever the social and economic constraints. Urbane and cosmopolitan, these two young men seem more critically conscious of the rhythms and functions of the global capitalist system than the aforementioned characters. Yet, they seem as perplexed as Ali and Balram when it comes to identifying and addressing the roots of their misery.

Is it possible to read the puzzling absence of utopian collective visions in these fictional works etiologically, as symptoms of more pervasive fetishistic disavowals of political alternatives? How are we to tie the stories of a rural Bangladeshi *moulvi*,[1] a ruthless Indian upstart, and two young and aspiring Pakistani migrants into a seamless narrative without surrendering the key cognates of their cultural difference? Although the practitioners of South Asian literary postcoloniality often fall back on the trenches of Nietzschean and Heideggerian varieties of difference when faced with such questions, this book has opted to pursue a different direction—one that has placed it on the path of a historical materialist study of homology. This book is not about the essential difference between one form of identity and another, least of all about the cultural distance between Bangladesh, India, and Pakistan—the nation states that are the points of references of these works. What this work seeks to understand, instead, is how the pervasive absence of utopian alternatives in contemporary South Asian fiction corresponds to the much larger question of neoliberal domination, and how the tropes used in literature point toward an erasure of unarticulated utopian visions which, after being negated, have nevertheless found their way into the literary unconscious. Almost inconspicuous and buried under the rubble of manifest thematic considerations, the vanishing trails of negated utopian impulses can lead us to discover the mediating content of the global capitalist system, sedimented in the particular forms of antagonisms and appearances. The objective of this work is to peel off the veils of fetishisms that get attached to specific modalities of representations and document how such representations mask the fundamental struggle between labor and capital. To be more precise, this book is a foray into literature's political unconscious—a dive into its concealed content of negated utopian dreams. It seeks to unearth the traces of literature's traumatic encounter with the processes of production and expropriation, both of which often get pushed under the rug by the toils of daily lives, by the fetishism of commodities, and by the rubble and clatter of academic discussions.

Allegory and the Novel

In his pioneering essay "Third-World Literature in the Era of Multinational Capitalism," Fredric Jameson demonstrates how works belonging to disparate cultures and languages can be effectively read as national allegories, tropologically and symptomatically registering the nation's struggles within a capitalist and imperialist world order. Published almost three decades ago, Jameson's essay points toward the irrepressible juncture between literature and national consciousness, exemplified in the manner in which Chinese fiction writer Lu Xun's "Diary of a Madman" and Senegalese writer and filmmaker Ousmane Sembène's *Xala* tropologize the nation's ordeals. Of course, the idea of all third-world texts being "national allegories" ("Third-world literature" 69)—an idea that Jameson emphatically foregrounds—appears essentialist when we consider how cognitive mappings of such varieties divest almost all first-world metropolitan texts of the desire and propensity to engage with the nation.

Despite Neil Lazarus's passionate defense of Jameson's national allegory hypothesis in the second chapter of *The Postcolonial Unconscious* (2011)—a defense that drives him toward debunking the key tenets of Aijaz Ahmed's critique of Jameson's key propositions—it is important that we not discount the merit of Ahmad's observation that "we live not in three worlds but in one" and that "this world includes the experience of colonialism and imperialism on both sides of Jameson's global divide" (*In Theory* 103). Lazarus's objection against Ahmed's critique of Jameson, it seems, stems not from what he identifies as a critique of "the categorical universalism of Jameson's hypothesis" (*Postcolonial Unconscious* 94) but rather from the very absence of such a schema. Even when invested in the project of delving deep into the unconscious of the subject, a writer cannot entirely obliterate the nation from the tissue of literary works as long as the nation remains the primary reference point of the interaction between the subject and society. A critic cannot place first- and third-world literary productions squarely on different spectrums of national imagination, unless one is advancing a category like national allegory to refer to a body of work corresponding to a distinctively oppositional literary structure of feeling engaged in the task of resisting colonial and imperial oppressions. Nation, in such cases, becomes a broad political platform in whose name the colonial/imperial power that denies nationhood is resisted. Jameson's taxonomy of the national allegory, perhaps, is a belated effort to arrest the anticolonial nationalist unconscious that can be located in the political and cultural mobilizations of the 1950s and 1960s; yet, the same concept, at least in the manner in which he has used it, cannot be advanced to adequately account for the gradually subsiding anticolonial sentiment of the 1980s, the time when his essay appeared. Perhaps Jameson is better served if, instead of homing in on national allegory, we direct our attention to "the primordial crimes of capitalism," and to "wage labor," "the ravages of the money form," and "the remorseless and impersonal rhythms of the market" (84)—phenomena that he refers to in the latter

4 Introduction

part of his essay but does not fully address. He misses the chance here to develop a deeper analysis of what phrases like "the primordial crimes of capitalism," "the remorseless and impersonal rhythms of the market," and "the ravages of the money form" signify in the context of the literary works he analyzes. Those concepts and phenomena offer us a more accurate mapping of the operations of "multinational capitalism" than does the notion of the national allegory, which Jameson sees as an essential property of "Third World" literature. At the very least, any substantive analysis of national allegory must begin with a historically specific account of capital's contradictory relation to the nation state.

In 1986, when Jameson's essay appeared in *Social Text*, profound changes were taking place in the world, not only in the United Kingdom and the United States but also in many other parts of the globe, especially in the Southern hemisphere. Those changes cannot be summed up as a return to the national space. If anything, these changes—a political-economic engineering that has come to be known commonly as neoliberalization—exhibited a globalist impulse, demonstrating a desire to facilitate quicker transportation of commodities and labor—a desire to batter down the barriers that stymie market expansion and hinder the movement of capital. This globalization also often involved imperial imposition, transfer of public property to private hands, forced labor, destruction of the social safety net, immiseration and the production of "surplus population" (processes that affected women and children the most), and absolute domination by the capitalist class in politics and culture. Such coercive impositions faced powerful resistance around the world, but the absence of a unitary political opposition did not engender the kind of global solidarity that was required to defeat a system and ideology that was so pervasive and hegemonic. It is not that Jameson was unaware of the profound transformation taking place around him; indeed, much of what he wrote since the 1980s demonstrates how intensely preoccupied he was at that time with themes such as globalization, late capitalism, and imperial impingements. Although musings about uneven development and the world system can be spotted in some parts of his "Third-World Literature" essay as well, his accent in it falls on the irrepressible presence of the nationalist unconscious in all "third-world" literary texts.

My objective here is not to critique an essay so demonstrably replete with brilliant insights but to establish that this same essay—often erroneously dismissed for its totalistic impulse—can be summoned into service to grasp the broader homology that exists among the fictions of our era. Such efforts, unsurprisingly, have already been made. In "Neoliberalism and Allegory," published in *Cultural Critique* in 2012, Betty Joseph utilizes Jameson's insights to arrest the historical shift that necessitates an attentive introspection of the neoliberal ideology and policies that have, after reshaping the state, normalized themselves in our daily lives today. "[It] is toward neoliberalism itself that allegory now attaches itself" (Joseph 91), she writes in the concluding section of her essay, implying that the era of national allegories, the era of Raja Rao and Salman Rushdie when it was still possible to "speak in a collective voice," has been irrevocably lost to an emergent *zeitgeist*. She contends that novels like *The White Tiger* (2008) demand a new analytical schema—one that involves diving into neoliberal discourses to locate how the fictional representation of such discourses verbalizes a critique of neoliberalism by satirizing its inconsistencies (Joseph 68–9). She reads Adiga's novel as a neoliberal allegory because its narrator speaks in a forked tongue, exposing the inexorable reality that many Indians encounter on a daily basis while also waxing lyrical about technological progress and prosperity. In Joseph's estimation, Adiga's work operates unconventionally, "not by putting the individual's story in terms of a national story but by putting one discourse in terms of another" (Joseph 72). It is in the novel's ventriloquism—that it presents the narrative of neoliberal success through "an illegitimate spokesman" like Balram—that the latent features of neoliberal allegory become manifestly visible.

The parlaying of one discourse on another, the narrative strategy that Joseph identifies as a key moment in *The White Tiger*'s allegorization of the neoliberal discourse, is not the only pathway that she traverses in her efforts to establish its credential as a critique of neoliberalism. The two other avenues of the novel's allegorical retelling involve the flattening of historical canvas, which, by borrowing from Jameson's re-reading of Walter Benjamin's "Thesis on History" and *The Arcades Project*, she calls "schizoid constellations" (Joseph 82), and the de-fetishization of the object, an idea she develops by re-engaging with Marx (Joseph 90).

Joseph's idea that neoliberal allegories speak ventriloquistically is not far from how allegory has been historically understood. As a mode of articulation, allegory is considered a masked speech, one whose exterior frame of reference contains a carefully concealed ulterior referent. Combination of two Greek roots—"*allos*" (other) and "*agoreuo*" (to speak openly, or to speak in an *agora* or marketplace)—allegory involves the articulation of something "other" than what has been explicitly verbalized (Mucci 298), pointing toward the overlaying of a manifest semantic item on an implicit subtext. The conventional description of allegory that sees it as a semantic attribute masking an implicit articulation is as important an element of literary allegories as is an ideological one that seeks to understand allegory through the conduit of structural mediations. One of the most admirable features of Jameson's later meditations on allegory, especially in his book *Allegory and Ideology* (2019), is his persistent reminder that allegory works ideologically and is as much an aspect of literary presentation as it is of interpretation. The tension and transaction between representation, value, and history, which he posits as the three different aspects of the writer's, the reader's, and the critic's perspectives about aesthetic processes (30), is indeed an elaboration of the split that exists between the three dimensions of capital's

6 Introduction

evolution represented by production, consumption, and reproduction (for further consumption). The traffic between the production of aesthetic works, their consumption, and their interpretation cannot take place in a historical or ideological vacuum, although efforts to reduce history to a mere backdrop or to turn the question of ideology into a mere instance of literary interpretation are underway in the academic circuits today. In *The Political Unconscious: Interpretation as a Socially Symbolic Act* (1982), a seminal work in the domain of literary criticism and theory, Jameson insists on the irrepressible presence of ideology in all forms of aesthetic productions and interpretations. This idea is echoed in *Allegory and Ideology* as well. When, for instance, Jameson proclaims that allegory "is always with us, in politics, in narratology, in daily life, and in "common sense" (*Allegory* 207), he is not merely gesturing toward the pliability and elasticity of language but is also emphasizing the necessity of noticing the stubborn presence of history and ideology in all forms of social experiences. Such an interpretation of allegory itself is historical materialist because its primary consideration is not how allegory operates as a genre or a semantic ploy but rather how it lends itself to the service to a historical analysis of objects and social relations, bringing literary analysis to bear upon the material world on whose foundations it is premised.

Such expansive understanding of the convention puts the Jamesonian elaboration of allegory at odds with the more restrictive construal of it by the Hungarian Marxist philosopher and critic György Lukács, who offers, in the first chapter of *The Meaning of Contemporary Realism* (1963), a searing critique of allegory as a modernist convention. In it, he imputes to modern allegory the responsibility of fetishizing particularity by pulling away from the universal, writing: "In realistic literature each descriptive detail is both individual and typical. Modern allegory, and modernist ideology, however, deny the typical. By destroying the coherence of the world, they reduce detail to the level of the mere particularity ..." (Lukács 43). Lukács's celebration of realism here, his disapproval of "modern allegory" as such, let us not forget, has its origin in his firmly held belief that realism and avant-gardist literature are mutually exclusive of one another, and the latter is guilty of reducing the objective world into a mere container in which the alienated and "petrified" modern subject struggles, wishing to escape "the dreariness of life under capitalism" (Lukács 29). The emptying of the objective world of its content and agency, which he identifies as the tell-tale sign of modernism's withdrawal into self-referential subjectivism whose philosophical grounds have been laid out by figures like Martin Heidegger, nudges him to dismiss modernist literature *en bloc*. He is particularly irked by Heidegger's coinage *Geworfenheitins Dasein*, "thrownness-into-being" (Lukács 20), which he critiques for its hapless fatalism, whose premise is the assumption that human beings are essentially lonely figures, accidentally thrown into existence. Pointing toward the limit of such an ahistoricist account of human existence, Lukács writes:

Man, thus conceived, is an ahistorical being … This negation of history takes two different forms in modernist literature. First, the hero is strictly confined within the limits of his own experience. There is not for him—and apparently not for his creator—any pre-existent reality beyond his own self, acting upon him or being acted upon by him. Secondly, the hero himself is without personal history. He is 'thrown-into-the-world': meaninglessly, unfathomably. He does not develop through contact with the world; he neither forms nor is formed by it. (Lukács 21)

This, then, is the backdrop in which Lukács's critique of the modernist allegory appears. His reservation against modernism stems from the notion that the individual who is fetishized in modernist literature—who is simultaneously its subject and object of reference—is an ahistorical being whose history of emergence and relation to society have been erased by the very authors who have sought to present the modernist individual as representative. If subjects are indeed subjects of history, then such subjects cannot be stripped of their relationships and agency, unless one sees the subject-object relationship as a determinate one without any possibility for transcendence. The fetishism of the particular, which expresses itself through modernism's habitual dismissal of "the typical," is what makes modernist literature overwhelmingly "style" oriented. Lukács, it seems, landed on the guiding matrix of postmodernist philosophy long before the prophets of postmodernism did and subjected it to the kind of criticism it deserved. If the subject is both "acting upon" and "being acted upon," then a category like *Geworfenheitins Dasein* is supposed to be too restrictive to account for such subject's active relationship to the world in which such subjects live and produce. What is omitted by the Heideggerian hermeneutics of the subject is the intentional state of subjecthood or being—a state that offers a more adequate account of the process of labor that allows such subjects to create with a specific objective in mind. Lukács, aware of the limits of Heideggerian fatalism, reinvokes the old Hegelian category of the universal to remind us of the limits of fetishism of the particular and invites us to take into account the homology that binds subjects and objects in a relationship.

Yet, his mistake seems to reside in his belief that the contradiction between "modernist allegory" and "realism" is an embodied one, clearly spelled out in the manner in which these two aesthetic traditions thematically address their objects of narration. The idea that allegory is "a problematic genre" because it declines to accept that there is "an immanent meaning to human existence" is an outgrowth of his conviction that, as a genre, "allegory lends itself par excellence to a description of man's alienation from objective reality" (*Lukács* 40). What Lukács fails to notice is that irrespective of the authorial intention, modernist literature's thematic presentation of alienation of the subject does not result in a withdrawal from the objective world; rather, such efforts allegorically represent the modern subject's struggle against a material world whose relations appear as fetters to

8 Introduction

these subjects. Under the rubble of James Joyce's "*monologue intérieur*" we hear the clatter of Buck Mulligan's mirror and razor (Joyce 349), the "seven books" that Stephen reads "two pages apiece" (Joyce 382), and the "grilled mutton kidneys" that Leopold Bloom likes for their "fine tang of faintly scented urine" (Joyce 393). The books, the mirror, the razor, and the grilled kidneys are markers of their consumers' relation to the objective world—a world whose mundaneness troubles them but whose perimeters they cannot transcend. As commodities, these are sensual objects, but their production and consumption are not devoid of the symbolism that corresponds to abstract value. There is a whole world of social relationships that lies behind these commodified objects—relationships that are indicative of the class and social position of the subjects who are consuming them and the people whose labor goes into making such objects consumable. The objects that modernist literature conjures up casually to allude to the world that characters like Bloom or Mulligan inhabit is not merely material but also allegorical, precisely because the physical existence of a commodity points toward the presence of labor or another (be it human labor or nature's) and is indicative of the relationship that has been erased in the object itself.

Contemporary Theories of Neoliberalism

The notion of allegory that this book posits is drawn from the idea that the relationship between the subject and the world—a world in which the subject produces, consumes, encounters hospitable or hostile communities, and dreams of political transformations—is not only material but also allegorical. Some of the familiar modes of appearances of capitalist relations—money and commodity, rural to urban movement, correspondence between race and class, gender and ecology—are its objects of exploration. This work scrutinizes how these forms of appearance conceal negated utopian dreams, and how the moments of concealment themselves, in turn, function symptomatically, as residues of the fetishistic disavowal of the desire for a radical political reorganization of society. It takes as its object not only the allegorical presentation of the massive class inequality that has opened up since neoliberalization became the *de rigueur* economic logic of the past three decades in South Asia, but also the narrativization of gender, race, and religious conflicts that have been heightened since the shift occurred. Allegory in this work is approached as a masking of social processes, especially of structural relations, whose presence is alluded to but not fully acknowledged in literary works because the subject of the allegorical speech is not fully aware of the allusiveness of the articulation. Although it may appear as though this book has abandoned the path of historical materialist critique in its pursuit of a symptomatic reading of the literary unconscious, the prisms through which it looks into literary works are themselves derived from the historical materialist tradition, especially from the reading of Marx's major works.

Two key conjunctions that this work intends to offer—ideas that may appear counter-intuitive to some—are, first of all, that even those writers who themselves are not avowed anti-capitalists in their political views leave behind a body of evidence of the processes of capitalist expropriation partly because such processes are woven into the fabric of life today; and, secondly, that the subject is always, albeit vaguely, aware of the fetishistic concealments of utopian visions even when the subject chooses to ignore the flashing of such potentials. The objective here, at least at the outset, is not to normatively pigeonhole representations by labelling them either as complicit or as radical but to show that allegorical representations allude to history and social relations irrespective of authorial intention because aesthetic productions themselves are conditioned by history and social relations. Yet, as will also become clear in the course of the discussion, this book is a critique, and not a celebration of many of the canonical works and authors belonging to the Anglophone South Asian literary tradition. Ahmad, on many occasions, has argued that Indian writing in English draws more attention than those written in other major Indian languages because of its complicit relation to the global capitalist/imperialist structure. Such an observation is more applicable to Bengali literature because some of the finest writers from the Bengal Delta—writers of the caliber of Manik Bandyopadhyay, Bibhutibhushan Bandyopadhyay, Syed Waliullah, Mahasweta Devi, Akhtaruzzaman Elias, and Debesh Roy—remain in the shadow while the light keeps shining on much lesser writers mimicking other mediocre writers from the Anglophone tradition. Given how uninclined some of the South Asian writers are to critique capitalism, it is certainly possible that the presentation of capitalism's inequality in their works is coincidental rather than fully conscious. Yet, the precise point of reading such works as neoliberal allegories is to venture beyond authorial intentions, to show that capitalist inequality continues to assert its stubborn presence even in the aesthetic productions of the system's most ardent admirers. The motive of this work, therefore, is not to critique specific authors for their aesthetic or ideological failures but to remind the readers that, irrespective of an author's intention, history and utopian political visions continue to float up in literary works despite the relentless efforts of capitalist institutions to fully submerge them.

One of the imperatives of reading literary works as allegories of the mode and relations of productions is identifying what the "this" and "now" of literary production implies. The now of the past four decades—the point of juncture when the works that I analyze here were published—is often described as the neoliberal era in South Asia. Of course, there are other nomenclatures that have been made available through a range of academic discussions as well, concepts that bear captivating titles such as "the Postmodern Era," "the Biopolitical Era," "Globalization," "the Anthropocene," "the Capitalocene," and so on, but the idea of the neoliberal is perhaps the most apt description of the changes that have taken place in the last four decades. Nevertheless, the effectiveness of the

10 Introduction

terminology lies not in its ability to grasp the totality of the social movement but rather in its usefulness in identifying what is new about our time. Our globalized world still runs on the engine of capitalist relations of production, and what is often described as the neoliberal era is but a phase within the capitalist *longue durée*. The plethora of works that offer an array of neologisms to shore up the belief that we live in an entirely new era marked by the arrival of a new juridical/political/economic subject are perhaps too taken up with the newness of our time to account for what is homologous about our collective existence. In *Undoing the Demos: Neoliberalism's Stealth Revolution* (2015), a seminal work in which U.S. feminist critic and political philosopher Wendy Brown yokes together Marxian and Foucauldian insights to critique neoliberalism, there is a passage that proclaims the "advantage of genealogical over dialectical history for grasping the present" (*Undoing* 52). This book will claim otherwise, not simply by attesting to the effectiveness of the Marxian dialectic but also by pointing toward the limits of the genealogical method, which, in its quest for multiplicity and rupture, often turns away from contradiction and historical continuity. Before discussing in detail how a genealogical anatomy of neoliberalism, in its pursuit of rupture and multiplicity, obfuscates generalized patterns of class oppression, let us first turn toward the theories of neoliberalism themselves to schematize what is at stake in the idea.

Alexander Rüstow, Friedrich von Hayek, Milton Friedman, James Buchanan, and other conservative economists and thinkers—all ardent supporters of neo-liberalization of economy—ressurected the ghost of nineteenth-century laissez-faire capitalism in the twentieth century, propounding the idea that neoliberalism was a vision of economic freedom, where personal freedom and the freedom of the market coexisted in perfect harmony, ushering in prosperity and compound growth. In his often-cited book *The Road to Serfdom* (2007), von Hayek proposes that "competition" should be the "principle of social organization" not simply because it is "the most efficient method known" but also because it can forestall "coercive or arbitrary intervention of authority" (*Road* 86). In succeeding paragraphs of the fourth chapter of his vastly popular book, he clarifies that the freedom that he envisages as the foundation of social organization predominantly means the freedom of "the parties in the market to sell and buy at any price at which they can find a partner" and freedom to "produce, sell, and buy" anything that "may be produced or sold" (*Road* 86).

The key discussions in Milton Friedman's *Capitalism and Freedom* (2004), like-wise, center around the "role of competitive capitalism" and the "organization of the bulk of the economic activity through private enterprise operating in a free market" (*Capitalism* 4). How the desire to set in motion the processes that were to ensure freedom transmogrified into military interventions and coup-de-tats in Asia, Africa, and South and Central America, and how the prophets of freedom—von Hayek, Friedman, Buchanan, and the rest of their ilk—metamorphosed into ardent admirers of dictators and fascist leaders are paradoxes that cannot be made sense of if we do not take into consideration how the neoliberal preoccupation with freedom itself is underwritten by its deep anxiety about socialism and working class politics. Hayek's long diatribe against socialism in the second and third chapters of *The Road to Serfdom*, where he postulates socialism as an antithesis of freedom, and Friedman's insistence on reducing the government to a rule maker and "umpire" in *Capitalism and Freedom*, where he envisages the world dictated by market necessities, are illustrative of the class component of the neoliberal doctrine. It is not for no reason that David Harvey has gone on to describe neoliberalization as "a project to achieve the restoration of class power" (*A Brief History of Neoliberalism* 16), for it seems as though what truly traumatized von Mises, von Hayek, and Friedman was not the emergence of fascist leaders like Mussolini and Hitler but rather the rise of socialist politics in Europe. That Hayek's best-known book began as a memo written to dispute the belief that fascism was an attempt to rescue "the dying gasp of a failed capitalist system" (Caldwell 1)—a belief that was mainly held by the European socialists of that era—is illustrative of the disdain that the pioneers of neoliberal economic doctrines harbored against working class politics.

At the point of its emergence, neoliberalism was still a marginal idea, held by a handful of academics whose ulterior motive was to assert their dissent against the Keynesian policies adopted by the governments of their countries. After stag-flation hit in many parts of the world in the 1970s, specifically in the United Kingdom, which had to be bailed out by the International Monetary Fund (IMF; Harvey, *Brief History* 12), and the United States, where an economic crisis had sunk in since the late 1960s, the neoliberal doctrines circulated by the influential academics of the Chicago School found a foothold in state policies across Europe and North America. By early 1990s, when the U.S.S.R. and the Eastern Block imploded, even social progressives and labor parties began to embrace neoliberal ideas of economic and political governance. Harvey notes how, after their election victories, democratic nominee Bill Clinton and labor appointee Tony Blair—both pitched as progressive liberals—gleefully embraced neoliberal poli-cies without any inhibition or qualm (*Brief History* 13).

One of the paradoxes surrounding neoliberalism is that this philosophy of freedom required the mediation of military dictators, religious fanatics, and social conservatives from the global south to acquire its hegemony in the world. Chile, under the dictatorship of Augusto Pinochet, submitted to neoliberal economic reforms, becoming the first laboratory for perfecting the hypothetical ideas that von Hayek and Friedman propounded. Friedman himself traveled to Santiago to oversee the transition, wrenching the control of the economic policies through his disciples when Chile's economy stagnated within two years after the coup (Fischer 320). In South Asia, likewise, aided by the U.S. imperialists, British neocolonialists, and the World Bank on the one hand and the local comprador politicians, economists, and military dictators on the other, neoliberalism began

12 Introduction

to tiptoe into the state economic policies in the late 1970s. World-Bank–proposed structural adjustment policies in the 1980s, Anu Muhammad and Lamia Karim note, put Bangladesh on the highway of free market economy, gradually transforming the war-ravaged country ruled by military dictators into a neoliberal state governed by comprador bureaucrats, corrupt politicians, and power-hungry military rulers (Karim 111–3; Muhammad 24–5).

In Pakistan, the labor and land reform programs that Zulfikar Ali Bhutto, who was the Prime Minister of Pakistan from 1973 to 1977, carried out to appease the left-leaning members of his party, were halted after his persecution, leading Pakistan to become a vassal state dependent on foreign aid and imperialist assistance. The bizarre quasi-religious state policies taken during General Zia-ul-Haq's reign were not whimsical steps taken out of piety or spiritualism, but rather calculated policies to beef up support for Haq's regime, which worked as a broker between the imperial United States and the local ruling classes (Talbot 230–233; Brown). Unlike Bangladesh and Pakistan, India's neoliberalization took a different trajectory, beginning in the 1990s with the opening of India's markets for corporate institutions and reaching a new height with Narendra Modi's BJP on the helm. As early as 1996, Aijaz Ahmad warned that India's market reform, instead of moving toward the traditional liberal developmental trajectory, was gyrating toward neoliberalization, turning the state into, in a modification of Marx's famous line from the *Manifesto*, a managing committee overseeing the interest of the national bourgeoisie (*Lineages of the Present* 213). That Ahmad's caveat was not a false alarm can be understood when one reads Arundhati Roy's *Walking with the Comrades*—a book that catalogues corporate atrocities in India's heartlands, especially in the areas populated by indigenous communities (33–4). Her second novel, *The Ministry of Utmost Happiness* (2017), reads like an extended elegy, lamenting the absence of the spaces, species, and communities lost to neoliberal encroachment.

Much like India and Bangladesh, Sri Lanka too was built on the principles of a welfare state system, but it began to sway to the direction of market capitalism when, in the late 1970s, J. R. Jayewardene's nationalist government began to implement market reform policies. Nira Wickremasinge's historical mapping of modern-day Sri Lanka in *Sri Lanka in the Modern Age: A History* (2014) documents how fractious nationalism spawned a three-decade-long Civil War between the north and the south, destroying the nation's hope for a prosperous future (Wickremasinge 317–8). Sri Lanka's adoption of neoliberal policies, which often meant carrying out massive gentrification programs with public money, has recently bankrupted the state, leaving it at the mercy of Chinese and Indian capital. Nepal's relation to international capital, it needs to be noted, is more complex in many ways. Predominantly an agrarian nation, it has seen intense industrialization in recent years, bearing proof of its integration into the global division of labor. Although its industrial production is still much smaller than its

Introduction **13**

agricultural production, Nepal's slow adoption of neoliberal policies is a fascinating example of how national politics can deter large-scale neoliberalization of a nation's economy. The formidable presence of socialist politics has been one of the reasons why neoliberal South Asia has not been able to rope it in. Butan, the smallest South Asian nation state, is still a monarchy, but many of its policies are modelled after welfare state initiatives, putting it in a category of its own. Its economy has so far resisted neoliberalization, but as recent activities bear proof, the efforts to connect Bhutan to the rest of the South Asia through agricultural exchange have intensified, leaving rooms for speculation that this small nation too may not be able to avert neoliberal annexation.

Unlike what it is in the U.S. and the U.K., neoliberalization in South Asia has mostly involved the dismantling of the welfare state and the transfer of public wealth to private accounts. India, Bangladesh, Nepal, Pakistan, and Sri Lanka have also witnessed the transfer of a massive amount of land and natural resources to corporations and powerful individuals—processes that have often resulted in forceful eviction and pauperization. In Bangladesh and Pakistan, military coups and political violence—bumping off a huge number of left activists—were required to clear the ground for the implementation of World-Bank–initiated neoliberal programs. In India, similar processes had different appearances, with more robust resistance from political, social, and intellectual alliances. Although appearances vary, neoliberalization in general has a singular content: more power and wealth for the capitalist class. One of the key features of the neoliberal economy has been the usurpation of the state and the juridical institutions for the manipulation of a particular group of people. In the United States, for instance, the initiative to ensure corporate power in state and federal government has come in the form of legal measures, such as the Supreme Court ruling on corporate personhood. However, the significance of such legal measures notwithstanding, the pivotal role of violent measures, such as the suppression of African American radicalism in the 1970s and 1980s, the so called "War on Drugs" and mass incarcerations of the 1990s, and the systematic assassinations of Civil Rights activists and anti-capitalists, cannot be underestimated. There is value, therefore, in seeing neoliberalization as "privatization," "financialization," "manipulation of crises," and "state representation," but it is also important to bear in mind that such forms of appearance are inseparable from the phenomenon of "restoration of class power" (Harvey, *Spaces of Global Capitalism*, 43–48) through extensive use of state and juridical violence. One must additionally factor in the catastrophic effect neoliberalization has had on the planet. The burgeoning eco-consciousness of our era is also a conscious or unconscious acknowledgement of neoliberal capital's dismantling of the traditionally guarded properties of the common, its relentless extraction of nature's properties—a phenomenon that Jason Moore has described as the "appropriation of cheap natures" (Moore 191).

14 Introduction

It is true that neoliberal ideologies—ideas such as corporate capitalism is the only alternative for the people of the world and that capitalism is the sole path to freedom—have gained traction with a large number of people, even among those whose lives have been squashed by neoliberal policies. It is also noteworthy that today, more than any other moment in history, it is also increasingly critiqued and questioned by many who see it as a threat to the well-being of human beings and the planet. There has always been strong resistance against neoliberalization, be it in the Global South or in the Metropole. The Zapatista uprising in Mexico, protests against IMF policies in Egypt and Tunisia, Kaansat and Fulbari protests in Bangladesh, indigenous mobilization against corporate land grabbing in India, and the Occupy Movement in the United States—all these movements and many others that exist in other locations of the world are illustrative of the global discontent against neoliberalization of economy and the social sphere. Academic critique of neoliberalism as an idea and as economic policy, in recent times, has poured in from all directions despite neoliberalization of academic institutions themselves. In literary studies, such critiques have been launched from two camps mainly—Marxist and Foucauldian—although the traffic and transaction between the two are noticeably frequent. Marxists tend to conjoin neoliberalism with capitalism, seeking to understand it through "financialization" (Harvey, *Spaces of Global Capitalism* 24), "accumulation by dispossession" (Zamora "When Exclusion Replaces Exploitation"; Harvey *Spaces* 43), naked imperial ambition (Foster, "The New Imperialism of Globalized Monopoly-Finance Capital"), and so on, stressing its relation to capital and class. Foucauldians, on the contrary, emphasize governmentality and juridical formations, arguing that neoliberalism can be best understood by the appearance of a new subject—the *homo œconomicus*—who declines to submit to the jurisdiction of the sovereignty of the state (Foucault, *The Birth of Biopolitics* 283) and approaches "everything" in transactional terms, "as a market" (Brown, *Undoing the Demos* 39).

The governmentalist approach to neoliberalism, where it is seen as the moment of arrival of a new economic subject, is culled from Foucault's lectures at the Collège de France in 1978–1979. After long editorial interventions, Foucault's lectures from 1978–1979 were finally published in the original French in 2004 and in English translation in 2006. Its publication in English marked a decisive moment in Foucault studies because his meditation on the subject had profound effect on those interested in legal and political philosophy, most notably on Wendy Brown, who collated Foucault's scattered ideas to hypothesize about neoliberalism's adverse effect on the democratic state and the liberal juridical system. The main tenet of Foucault's observation is that "neoliberalism" advances a new kind of subject, *homo œconomicus*, who threatens the foundation of juridical power—the power of the sovereign—by negating the sovereign's right to control "the economic field" (*Biopolitics* 292). This discussion about the economic subject's relationship to the juridical system is profound and insightful precisely because it anticipates the catastrophic outcomes of the introduction of an economic reason in other fields governed by their own sets of laws and conventions. Yet, the idea that neo-liberals are fundamentally different from other advocates of capitalism seems suspect when we consider that the maximization of surplus is built into the very being of capitalism; subjects belonging to two different moments within the historical unfolding of capitalism do not merely symptomatize ruptures but rather attest to the continuity of unequal relation between labor and capital as well. Foucault's conjecture about neoliberalism's disinclination to submit to any logic of governmentality, in addition to underscoring the intensification of the iron grip of capital, also testifies to the accumulation of class power—a phenomenon he disingenuously ignores in his efforts to draw attention to the novelty of the neoliberal governmental logic.

The French theorist's juridical phenomenology, it needs to be stressed, appears perceptive when one looks at it from the standpoint of governmentality. Neoliberalism does indeed impose on the state the logic of economy, but to what degrees this phenomenon is motivated by the mere desire for economic governance of the state is questionable because neoliberal states seem more interested in redistribution of collective wealth than in governance. That conflicts of all kinds—racial, gender, ethnic, religious, sexual, caste, environmental, etc.—have intensified in the past 40 years with the direct or indirect patronage from the neoliberal stateand that governance now has become synonymous with management of corporate interests through state brokered policies bear proof of neoliberal abdication of governance as such, not the opposite of it. What is equally problematic about his theorization of the neoliberal is that he does not factor capitalism into his broad considerations on economization, whose sublation of politics he flags as a dangerous propensity. Foucault's reluctance to specify what kind of economic relations feed into the neoliberal desire for the economization of the juridical/political leads him to hold the entire realm of the economic culpable of impinging upon other social/political/cultural/juridical domains, thus erroneously suggesting a separation between economy and other spheres of life. Just as Foucault's general theory of power in the first volume of *The History of Sexuality* propels him toward an amorphous theory of power (Said, "Foucault and the Imagination of Power" 241–42), so his general theory of economization of the juridical lands him on a subjectivist theory of neoliberalism incapable of specifying as to what kind of relation is responsible for the production of the *homo œconomicus* and why. Foucault's theory of neoliberalism, therefore, is established on an undialectical foundation that fails to notice how the birth of the *homo œconomicus* takes place in an overdetermined but contested universe where the economic subject is not merely a bearer of the neoliberal inscription but also is an active agent struggling against its dictates. That Foucault fails to foresee any resistance against the totalizing will of neoliberalism, that he

16 Introduction

empties the neoliberal world of any contestation, especially class contestation, exemplifies the limits of his subjectivist construct.

Much like Foucault, who shows little interest in the question of class struggle in his cognitive mapping of the neoliberal, so Wendy Brown exhibits little concern for the actual sites of oppression and exploitation in her widely circulated book *Undoing the Demos* (2015). For Brown, the most important aspect of the meteoric rise of neoliberalism is the question of the arrival of a "normative reason" that has the potential for becoming a "governing rationality" (30), and not the reorganization of space and society according to the expansionist logic of neoliberal capital. Although, unlike Foucault, Brown acknowledges the significance of the Marxist critiques of neoliberalism and aligns herself with such analyses, she nevertheless persists with the idea that the most productive way of understanding it is through the modality of subject formation. Explaining why she prefers the Foucauldian frame over the others, she writes:

> In contrast with an understanding neoliberalism as a set of state policies, a phase of capitalism, or an ideology that set loose the market to restore profitability for a capitalist class, I join Michel Foucault and others in conceiving neoliberalism as an order of normative reason that, when it becomes attendant, takes shape as a governing rationality extending a specific formulation of economic values, practices, and metrics to every dimension of human life. (*Undoing* 30)

For Brown, then, what is of importance is the phenomenon that neoliberalism, when it becomes a governing rationality, expands its horizon beyond the economic and exerts its tentacular presence in "every dimension of human life." Both Foucault and Brown, it seems, are particularly alarmed by neoliberalism because it has the ability to spill over to other domains of human life and sublate those into its own expanding horizon. Following Foucault, she too identifies the *"homo oeconomicus"* as the embodied manifestation of neoliberalism. What is novel about our era, she maintains, is that "we are everywhere *homo oeconomicus* and only *homo oeconomicus*" (*Undoing* 33). Unlike the figure of the same in the 18th century, today's *homo oeconomicus* is distinguishable for its desire to govern "itself [as] a firm," specifically "as human capital across all spheres of life" (*Undoing* 34–5). When "everything is capital," she writes, "labor disappears as a category, as does its collective form, class, taking with it the analytic basis for alienation, exploitation, and association among laborers" (*Undoing* 38).

Brown's taxonomy of the human capital, thus, impels her not only to drown out all forms of class solidarity but also dissent. If all of us are indeed living breathing human capitals, solely invested in self-promotion and transactional relationships, there is no room in our consciousness and society for transgressive and self-negating activities. As capital embodied, our only destiny is to compete with other human capitals, seeking to exert our domination over those who have internalized the same worldviews. Brown's choice, her desire to examine neoliberalism by adhering to a genealogical method, of course, affords her the ability to locate what is new about neoliberalism—its governmentalist logic and the transactional propensity of the subject it produces—but it also blurs her vision of the dialectical conflict between the neoliberal subject and the environment and institutions that the person is surrounded by, especially between the subject and the law that such subjects find restrictive. What genealogy also withholds from her is the dramatic conflict between the dominant and the dominated, whose manifold appearances point toward a unified logic of organizing society. More importantly, what genealogy's "discreet and apparently insignificant truths" (Foucault, "Nietzsche, Genealogy, Truth" 77) are unable to offer her is a proper account of the dialectical relation between continuity and disjuncture, something that grand old Marx alluded to when he described the persistent presence of "dead generations" in the lives of those who occupy the here and now as the "process of world-historical necromancy" ("The Eighteenth Brumaire of Louis Bonaparte" 146–7).

South Asian Fiction as Neoliberal Allegory

It is easy to understand how figures like Afaz Ali, the protagonist of Elias's short story "Kanna," raise doubts about the efficacy of the type of subjectivist hermeneutics that Foucault and Brown have sought to pursue in their works. Although Ali is constantly forced to think of money, to the extent that his efforts to earn money look desperate, his reasons for doing so are not bound to his desire for self-enrichment. As the objective world around him succumbs to the culture of profiteering, his expectation from society remains simple: escaping his internment in his workplace—a graveyard located in the city of Dhaka where he is a petty *moulvi*—and returning to his family who reside far away from the capital city, in rural Bakerganj. A subjectivist theory of neoliberalism, the kind that has been advanced by Foucault and Brown, fails to account for Afaz's desperate pursuit of money, for what motivates him to earn money is not his desire to become successful—to become entrepreneurial and advance his knowledge for self-enrichment, thus becoming a human capital—but rather the necessity to escape the trap of debt. In Elias's story, what allows us to peer into the neoliberally conditioned world, is the transformation of the objective conditions of subjection, not the changes in the protagonist's subjectivity. It is the material relation between labor and capital as well as the emergence of the monetized culture that offers us a better theoretical grasp of the effects of neoliberalism, not a governmentalist theory of subjectivity.

Likewise, when we read Kamila Shamsie's *Home Fire* (2017), which explores the traumas and tribulations of Pakistani Muslims living in the United Kingdom,

18 Introduction

subjectivity falls comically short of accounting for the love, empathy, and helplessness its central characters feel for one another. Neither Eamonn nor Aneeka, hapless romantics who are ready to sacrifice their own lives for their loved ones, fit into the frames that the notion of *homo œconomicus* offers. One has to extend one's understanding beyond the arc of subjectivity to locate the presence of laws, institutions, discourses, commodities, and so on that evocatively summon into existence the institutions against whose norms and dictates Isma and her family are struggling. In order to understand the neoliberalized world better, one should not solely pivot on the subject but also carefully examine the tension and the transaction between the subjective and the objective world, so a more dialectical understanding of the relationship between the subject, objects, commodities, institutions, and other non-human denominators can emerge.

To understand how neoliberal allegories often operate in South Asian literature, then, we need to adopt a critical position that attaches the same importance to both the subject and the object. Additionally, it is important that we historicize these works to understand the dialectical contradiction that underlies allegorical presentation itself. For instance, many of the fictional works written in the 1990s are allegorical presentations of neoliberal structure of feeling—anticipations and critiques of the ascending neoliberal order—rather than the presentation of an empirically experienced reality, whereas the ones written in the 21st century are more unabashed critiques of the effects of neoliberalization. Bangladeshi novels written in the late 1980s and early 1990s are replete with moments that depict an obsessive anxiety about monetization and corruption—nervousness that is at once peculiar, pervasive, and profound. The new managerial class, entrepreneurs, and political beneficiaries of military dictatorship appear in these fictions as upstarts who threaten the foundation of the nation and its culture, about to swallow the whole of the nation's wealth. Elias's remarkable short story "Milir Haate Sten gun" (The Sten Gun in Mili's Hand), Shahidul Zahir's novella *Abu Ibrahimer Mrittu* (Abu Ibrahim's Death), Nasrin Jahan's brilliant work *Urukku* (The Woman Who Flew), and Jyotiprakash Dutta's short story "Gram O' Shohor Unnoyoner Golpo" ("A Story of Rural and Urban Development") thematically explore the struggles of ordinary women and men against more powerful and corrupt entrepreneurial individuals. Similarly, all three of Ahmed Sofa's fine novels from the late 1990s—*Ekjon Ali Kenaner Utthanpoton* (The Rise and Fall of One Ali Kenan) (1988), *Moronbilash* (Death Fantasy) (1989), and *Gabhi Bittanto* (*The Chronicle of the Cow*) (1995)—are depictions of the rise and ungainly fall of opportunistic and exceptionally violent figures whose emergence coincides with the corrosion of the body politic. *Bittanto*, specifically, exposes the unhealthy liaison between higher education and class power by wittily transferring knowledge into a metaphorical entity: a cow. The "miraculous" ("Bittanto" 360) rise of Abu Zunayed, a meek and introverted chemistry professor who unexpectedly becomes the Vice Chancellor of an

Introduction   **19**

eminent educational institution, is the object of Sofa's satiric gaze here. Zunayed's bizarre affection for the cow that he receives as a present from a construction businessman symbolically represents the unethical, transactional relationship between Bangladesh's intellectuals and its ruling elite, the national bourgeoisie.[2] While Zunayed's accidental rise implies a definitive cultural shift marking the inscription of the academic within the neoliberal lifeworld, the quiet efficiency of Seikh Tobarak Ali—the construction mogul who monopolizes the university's construction works by bribing and rewarding different groups who have stakes in that institution's power hierarchy—is a reaffirmation of the power of the nationalist bourgeoise that has surreptitiously taken over the state and its economy.

Similar prescient alertness about the changes in society can be noticed in Nepalese fiction writer Samrat Upadhyay's short story "The Good Shopkeeper." On its face, it seems to have very little to do with neoliberal form or content. A realist short story narrating the crisis of an old-fashioned accountant's life, "The Good Shopkeeper" registers little formal challenge. Its plot also seems far re-moved from a critical presentation of neoliberalism's economic or political programs. Upadhyay's Kathmandu is not a space of intense capitalist activity marked by rural to urban migration, nor a fast-paced city characterized by postmodernist culture and newly erected malls and apartments. The chaotic madness and greed that characterizes Adiga's *The White Tiger*'s Delhi or Naqvi's *Home Boy*'s New York City, for instance, are also absent in Upadhyay's narrator's Kathmandu. His tone, throughout the narration, remains subdued, echoing the city's relatively calm and slow-paced life, its unpretentious simplicity, and its quasi-feudal culture. Nepal at that time was still formally a monarchy, although its constitutional reform was carried out in 1990. And yet, even here, we detect traces of the manifest features of neoliberalism.

The story's plot moves around the misfortune of an old-school accountant. Having been let go by his firm, Pramod, the protagonist of Upadhyay's story, sees his coherent life fall apart and his hopes dwindle. Unable to land another job—a thing difficult to come by in Kathmandu—he seeks comfort in the temples of the city. What is rendered visible through Pramod's numerous visits to "Shambhu-da," his wife's prosperous cousin, is the structure of favoritism; jobs are only available if one has an influential guardian ready to use his political/financial influence to find one a position. Pramod's recurrent visits to his powerful relative, however, yield nothing substantial, and he grows bitter as he struggles to find a job. His wife, who also struggles heavily with their seven-month-old daughter, advises him to sell a plot of land they own and set up a shop. Pramod, thinking shopkeeping is beneath his social class, rudely declines to do so, despite his wife's entreating and despite his own repeated social humili-ation. Deeply frustrated and vegetating in the parks of Kathmandu, he meets a "young woman" at the city park—a woman far below his social rank, who works

20 Introduction

in an affluent house as a "servant" (10). Pramod's relationship with the "servant woman" can be interpreted in a number of ways, most effectively as his patriarchal revenge on his wife as well as a neurotic reaction against his self-perceived emasculation through joblessness. His relationship with the maid can also be seen as a symbolic prefiguration of being declassed, which takes a fetishistic form expressing itself through the symptom of his ritualistic vegetation at the park and lazy afternoons spent inside her tiny room. Read as such, "The Good Shopkeeper" appears to stage an anachronistic feudal fantasy, mirroring the persistence of the feudal life that the city was still caught up in, the monarchy that was still ornamentally present when the story was written.

Yet, as I would like to argue here, a new schema emerges when this story is read as an allegory of Nepal's inscription in the global capitalist structure. Pramod, we are told, has his job to "a young man who knows computers" (5). We are also given hints about Nepal's emerging social structure when Pramod, wary of Shambhu-da's avoidance, imagines himself "as a feudal landlord, like one of the men who used to run the farmlands of the country only twenty years earlier," punishing him (8). This moment, which appears as fantasy, is evocative of Pramod's yearning for a long-gone feudal past, when society was hierarchically organized and where people like Shambhu-da had little relevance. It is against this backdrop that Upadhyay's story attains its allegorical relevance. Pramod's acceptance of his future existence as a shopkeeper allegorically represents Nepal's acceptance of its new class and social structure dominated not by landlords who ran the farmlands 20 years ago but by people like Shambhu-da whose newfound wealth comes from "shady businesses" and construction jobs in the city (2). Likewise, the specter of computer-educated accountants replacing old school clerks also implies the nation's changing technological landscape, moving in synchrony with the global technological changes. Written in the late 1990s when the effects of neoliberal global restructuring in Nepal was still in its nascent stage, Upadhyay's story bears witness to impending social and technological transformations whose contours were still too distant to make out. It is Shambhu-da who mediates that distant horizon symptomatically embodying the emerging class, which will accumulate through private trade but is also willing to employ violence, theft, and dispossession as a means to secure wealth. What is deeply suggestive here is that the victim of Shambhu-da's violence is a policeman. It is, after all, the body of the semi-feudal welfare state that the country must dump before entering the circuit of late capitalism run by advanced computing machines.

If Upadhyay's story allegorizes neoliberalism by absorbing all the trivialities of a changing material world and by projecting onto the body of the nation the shadow of a distant world whose political and economic transformations are affecting lives in a relatively quiet part of the globe, Amitav Ghosh's *Ibis* trilogy critiques neoliberalism more overtly, by exposing the vacuousness of the rhetoric

Introduction **21**

of freedom and invisible hand of the market—neoliberalism's ideological foundations. The trilogy does so not by directly engaging with the present moment but by reimagining a turbulent period of the 19th century, which, despite its apparent historical remove, functions as a mirror image of the world in which we live today. Ghosh started writing his trilogy in 2004, soon after the beginning of the Iraq War, and finished it in 2014, more than six years after the great financial crisis of 2008. At the center of its narrative stands a ship and its occupants, whose lives the trilogy's intricate plot follows. One of the characters that Ghosh's novels closely pursue is the schooner's carpenter from Baltimore, Zachary Reid. It is his remarkable transformation from being a mere carpenter to a partner in the shipping firm that signifies the imperial cooperation in the form of Euro-American co-authorship in the Opium War, thus anticipating the Iraq War in whose aftermath the novel was written. Reid's partnership with the British trader Benjamin Burnham also suggestively points toward the expanding brotherhood of free-trade ideologues who have the power to dictate what course their nations may take and against whom their nation must wage a war. Reid thus holds the key to the novel's allegorical presentation of the pre-Iraq War political climate through the trope of the Opium War, whose re-narration allows us to see the connection between the present and the past.

Ghosh himself was interested in tracking this homology, this correspondence between what happened before the beginning of the Opium War and what happened almost two centuries later. How free trade became the rallying cry for the opium traders has been described by Ghosh in an interview, where he suggests that what inspired him to write the trilogy was the strange semblance between the past and the present. This interview, where Ghosh gestures toward the axis between imperial war and free trade, clearly lays out the connection between The first Opium War and the second Iraq War. Noting the strange similarity and how it inspired him to write the trilogy, he states:

> I started writing this trilogy in 2004, soon after the start of the Iraq War; and the Iraq War was of course fought in the name of freedom and free trade and so on and so forth. When I looked at the historical material on the Opium War it soon became clear that there were many similarities between that war and the Iraq War of 2003; it extends to the point where it's almost uncanny. ("The Opium Wars, Neoliberalism, and the Anthropocene")

When we read Ghosh's interview, the correspondence between the past and the present, Free Trade imperialism[3] and neoliberalism, and 19th-century primitive accumulation and the 21st century "accumulation by dispossession" (Harvey, *Spaces of Global Capitalism* 91–92) becomes clear. If, to travesty Fredric Jameson, the object of allegory is not meaning but structure itself (*Allegory and Ideology* 10), these transhistorical homologies[4] gesture toward a broader structural relation

22 Introduction

between then and now—a relationship that allows us to see these multiple temporalities as coexisting moments within the broad historical expanse of capitalist modernity, where expropriation, exploitation, imperialism, and war exist as concurrent processes of accumulation.

To understand why Ghosh's trilogy is a more direct take on neoliberalism, let us first turn to the most explicit feature of the trilogy's critique—rhetorical similitude. In her recent work *In the Ruins of Neoliberalism* (2019), Brown shows how the neoliberal discourse of free market economy draws its inspiration from Hayek's insistence on the conjunction between the market and morality, which now features in most conservative discussions about "God, family, nation and free enterprise" (*Ruins* 89). In *River of Smoke* (2011), the second novel of the trilogy, we see similar rhetorical strategies from Benjamin Burnham, the owner of the *Ibis*. When the Chinese, determined to prosecute those Hong merchants who persist with the opium trade, make their intentions public, Burnham, who hears the news from a fellow British trader, is infuriated, calling the Chinese commissioner "a monster" (*River* 431). Hearing Burnham's comment, Mr. King, an American businessman, quips whether Burnham sees anything monstrous in his own actions. The latter responds:

> No, sir … [b]ecause it is not my hand that passes sentence upon those who choose the indulgence of opium. It is the work of another, invisible, omnipotent: it is the hand of freedom, of the market, of the spirit of liberty itself, which is none other than the breath of God. (*River* 432)

This idea that no mortal has the authority to intervene in the market because its freedom has been warranted by God himself validates Foucault's observation that neo-liberals do not accept the jurisdiction of the sovereign in the matter of trade. To them, the market exists outside political jurisdiction and, therefore, cannot be governed by the same laws that operate in the nation or society.

By invoking the rhetoric of the free hand of the market, Burnham is not indeed leaning toward Adam Smith and classical liberalism, whose worldviews remained more or less secular; he is, rather, aligning himself with the Evangelicals and the moralists like Hayek, who sought to connect freedom of the market with Christianity. It is there that the novel's critique of neoliberalism explicitly comes to view. By putting the discourse of neoliberalism in the mouth of Burnham—a conservative British free trader—Ghosh is performing what Adiga does in his first novel: exposing the duplicity of neoliberal discourse by putting it in the mouth of an unworthy practitioner. The difference between the two novels lies in the manner in which these two preachers of neoliberalism practice their own preaching. Whereas Balram, Adiga's quizzical protagonist, practices it to the best of his ability by remaining true to the neoliberal mantra of entrepreneurship, which proclaims that our relationships are all transactional, Burnham applies his credo selectively, validating the premises of the Marxist interpreters of neoliberalism, who claim that neoliberalism is a rhetorical empty shell underwritten by class interest and imperial ambition.[5] Two examples, hopefully, will sufficiently explain this point. In *Sea of Poppies*, we see Burnham quickly and efficiently shelving the costs of economic loss on the shoulders of his local partners (*Sea* 80), thus bending the laws to dodge the cost of his own business decisions. In *River of Smoke* (2011), the British traders collectively change the rules of business so they can monopolize the shipbuilding trade (*Sea* 422), putting the gospel of God's free hand to rest in a quiet corner. Both instances illustrate how the trilogy effectively sees free market ideology as a discourse underwritten by class and imperial relations of power, as rhetorical exercises they are not only rehearsed sporadically but also applied unevenly, making sure that concentration of capital in the hands of the imperialists is accompanied by a surfeit of logic that defends their right to accumulate wealth freely.

Ghosh's trilogy can be approached through another route as well—the way of the object. Once we approach these novels through the trope of opium, which serves as a master metaphor in them, their relationship to capitalist modernity becomes clear, allowing us to read the trilogy as an allegorical exposé not only of the capitalist production process itself, which is marked by inequality and decrepitude, but also of the risk of commodity circulation, whose disruption may spawn crises. As value in motion, the commodity form must transform into money as fast as possible; any delay in commodity's exchange and conversion into the money form has the capacity to generate a full-blown economic crisis. Such a crisis will intensify the possibility of war and conflict. In *Sea of Poppies*, the crisis ushered in by the deprecation of value of "American bills of exchange," results in the reduction of the price of opium, forcing the Burnham Bros. to face financial loss for the first time in its history (*Sea* 80). It is this loss that sets Benjamin Burnham to encroach on Raja Neel Ratan Halder's estate, driving the latter into exile. In *River of Smoke*, a chain of crises is unleashed when the Chinese government bans the sale of opium, resulting in a log of unsold opium, which leads the British opium merchants to wage war on the Chinese. The tragic death of the Bombay merchant Bahram is the consequence of the loss emanating from the unrealized surplus value of opium—an economic loss that drives him toward frustration and then addiction, finally causing his death (*River* 503–510). *Flood of Fire*, the last novel of the *Ibis* trilogy, can be read as an allegory of overcoming the crisis of conversion by waging war and expanding the market even further. What is laid bare in the process is that war is a necessary strategy for overcoming capitalism's crises. The entire trilogy, thus, can be read as a story of capitalism's crisis of overproduction and price deprecation, and the violent means through which capitalism overcomes its crisis, but does so in a manner that posits the contradictions at a higher stage.

24 Introduction

In *Capital Volume II*, Karl Marx writes how, once converted into commodity, capital must perform its "commodity functions" before returning to its owner in money form (*Capital II* 122). The inability to do so, writes the German revolutionary, leads toward calamity and stagnation. Marx identifies various reasons for capitalism's crises, most notably the delay in moving from one circuit of capital to another. "If capital," he writes,

> comes to a stand still in the first phase, *M-C*, money capital forms into a hoard; if this happens in the production phase, the means of production cease to function and labor-power remains unoccupied; if in the last phase, *C'-M'*, unsaleable stocks of commodities obstruct the flow of circulation. (*Capital II* 133)

The crisis that unfolds in the *Ibis* trilogy is the crisis of the third stage, when "unsalable stocks of commodities" begin to pile up because the Chinese decline to allow their markets to be swamped by opium. The question that is raised in the process is not about the essence of opium and its objecthood, but rather how its valorization through production and exchange allows this object to become a commodity. It is here, in its willingness to tell how the commoditization of poppy leads toward crisis and war, the destruction of life as well as the environment, that Ghosh's trilogy's critical tenor is heard most clearly.

Among the many discussions that are available on the trilogy, only a handful pay adequate attention to its representation of capitalism, and none on its relationship to neoliberalism. Only a small number of research works have taken note of the correspondence between past and present in Ghosh's trilogy, especially of its vexed relationship with our own time. Kanika Batra's otherwise excellent ecological reading of the second volume of Ghosh's trilogy in "Reading Urban Ecology through *River of Smoke*," for instance, notices the mirroring of the present onto the past (Batra 323), but displays little interest in stretching her analyses beyond hybrid formations and postmodern style when it comes to explaining what that present looks like. Her ecological reading, therefore, goes only as far as a liberal ecocritical reading can proceed, pointing toward the novel's deft presentation of city botany, eschewing the more troubled path of political ecology that would have allowed her to connect urban ecology with capitalism's expansion in the 19th century. Correspondingly, her essay remains committed to the process of locating hybridity and postmodern aesthetic forms in the novel, omitting from discussion the very conditions that facilitate hybrid social transactions through trade and cultural exchange. Binayak Roy's "Exploring the Orient from Within," likewise, characterizes Ghosh's novel as a "meta-form" traversing disciplinary boundaries and effortlessly navigating the line of demarcation separating history and fiction (Roy 1). How a "meta-form" enacts a system of reference and how the formal features of novels like *Sea of*

Poppies and *River of Smoke* correspond to their thematic preoccupation remain almost unexplored in Roy's essay, illustrating, once more, that Postcolonial Studies is habitually disinclined to factor in class and capital in its examination of history and culture. That he belauds Ghosh's novels' "particularist universalism" and provincialization of "Eurocentrism" (Roy 5) but lets slip how the interwoven world of commodities and cultures are made possible by the spectral mediation of capital cannot be merely coincidental, for such patterns themselves symptomatize preferences.

There are notable exceptions, of course, but such hesitations also raise questions about contemporary South Asian academics' relationship to capital. The omission of capital and class can be construed as the discipline's inability to free itself from its own (neo)liberal bias and inscription. The general lack of interest among the practitioners of postcolonial studies to address the question of class exploitation has been pointed out by a host of thinkers on the left, most notably by Aijaz Ahmad, Arif Dirlik, and E. San Juan Jr., in the 1990s, during the heydays of postcolonialism. More recently, Vivek Chibber has explained how the discipline of postcolonial studies began its ascension as an academic discipline in the Metropolitan West at a moment when working class politics and socialist states in much of the Global South were upended by the forces of market capitalism (Chibber 2). Despite postcolonialism's pedigree of left politics—Edward Said, the discipline's most eminent figure, mentions in the "Afterword" of *Orientalism* that thinkers such as "Anwar Abdel Malek, Samir Amin, and C. L. R. James" were the forerunners of postcolonialism (*Orientalism* 349)—it began, at the turn of the century, to quickly shed its aticolonial/anticapitalist pedigree to initiate the *fin de siècle* "cultural turn" of theory (Chibber 1). Sumit Sarker, a prominent member of the Subaltern Studies group, which itself represents one of the most influential voices within the postcolonial tradition, has bewailed the group's gradual move away from its Marxist/Gramscian pedigree to embrace Foucauldian discourse analysis theory (Sarker 300). To Sarker, such a distancing marks the group's domestication within the metropolitan postmodernist circles, not a resurgence (Sarker 300–301). Gayatri Spivak, who, in the 1980s, help steer the Subaltern Studies group on the track of postmodern/deconstructivist thought, later complained about Postcolonial Studies' complicity, claiming that the fetishistic retreat into colonial discourse analysis in the era of "financialization of the globe" can be decoded as a symptom the diasporic postcolonial academic's complicit participation in the capitalist accumulation process (Spivak 3).

Mostly articulated in the late 1990s, when neoliberal economic policies and a monetized culture began to flex muscles in academic institutions, these critiques blurt out deep anxieties about postcolonial studies' capitulation to neoliberal capital. They also point toward the conjuncture between the academic postmodernism and cosmopolitan liberal worldviews. This chapter has tried to demonstrate through short textual readings of Upadhyay and Ghosh that a radical

26 Introduction

critique of contemporary hegemonic practices does not require one to commit to the theories of subjectivity to explain what is wrong about the contemporary world. Nor is there any urgent necessity to sidestep the question of class oppression to draw attention to hybrid formations and postmodern postures because even liberal writers such as Upadhyay and Adiga, and non-aligned critics of imperialism such as Ghosh, Shamsie and Hamid, cannot mop up from their narrative canvas the ravages of neoliberalism. One of the objectives of this book is to establish that it is possible to bridge the conjectured distance between aesthetics and political/economic realities. The aesthetic itself is political, although it is important to cautiously forewarn that the politics of the text is not a direct outgrowth of the author's worldviews, nor is it a mere echo of the political humdrums outside. However desperate one may be to sidestep the question of determination, one cannot ignore, let alone escape, the traces of historical conditioning. Indeed, the desire to escape the processes of historical determinations by willfully disengaging from the sites of struggle more forcefully establishes the presence of socio-economic inscription in the author and the text. Hence the usefulness of allegoresis. In a world conditioned by neoliberal policies and capitalist relations, cultural and aesthetic productions are bound to bear the traces of these conditionings; it is also only expected that the hegemonic ideas will conceal themselves and erase the tracks of their normalization within institutions and epistemological practices. It is here that an allegorical reading proves itself useful, for to do so is to draw out to the surface what the historical dominant tries to kick under the rug and conceal.

Conclusion: The Map of the Work

Allegories, as has been made clear through the preceding discussions, is an attempt to read literary productions through the lens of class struggle, although the processes through which such a reading has been carried out remains steeped in the jargons and vocabularies of various tenets of contemporary critical discourses. The readings that have been advanced in it are deeply influenced by the major tenets of Marxist thought. Although the name of Marx has become an anathema in certain cicles of postcolonial academics, this book strongly maintains that neoliberalism's economization of the cultural sphere mandates a close reading of Marx, especially of his seminal work *Capital*, because in the absence of a substantive discussion of capital, any examination of neoliberalism is destined to become anemic. Almost all the chapters of this book draw upon the rich foundation provided by Marx to explain how neoliberalism's entrenched visions are manifestations of something more fundamental, deeply rooted in the historical development of capitalism itself. Since more detailed discussions are advanced in the rest of the chapters, let us quickly consider how the book is schematically organized.

Introduction **27**

The first chapter of this book advances a reading of a relatively ignored short story by Akhtaruzzaman Elias, who is deemed by many literary scholars as the finest fiction writer from Bangladesh. If the *Ibis* trilogy successfully portrays the crisis of converting the commodity form into money form, Elias's short story "Kanna" depicts, in depth and breadth, the crisis of the money form itself. Marx, in the first chapter of *Capital Volume I*, describes the commodity as a "social hieroglyphic" (*Capital I*, 167) whose value form conceals the exploitative relation under which commodity is produced. Abstract labor, the quantification of which allows the value form to emerge, is the reason why it becomes possible to mediate all products of labor as values. It is the same thing that contributes to the fetish character of commodity. Private labor, which appears as the aggregate labor of society through abstract value and exchange, is what results in the "material relations between persons and social relations between things" (*Capital I* 166). The agency of the commodity—its power to mediate social relations—attains material form in Elias's "Kanna." This chapter explains how the story allegorizes money's agency and mediating power by drawing attention to its protagonist's subjugated affect. The protagonist, despite losing his son to a rather innocuous disease, is unable to mourn for his loss because of his debt, which can be read allegorically as a depiction of the symbolic power of money in a capitalist society. Particularly because this story was written at a historical moment when neo-liberalism had just begun to set in, I read this depiction as an example of the structure of feeling that was pervasive at that time. That Elias's protagonist fails to perform his responsibility as a father, not because of his lack of inclination but because of material necessity, I argue here, is evocative of a momentous shift in the objective conditions against whose norms Ali is wrestling.

The second chapter peers into Aravind Adiga's Booker winning novel *The White Tiger* to argue that uneven geographical relation is central to the novel's depictions of space. An important element of Marxist critiques of capitalism, uneven development has been explored using both temporal and spatial frames. Earlier proponents of the theory, such as Andre Gunder Frank and Immanuel Wallerstein, posited uneven geographical relations as the temporal progression of capitalism through spatial conflict and contradiction. They also offered to see it through a World Systems theory where national competition was subjugated under the capitalist world system in which a few capitalist centers enjoyed structural privilege over both semi-peripheral and peripheral nations. *The White Tiger*, which is often read as a satirical novel critiquing neoliberal India, pro-blematizes not only the dominant discussions about space under neoliberal capital but also the Indian nation's relation to its internal and external spaces. Critiquing some of the Foucauldian readings of the novel, which advances the idea that the relation between India's privileged and less privileged spaces is a temporal one, I argue in this chapter that capitalism space itself is developed unevenly, ensuring that the infrastructural development of one space necessitates the retardation or

28 Introduction

restriction of development in peripheral regions. As such, uneven geographical relations mirror capitalism's own fundamental contradiction in which capital enjoys privilege over labor. It is this relationship that mediates spatial relationship under capitalism. My reading of Adiga's novel in the second chapter is distilled through Marx's discussions about subsumption, for witout a recourse to the German thinker's meditation on the annexation of space under the logic of capital, one cannot adequately explain as to how the production of uneven geography is anchored in capital's uneven relation to labor.

In chapter three, I advance a reading of two fictions whose protagonists, unable to swallow the humiliation and restriction imposed on them after the terror attacks of September 11, decide to leave New York City and return to their cities of origin in Pakistan. On the surface, both novels appear to tell stories of struggles of Muslim men in NYC in the climate of antipathy. As has been pointed out by some critics, these novels expose the paradigms of precariousness in the United States, where the Manichean rhetoric that pits Muslims against the rest of the nation unleashes a normative culture whose logics move around the effusion of empathy for a selective group of people and antipathy for those who are cast as enemies. The young narrators, who also suffer losses and are left to weather the growing hostility on their own, both blame the city for withdrawing its hospitality. To them, NYC appears as an inhospitable city, an uninhabitable city, whose transformation is marked by nationalist and xenophobic zealotry. However, another narrative, which is less pronounced but equally powerful, begins to emerge from the shadows—a narrative that describes the city's cabbies, its prostitutes, and its less prosperous migrant population. It is this other narrative of the city's working class and surplus population that allows us to grasp the systemic exclusion that preceded the transformation, leaving us with ghostly demarcation of the city's neoliberally organized life. In my discussion on the two novels, I try to exhume this enfolded parallel narrative and put it in conversation with the dominant one which is committed to the task of initiating a dialogue about Muslim precariousness. Instead of reading these works as mere representations of racial and religious marginality, I try to locate in them attentive prefigurations of systemic production of immiserated people—people who are describebed in *Capital Volume One* as the "reserve army of capital" (*Capital I* 785). I also note how, instead of producing an awareness of systemic inequality, precariousness propel the narrators of these novels to fetishistically cast their marginality as an outcome of racial and religious oppression, not as a common condition produced by global capitalist system's drive for surplus.

In recent years, what has become acutely obvious is that the decades of implementing neoliberal policies have hurled us into a terrible economic and ecological crisis, the likes of which the world has never known. According to the 2019 Oxfam report, the wealthiest 26 people own more wealth than the bottom 50 percent of the world's population, more than what 3.5 billion people own.

The unprecedented gap between the rich and the poor has started catapulting into a massive social crisis today, spawning in the process an acutely divided world. What has also become apparent after the financial crisis of 2008 is that the social and economic cost of the failure of large corporations and financial institutions now must be borne collectively by the rest of the population. Dumping financial responsibility on the shoulders of ordinary folks and young people in the form of debt and corporate bailout has become the steroid that capitalism rests on for managing its crisis. As the global surplus population, most of whom are refugees, increases, neoliberalism's strategies for exploiting labor grow more sophisticated and draconian. The same attitude is noticed in relation to nature and climate. Mining, fracking, burning of fossil fuel, poisoning of rivers, decapitation of hills, burning of forests, production of industrial waste—all seem to point toward capitalism's reluctance to change and adopt technologies that are less harmful for the planet. Human-induced pollution has resulted in the increase of surface and ocean temperature, causing largescale damages not only to people but also to a large number of other species. What has accompanied the twin crises of neoliberalism is xenophobic fascism, which, aided by the platforms provided by the neoliberal corporations, has become a part of the mainstream. Production and management of fractiousness and rage within the population has emerged as one of the key strategies for maintaining the status quo.

The fourth and concluding chapter of this book offers to read those contemporary fictions that thematically explore the crises of neoliberalism and, simultaneously, imagine a world beyond its control. In Amitav Ghosh's *Gun Island* (2019), a novel thematizing environmental crisis and the threat to the planet, an old Bengali myth is reconstructed to launch an adventure that moves through four continents, unveiling the trail of global ecological devastation. Ghosh's novel explores the global production of refugees either through natural catastrophes or through social crises, especially through imperialist wars. In Arundhati Roy's *The Ministry of Utmost Happiness* (2017), the costs of India's religious and nationalist fundamentalisms are recounted, laying bare the processes of local manufacturing and management of the surplus population. What is also depicted in Roy's novel is the courage and resistance of the social outcast. Instead of only looking into the strategies through which the state, its corporations, and the state-favored religion oppress and traumatize people, *The Ministry* also sheds light on the ways in which the victims of religious and corporate oppressions produce counter-sites so as to develop, out of the ashes of destruction, a counterculture imbued with utopian visions and qualities.

Taken together, the novels that I describe here as allegories of neoliberalism, ask some probing questions about our world and the conditions we live under. They tell us how money and capital build a self-centered universe where the pursuit of happiness gets subsumed by the desire to possess unlimited wealth. They also show how the processes of capital accumulation create a disturbingly

30 Introduction

unequal and splintered world, where war and oppression exist not as exceptions but as the very foundations of polity and social life. Neoliberalism's war on the poor extends far beyond human society and reaches the quiet corners of the planet, where its search for compound growth decimates the web of life and drives plants and spices toward extinction. Since almost all the novels discussed here deal with trauma and struggle, it is difficult to avoid the pessimistic overtone of their themes and representations. Yet, as I point out in my readings, the overlaid sense of grief and pessimism that we encounter in these literary works is simultaneously underwritten by a nascent optimism about the future. What initially appear as idiosyncratic impractical acts of defiance are indeed complex expressions of a utopian desire for a better society, which, having found no collective outlet, has sought to express themselves as a trivial private action. These works, thus, gesture toward our collective utopian potential, narrativizing the constant efforts of the oppressed to rebuild the society from below. The gloomy prognoses of the neoliberal assault on life, this work emphatically maintains, is not simply a pessimistic call for resignation but also a masked articulation of optimism and possibility, a precognition of the necessity to pull ourselves from the ravages of neoliberalism.

Notes

1 A mawlawi or *moulvi* is an honorific title given to someone who works in a mosque and conducts prayers. In Bangladesh, only a handful of *moulvi* are affluent because of their associations with powerful people and/or institutions. Most mawlawis live in rural areas, often far away from family and home, and struggle to make ends meet because their livelihoods depend on charities given to the mosque or the institution they are attached to. Afaz Ali, the protagonist of Elias's short story, is from a remote village located in the south-western part of Bangladesh. He earns his living from a graveyard (*gorosthan*), which has, as is typical, a mosque within its premise—a mosque that takes care of the graves, renders service before and after the burial, and conducts regular prayers five times a day. Ali works as a senior *moulvi* in that mosque. As is the custom in Bangladesh (also in other countries of South Asia), he leads emotionally charged *monajat* (after-burial prayer for the deceased) in Arabic, Urdu, and the mother tongue.

2 Seikh Tobarak Ali, who presents Abu Zunayed the cow, is a "contractor" who has absolute monopoly over the university's construction work. He maintains his control over the contracts by bribing both the government as well as the opposition party members, bureaucrats, student leaders, engineers, staff, and faculty members ("Gavi Bittanto" 402–3). He describes himself as a "businessman who began his career as a contractor and is still there" ("Bittanto" 404). A merchant himself, Ali is deeply skeptical about the profitability and utility of large-scale industry. His plan for the future includes expanding his construction business and investing in land, which, he believes, will yield huge profit. Ali fits perfectly within Fanon's description of "the national bourgeoise" who operate like "small-time racketeer[s]" and lack "ambition" and inventiveness (Fanon 101). In his drunken confession, Ali expresses his frustration at "mountebanks" who loan money from banks claiming they would set up industries but use the money in unproductive activities ("Bittanto" 403–4). The indolent and dependent bourgeoisie of postcolonial Africa, who is the object of Fanon's scorn and

ridicule in *The Wretched of the Earth*, is a familiar figure not only in Sofa's works but also in Akhtaruzzaman Elias's. Aware as they have been about the corrosive effect of the governance of a lazy and dependent national bourgeoise, both Sofa and Elias depict the national bourgeoise with Fanonian displeasure.

3 In their essay titled "The Imperialism of Free Trade," Gallagher and Robinson contend that 19th-century imperialism was characterized by the desire to establish a market for free trade. They seek to separate the imperialism of the earlier stages from the kind that came into being in the 19th century. Bernard Semmel, after Gallagher and Robinson, has also contributed to the discussion about the role free trade played in the imperialist wars and policies of the 19th century, suggesting those who see free trade as fundamentally opposed to imperialism are historically incorrect. While I am not entirely convinced by their stagist approach toward history and empire, I find their term useful in reading Ghosh's trilogy, where he draws an analogy between the past and the present. See Gallagher and Robinson's "The Imperialism of Free Trade" and Semmel's *The Rise of Free Trade Imperialism* for further elaboration of the distinction.

4 They are transhistorical in the sense of different time periods, but not in the sense of equating human history over all time. That is, the novels describe the moment of emergence for a capitalist world market dominated by the free traders, and its reincarnation at a later moment of capital's recreation, neoliberalism.

5 It is important to remember here how contemporary Marxist thinkers such as Harvey, Patnaik, and Bellamy Foster have persistently argued that neoliberalism's commitment to the freedom of the market remains shallow. Especially in the last decade and a half it has become evident that those who preach neoliberalism also seem eager to use state intervention the moment capitalist class is in trouble. It is only in the case of the workers and less powerful nations that the strong state must withhold its generous institutions from intervening in the market. See Harvey's "Neoliberalism as Creative Destruction," Patnaik's "The State under Neo-Liberalism" and "Trends of Center-State Relations in India Under the Neo-Liberal Regime," and John Bellamy Foster's "The New Imperialism of Globalized Monopoly-Finance Capital" for further discussion on this topic.

2

"KANNA" AND THE MONETIZATION OF AFFECT

Introduction

In the previous chapter, we have noticed how subjectivist elaborations of neo-liberalism struggle to account for those who are not enterprising, whose relation to neoliberalism remains equivocal. In this chapter we will look further into the issue, noting how the fetishistic overemphasis on the appearance of a new economic subject, the *homo œconomicus*, leads the subjectivist descriptions of neoliberalism to undervalue the material conditions that affect the manner in which the subject governs himself. Money, in such explorations, is often cate-gorized as an outgrowth and consequence of the neoliberal subject's pursuit of self-enrichment, and not the opposite, i.e. the subject being the effect of money's power. Although monetization (and through it financialization as well) and commoditization remain two of the most visible symptoms of neoliberal capi-talism's hegemonic presence in the world, in the Foucauldian theories these two important historical phenomena are pushed to the margins, as if they are mere consequences of a new logic of governance. This chapter will shed some light on the undermining of object relations in contemporary discussions of neoliberalism by zooming in on literary representation of money, specifically on its capacity for social mediation. Neoliberal capitalism, which often means the monetization of the body politic and culture, is better accounted for by a historical materialist examination of money's penetration into the fabric of our innermost world—the world of emotions and affect, the domains that are often conjectured to exist outside its mediation. This chapter will contradict the subjectivist phenome-nology that accords preponderence to the logic of governance. It will claim that in the era of neoliberal capitalism—a historical moment in which monetary

DOI: 10.4324/9781003324768-2

"Kanna" and the Monetization of Affect **33**

representation of capital has reached a more complex stage—money often conditions not only our social existence and relations but also our innermost feelings, a phenomenon that does not symptomatize the subject's subscription to an ideology but rather the fetishistic power of the object.

A number of contemporary Bangladeshi fictions, we have noticed in the introductory chapter, have made available the qualm and utter helplessness that the subject experiences in a neoliberally conditioned world dictated by the power of money. Ahmed Sofa's novel *Moron Bilash*, for instance, depicts the extent to which money is able to incite excessive greed, prompting people to pursue it at all costs, even by resorting to pillage and murder. Shahidul Zahir's beautifully written novella *Abu Ibrahimer Mrittu*, likewise, records the subject's struggle against an acutely corrupt sociopolitical environment. Although the novel's protagonist eventually triumphs greed, he nevertheless tragically loses his life to muggers who stab and kill him for money. Abu Ibrahim's personal honesty does not deter his killers fromseeking to to enrich themselves by robbing him.

Nasrin Jahan's first novel *Urukku* (1993) [The Girl Who Flew], by contrast, brings to light the affective aspect of money relations, showing how it triggers acute unhappiness in the minds of those who do not possess this coveted commodity. Jahan's novel tracks the musings of a young woman named Nina, whose material struggles spill over into her deepest fears and emotions. Separated from her unfaithful husband and hounded by the untimely death of her infant daughter, she grinds through the hostile city life unable to shelter her from a host of agonizing experiences. The recurrence of a series of evocative imageries of money—some of which relate to the protagonist's childhood—makes Jahan's novel one of the most compelling explorations of the subject's battle against monetized patriarchal society. The entire novel is laden with moments that point toward the intersection between money and patriarchy, hilighting in the process the nexus between wealth inequality and gender inequality. Reflecting on her past, especially on the continuity of material strife throughout her life, *Urukku*'s protagonist Nina reveals the following at the beginning of the novel:

> Much like what it was at my father's, the main issue at my husband's house was money. I grew exhausted managing things at my father's house, trying to cover this with that. When I came to my husband's, I saw the unrelenting repetition of the same. We often did not have water in the tap. Loadshedding was our area's inseparable mate. Often it seemed as if the sun had taken permanent residence on my tiny little roof. I was angry all the time. (Jahan 15)

It does not require much introspection to locate the relationship between the first and the last sentence of this extract. A causal relation between money (the lack of it, thereof) and unhappiness has been drawn here, showing how one triggers the other. Nina's inner state, at least in this case, is vastly influenced by the material

34 "Kanna" and the Monetization of Affect

condition in which she has been thrust. Want of money, constant struggle to make ends meet, dingy one-room-apartment, lack of water and sanitization, lack of electricity, and the relentless sun overhead—all point toward the convergence between materiality and anger, between want of money and negative emotions. The latter part of the novel records her desperate attempts to harness her intractable poverty through borrowing, additional work, and supplication to an affluent distant relative for money. Her desperation is perhaps indicative of her subjective disposition, the kind that may allow the critics to label her as an entrepreneurial human, but what it also powerfully highlights is how the world—the monetized and commoditized world, to be specific—demands such responses from her. Is there not a correlation between her angst and money, as there is between her rage and patriarchal oppression? Given how emphatic she is in her insinuation that money is one of the major sources of her unhappiness, should we not look intently into that conjunction, examining what makes money figure in her imagination that way?

The relationship between money and affect/emotions has been explored equally compellingly in Akhtaruzzaman Elias's story "Kanna" as well—a story that ekes out a grieving father's emotional and material strife to illustrate how money is not only able to stir greed but also throttle emotions. What we are summoned to account for in it is not merely money's power within the capitalist system but also its protagonist's obsequiousness in front of this quintessential capitalist commodity that has the power to torment and torture him. In *Urukku*, money provokes unhappiness, while in "Kanna" money stifles emotions, coming between the subject and his loss. The agency of the commodity, which has a visceral presence in Elias's short story, tells the often-omitted story of the object's hegemonic presence in the subject's social universe, thus urging us to pay close attention to the object's mediation of the subject's interior conditions.

Written in 1994 and published in a posthumous collection titled *Jaal Shopno Shopner Jaal* [Dream's Trap, Trap's Dream], "Kanna's" story develops around the tragic experience of Afaz Ali, who, despite losing his elder son—who he sees as his only hope for escaping grueling poverty—is compelled to return to work, ignoring his personal loss. Although immensely aggrieved, he is unable to mourn for his lost son because the debt that he has accumulated to get his son a job constantly disrupts his mourning, forcing him to eventually vent his grief vicariously, through another figure.[1] On the surface, Afaz's hasty departure without conducting a proper *monajat*[1] to return to his workplace gives weight to the consideration that he is a *homo œconomicus*, an "economic man" and a "subject of interest" (Foucault 274) who prioritizes economic gain over personal losses. Ali, as we will see in the course of our discussion, is not a neoliberal subject because he is convinced that economic reason must at all times be prioritized, but rather, as the story implies, is a neoliberal subject because he lives in a society that demands from him a practical response at a moment when his life is shattered by tragedy. Money in Elias's story becomes the master-trope signifying the power of commodities in a world organized by the values and dictates of capitalism. Its objecthood notwithstanding, money has agency in the story, tormenting Ali, plunging him into further trauma and confusion.

The personhood of money and the objecthood of Ali, may appear a little odd when we try to account for the predicament of the *moulvi* using the insights afforded by governmentalist theories.[2] Yet, for anyone who is familiar with Marx's concept of commodity fetishism, this moment will be a familiar evocation, a reminder of the "socio-natural properties" of a commodity (*Capital I,* 165), the phenomenon that describes the process through which the object wrests control from its producer once it enters the market as a commodity. As an object that stands as a representation of all value forms—an object without which no commodity exchange can take place—money wields enormous power in an economic system like capitalism, which attaches more importance to the systematic production of commodities than to the active and living creative energy (labor) that produces them. As Marx's discussions on money make apparent, the reduction of the subject is built into the system of production of commodities itself and is not an aberration but rather a norm in such a productive system. It is this normative aspect of the capitalist system that we encounter when we read Elias's story. As this chapter will demonstrate through a detour through Marx's meditations on the money form, the monetary mediation of grief and emotions is not a mere coincidence but an illustration of the normative privilege it enjoys within the capitalist system. Ali's capitulation to money, especially his suppression of emotion and grief, attest to the agency of objects and commodities, while also illustrating the subjugation of the subject in the self-referential world of commodities. The story thus exists as a reminder of disrupting presence of the object in our heavily commoditized world, urging us to seriously factor in the object's power as we embark on a critique of neoliberalism.

Marx, Money, Capitalism

In many of his most familiar works, Marx describes money not only as a commodity facilitating exchange but also as a repository of wealth and power, an engine behind the global commodity production process. In *Economic and Philosophical Manuscripts of 1844*, preparatory notes that were discovered many years after Marx's death, the German revolutionary refers to money as "an object of eminent possession"—a universal mediator between "man's need and the object" (*Manuscripts* 136). In bourgeois society, money's power is unlimited because in it, unlike in societies where commodities were exchanged directly, commodity exchange faces no external barrier tied to utility. The "omnipotence" of money, Marx notes, comes not just from money's capacity for mediation but also from its power to give concrete appearance to "abstract" value. That the possessor of money can access anything that has exchange value testifies to money's privileged status among commodities. Yet, despite its status as the universal mediator, money itself is a confounding object whose essence contradicts its social appearance. Emphasizing money's capacity to "overturn" and "confound" the "individual" as well as "society," Marx points out that money's omnipotence engenders an "upside-down" world in which commodity becomes the mediator of all relationships (*Manuscripts* 139–40). Since money is not a mediator of any specific kind of object or quality but for everything that has the potential to be exchanged, money's purchasing power appears as the power of the individual who possesses it, who, with the help of money, can buy what s/he does not possess (*Manuscripts* 140). Although Marx's early awareness of money's unfettered power over human beings and other commodities allows us to construe as to how bourgeois society fetishizes money, the process through which money attains its "omnipotence" is only nebulously present in the pages of *Economic and Philosophic Manuscripts*. It is in his later works that Marx revisits the problem of the money form to account for its power in bourgeois society by expanding the idea of exchange value.

In both *Grundrisse* and *Capital Volume I*, we see Marx developing an analytical schema of money—a historical anatomy of sorts—through a detailed discussion of money's historical emergence and its contradiction. In both volumes, he carefully details how money attains its power and value, its fetishistic form. In *Grundrisse*, Marx's notes from 1858–59, which were compiled and published posthumously, money is given the kind of apposite philosophical attention it deserves, probing deeply into its social being. He begins the second part of his notes on money by suggesting that since exchange value forms the substance of money and exchange value is wealth, money too is the "embodied form of wealth" (*Grundrisse* 221). Yet—and this is where Marx differs from other prominent theorists of money, most notably from Ricardo (Brunhoff xiii)—he also reminds us that money is a mere representation, "the general representative of wealth" in bourgeois society (*Grundrisse* 221). On the one hand, money is the concrete manifestation of exchange value and wealth whose historical development can be traced at various moments in history and, on the other, it is a representation—an abstraction—whose material presence is underwritten by an immaterial social imagination specific to commodity-producing economic systems (*Grundrisse* 225–226; Harvey, *Seventeen Contradictions and the End of Capitalism* 26–27). Having identified money's historical contradiction in this manner, Marx then draws attention to money's fetishistic character—its sociality—which results in the reification of its owner, whose access to the world of commodities is mediated by money. Money does not spell out a specific relation to its owner; rather, its relation to its possessor remains vague and abstract, as amorphous the spectral process through which private labor is given social character through commodity production and exchange. As a general

"Kanna" and the Monetization of Affect **37**

medium for exchange, money grantsits possessor access to all the commodities s/he has not produced. In other words, the agency of the possessor of money is the agency of money itself; while money attains vitality and agency in a commodity-producing society, allowing its possessor limitless access to commodities, the owner of money loses his own agency and is subjected to money's power. This is how Marx puts it in *Grundrisse*:

> *Money, however, as the individual* of general wealth, as something emerging from circulation and representing the general quality, as a *merely social result*, does not at all presuppose an individual relation to its owner; possession of it is not the development of any particular essential aspect of its individuality; but rather possession of what lacks individuality, since this social [relation] exists at the same time as a sensuous, external object which can be mechanically seized, and lost in the same manner. Its relation to the individual thus appears as a purely accidental one; while this relation t o a thing having no connection to his individuality gives him, at the same time, by virtue of the thing's character, a general power over society, over the whole world of gratifications, labours, etc. ... The possession of money places me in exactly the same relationship towards wealth (social) as the philosophers' stone would towards the sciences. (*Grundrisse* 222)

This early meditation on the reifying power of money becomes the more elaborate and penetrating analysis of commodity fetish in Marx's finest work *Capital Vol. I: A Critique of Political Economy*. In its first chapter, he explains how commodity's sociality spawns a magical world where commodities socialize and interact with one another and living labor is abstracted and commodified so that commodity exchange can take place. The dual process whereby, on the one hand, the workers are reified through the abstraction of labor and, on the other, commodities are made social through the process of exchange is what Marx calls fetishism of the commodity (*Capital I*, 163–65). In the third chapter of the same work, Marx delves deeper into the realm of money's reifying capacity by stressing the idea that without the mediation of money, commodity production and exchange at a global scale would not have been possible. While other commodities are merely "particular equivalents for money," money itself is "their universal equivalent," and its relationship to other commodities is the relationship of a universal standard to a local/par-ticular form (*Capital I*, 184). It is not that money's preponderance among commodities brackets it out from other commodities; on the contrary, it allows money to emerge as the *de jure* representative of other commodities, a "reflection" of the "relations between all other commodities" (*Capital I*, 184). Hence, Marx's supposition that the "riddle of the money fetish is therefore the riddle of the commodity fetish" (*Capital I*, 187).

38 "Kanna" and the Monetization of Affect

The German revolutionary's conjecture about identical sources of fetishism should not lead us to conclude that Marx has failed to draw a line of distinction between the fetishism of money and the fetishism of commodities. In all his major works, specifically in his writings on political economy, Marx shows an extra-ordinary awareness about money's capacity for inciting greed and violence. All commodities (of which money is the most prominent example), Marx argues in the first chapter of *Capital*, bear the traces of violent erasure of concrete labor, i.e. the ironing out of the qualitative difference between one kind of labor and another, and the forceful imposition of quantitative homogeniety by normativizing different types of skills. Once entering the market as commodities, exchange values wipe out the traces of the specific kind of labor that has produced them and, instead of being controlled by human beings, start controlling them (*Capital I*, 167–68). Marx elaborately discusses the process through which commoditized societies turn workers into mere appendages of the tools they work with in a remarkably insightful chapter of the same book titled "Machinery and Large-Scale Industry." Nevertheless, unlike *Grundrisse*, where he singles out money for its capacity to drive people toward greed and injustice (*Grundrisse* 222–24), and where he contends that money form itself is the cause of such depravation, in *Capital Volume I*, Marx pays more attention to the inherent anomaly of the capitalist mode of production itself, thus leaning toward the position that the monetary economy under capitalism deflects capitalism's own unequal relation to labor, engendering constant crises, while also simultaneously generating a temporary equilibrium, only to produce new volatilities and crises (*Capital I*, 243–44). In other words, money under capitalism, not only mirrors capitalism's structural inequality (between labor and capital and between those who possess money/capital and those who do not) but also bespeaks its fundamental crises and convulsions, symptomally bearing the traces of capital's conditioning effects on its being.

An important corollary of Marx's theory of money is the idea that the historical trajectory of money predates the historical emergence of capitalism. On the face, this idea appears to imply that money operates differently under capitalism, that its monetary system has a different form and function under the capitalist mode of production. Yet, when one pays close attention to his discussion of the historical emergence of money, one comes to understand that what the German thinker is preoccupied with is not only history but also potentiality; in Marx's reckoning, capitalist economy is a money economy not only because "the precondition for bourgeois society" is the production of "exchange value, i.e. money" (*Grundrisse* 225) but also because money's full potential can only be materialized within a commodity producing [a] global system like capitalism (*Grundrisse* 227). This conjuncture properly explains why he describes money as "a social relation of production" (Qtd. in Brunhoff 20). Just as capital is a social relation held together by the contradiction between living

"Kanna" and the Monetization of Affect **39**

labor and dead labor, money too is a social relation underwritten by inequality and oppression. Marx's observation about money mirroring social relation has been further explored by a host of Marxist thinkers, most notably by Rosa Luxemburg, Prabhat Patnaik, and David Harvey, who maintain that money under capitalism exude the same class bias that the system is known to harbor. While Luxemburg convincingly argues that the worker is the mere possessor of money, for the commodity has a tendency to return to the class that through its control over economic system and the state, Patnaik and Harvey insist on noticing the propinquity of money to class power and violence.

In his insightful work *The Value of Money*, Prabhat Patnaik categorically refers to the systemic inequality residing at the heart of capitalist monetary economy by claiming that "[t]he stability of the value of money is based on the persistence" of the "unequal and oppressive" relations that underlie "a modern monetary economy" (*The Value* xvi). Equally conscious of money's ability to incite greed and violence, David Harvey writes the following in *Seventeen Contradictions and the End of Capitalism*:

> [T]he fact that money permits social power to be appropriated and exclusively utilized by private persons places money at the center of a wide range of noxious human behaviours—lust and greed for money power inevitably become central features in the body politic of capitalism … what is certain is that the rise of the money form and the capacity for its private appropriation has created a space for the proliferation of human behaviours that are anything but virtuous and noble. (*Seventeen Contradictions* 33)

Money's ability to incite "a wide range of noxious human behaviours," let us not forget, is not a property of money itself, but rather is an effect of the system that has been built around the idea of the primacy of capital over labor. In other words, money's ability to mediate wealth and commodity, and through them social relations as well, is not its own property; it has been vested such power by the capitalist system itself because the massive number of commodities that it produces requires the mediation of an object that can attest to those commodities' value on a global scale. Simply put, the power of money is the power of capital, although, as a commodity mediating value and exchange, it has always incited greed and violence, subjecting human beings to trauma and oppression. Money's ability to torment human beings, however, further illustrates how it can strip human beings of their "humanity," bestowing on them objecthood as the object attains the agency of the class that is in possession of money and capital. "Kanna" depicts this propensity of money by rendering the metaphorical attribute concrete. Let us now turn to the story to have a clear glimpse of its exploration of the relationship between Ali, his emotions, and money—a relationship that allows us to grasp the omnipotence of money in the era of neoliberal capitalism.

"Kanna" and the Monetization of Consciousness

"Kanna" begins with the scene of Afaz Ali conducting a *monajat*[3] for a recently deceased person. While reciting a verse from the Quran, he notices, "out of the corner of his eye,"[4] a man in a "green sweater and green-yellow checkered lungi," hanging about in the graveyard ("Kanna" 376). When Ali recognizes Monu Mian, he becomes bitter, thinking he has come all the way down from his native village to hound him for money. Afaz owes Mian's father 5,000 taka—a sum he has used bribing an officer who has promised his son a job. Noticing that Mian has intruded into his workplace, he gets ruffled, unable to focus on the prayer he is engaged in. He also makes a serious mistake, which dampens his mood even further. Instead of uttering the name of the deceased "Hayat Hosen Khan" in the *monajat*, he mistakenly blurts out his elder son Habibullah's name. Afaz is "embarrassed" for the obvious mistake, but what bothers him even more is the thought that the error may be a premonition in disguise, a hint of the danger that looms over his son's head ("Kanna" 378).

When Ali finally manages to talk to Monu Mian after *Asar*[5] prayer, the latter informs him that he must leave right away because Habibullah is down with *"daast,"* severe diarrhea. Ali shrugs off Mian's insistence, for diarrhea, in the late 20th century, is not the same terrifying epidemic it once used to be. He indignantly quips: "Have you come all the way down [from Krishnakathi] to give me the news of his diarrhea? Has the government built the hospital in Bakerganj for you guys to watch bioscope there?" ("Kanna" 383). Ali's frustration is as much the fruit of his inability to process the absurd possibility of losing his son to diarrhea, a non-threatening illness, as it is of his reluctance to leave his workplace right before the pick of the season. It is a derivative anger, emanating from a source that has very little to do with the person it is directed at. Underwriting this anger is the rural destitution that has drawn Ali out of his familiar community, imprisoning him in the city where he lives alone, without family. The trauma of displacement becomes evident when we zoom in on Ali's description of his own isolation. He compares his condition to "being buried alive in a graveyard" and hopes his son would help him escape this deathlike displacement[6] ("Kanna" 380). This brief moment—indicative of the story's narrative economy and precise diction—touches upon the *locus classicus* of urban to rural movement. As we will also see in the discussion about *The White Tiger* in the next chapter, rural unemployment, lack of infrastructure, and corruption all play pivotal roles in uprooting people from their communities. Elias's story chronicles the familiar tale of rural immiseration driving people out of their peripheral rural communities and amassing them in specific urban locations. It is here that Afaz Ali's story attains its allegorical character, representing as it does the global story of capital's

"Kanna" and the Monetization of Affect **41**

expropriation of cheap labor, as told through the antithesis of town and country.[7] What is unique about Ali's labor, however, is that its product is immaterial, affective. He has not traveled to the city to sell his labor power in a factory that produces commodities; his work involves caring for the dead, and thus providing the emotional support to the wealthy whose family members are buried in the graveyard. Although Ali's poverty is not directly discussed in the story, it is quite evident from the circumstances that what uprooted him from his community is material necessity, not a desire to outdo others.

When Mian convinces Ali to leave for his village home urgently, the latter reluctantly puts his work aside, hastily leaving for Krishnakathi, his birthplace. But when Ali is close to his village, a fellow villager informs them that Habibullah's burial has already taken place. The news of his son's death strikes Ali hard, leaving him speechless. As he gets on a rickshaw to grab a boat that will take him home, he sits there unmoving "looking blankly at the way forward" ("Kanna" 385–6). Although versed in prayers for the dead, he fails to utter a single word until at the end of his boat trip, when he suddenly starts muttering "*astagfirullah*" ["I ask Allah for forgiveness"], thinking of the punishment sinners receive inside their graves. When he reaches home, he is comforted by his father-in-law, who tells him that diarrhea has suddenly become an epidemic in "the south," claiming several lives. "The young new doctor" at the local hospital, who is treating several hundreds of people alone, is doing his best without saline and medicine ("Kanna" 386).

The chasm between the wealthy urban locations and destitute peripheral ones is more compellingly explored in the next episode of the story. When Ali goes to visit his son's grave in the local graveyard, he is so appalled by its condition that he "slightly stumbles" as he begins to recite from *the Quran.* "What a mess," he thinks to himself. "Don't Allah's holy words become dirty if one recites them in such an [unclean] place!" He likens the graveyard to a slaughterhouse, a dumping ground of dead animals. The repelling smells of "women's defecation," "unearthed body-parts," and "the medicinal odors of trees and plants" assault his senses with such vicious ferocity that his legs begin to wobble. Although he finishes reciting a section from the *Quran*, he comes back without finishing the *monajat*, without praying to Allah for his son's deliverance. While the odious smell plays a role, what also seems to have steered his decision to flee from the sordid burial ground is a bodily apprehension of his material destitution. Before abandoning his *monajat*, Ali feels on the skin of his neck the hot "breathing of Abdul Kuddus Howlader," from whom he has borrowed money ("Kanna" 387). The feeling of losing his only hope for freedom from his entrapment in the affluent people's graveyard leaves the story's protagonist so traumatized that he is unable to raise his hands up for prayer. The scene of Ali's perplexity and grief, further compounded by his

42 "Kanna" and the Monetization of Affect

realization that he may never escape the trap of credit, is described in the following manner:

> As soon as he clasps his hands together to pray for his dead son's deliverance, he feels the hot breathing of Abdul Kuddus Howlader on his neck. The thin skin of his thick neck gets singed. The path to pay back the borrowed sum in monthly instalments through his son's salary is now shut forever. How sad! His own son lent him no assistance. The salty sea breeze that comes from the river over the canal allows a thin cloud to develop in Ali's eyes. But Abdul Kuddus Howlader's breath-infused local breeze soaks it up. Since the moisture of his throat is also lost, he fails to petition for anything [to Allah] despite bringing his hands up. On his way back from the graveyard, even his blood begins to dry up. Still, in his cadaverous frame he gathers enough strength to begin a conversation with Monu Mian. But he fails to remember what he wanted to say. ("Kanna" 387)

This brilliant passage, where sensory apprehension, affect, and economic life all seem to intersect without clear separation, is a fine example of Elias's complex rendition of social realism. Without even drawing a parallel between the neatly arranged and flower-adorned graveyard of Dhaka, where Ali works ("Kanna" 377), and the "dumping ground of dead bodies," where his son is laid to rest ("Kanna" 386), the narrator of this story conjures up the topological disjuncture between the rural and the urban by masterfully manipulating sensory metaphors. The stacking up of visual, olfactory, somatosensory, and gustatory images in succession not only points toward the strong connection between feeling and emotion but also emphatically proclaims that there exists a double bind between the affective and the economic. The ventriloquism of the economic conditioning of affect can be effectively exhumed in the figurative singing of Ali's neck, metaphorically capturing the disrupting persistence of economic reality in daily life. In what seems like a straightforward moment of grief and olfactory disgust, the thing that constantly disrupts and defers Ali's ritualistic performance of grief—the *monajat* or the prayer for forgiveness to Allah—is the consideration that he has borrowed money from Mian's father and that he must now return this sum on his own, without any help from his son.

The relation between money and affect/emotion, which appears to be a recurring feature of this story, can, as well, be traced back to an earlier moment in the text. When Monu Mian first informs Ali about his son's health, when it first dawns on him that his son's life may be at risk, he is so distraught that he suddenly sits down on the "stone railing" of a grave. A thorn from a rose bush—a plant that his assistant has planted under his supervision—pricks his "thick" neck. The sensation on his skin reminds him of a time when the infant Habibullah sat there, giving him similar sensations in the same spot. It also seems to Ali as if the sharp corners of the borrowed 5,000 taka are pricking him in that spot. Physical pain, affect, and financial loss merge into one another, forcing us to reconsider the

"Kanna" and the Monetization of Affect **43**

social and economic conditionings of affect. This is how Elias's narrator discusses Ali's overlapping emotions and feelings:

> What has he [Monu Mian] seen? Is this why, few moments ago, during the *monajat* of the man buried in [grave] number 12345, Allah has made him ask for his son's deliverance in advance? Afaz Ali suddenly sits down on the wide and smooth stone railing of number 7769 and a thorn from a rose bush, which Sharif Mridha planted under his supervision, pricks his neck. His neck is thick, but his skin isn't, so the prick leads to pain. Simultaneously, this area of his body, where many years ago infant Habibullah sat and swung his legs, tickles. Just above that part of his neck scratch the notes making up 5000 takas—the amount he borrowed for bribing [the officer] for Habibullah's job. The prick of the rose thorn remains, but the swinging of Habibullah's small feet fades under the weight of money. ("Kanna" 383)

Although evocative of Ali's premonitory feeling about his son's death, this passage stops from naming his feeling before and after the prick. Ali's is a feeling that cannot be named.[8] It emerges out of his body, when subtle physical pain begins to transmute into memories of his son's childhood; the same bodily sensation alerts us about his financial loss, eventually harking back, once again, to the touch of his son's vanishing small feet. Touch plays an important role here. The prick of the rose thorn, the memory of the sensation of carrying infant Habibullah on his back, and the sharp touch of pointed corners of paper money—all seem to direct toward the multiplicity contained within a single bodily sensation. However, what is particularly impressive about this passage is its depiction of the primacy of economic reason over affective affinities in Afaz Ali's life—an idea that is subtly gestured toward by the vanishing feet of Habibullah, which get crushed under the weight of economic considerations.

The fading of the affective—bodily sensation resulting from memory and emotion—under the "weight" of material concern that recurs in the story is evocative of the cultural and economic transformation of Bangladesh. In *Khoabnama* (1997), Elias's epic novel, the epochal transformation of rural Bengal is expressed through the symbolic loss of *Khoabnama*—the book of dreams. From the custody of dreamers and mystics who have been the traditional keepers of the secret art, the book ends up in the possession of the emerging national bourgeoisie—a group predominantly comprised of entrepreneurs and landowners—in the aftermath of the partition of the subcontinent. The loss of the book of dream marks, on the one hand, the loss of rural and agrarian Bengal's control over its own destiny and, on the other, the consolidation of power in the hands of the nation's elites. What is also present in the schematization of this collective loss is a deep sense of tragedy derived from the betrayal of the nationalist bourgeoisie, who, having failed to bring in radical political and

44 "Kanna" and the Monetization of Affect

economic transformations, resort to violence and intrigue to cling on to their newfound power. The shadow of the present looms large over the novel's re-imagination of the past[9]: the treason of the bourgeoisie, which is one of the key themes in the novel, is as much a reimagination of the popular history of the *Tevaga* and the anticolonial independence movements as it is a projection of the contemporary predicament on a distant past. The disappointment of the post-Ershad neoliberal era, which marks another failure of nationalist politics in Bangladesh, casts a long shadow on this novel's imagination of history and temporality. The dialectical transaction between the present and the past—most notably present in *Khoabnama*'s depiction of past myths constantly informing and inspiring present moments of insurrection—enacts a circular vision of time where history is shown to repeat itself in another form. What also seems to repeat itself in Elias's fictions is the loss of revolutionary insurrection to petty bourgeois nationalist politics. In *Chilekothar Sepoy,* too, we notice the wily petty bourgeois nationalists derailing a revolutionary uprising by appropriating its rigor for their own benefit. In "Kanna," no thematic engagement with Bangladesh's long history of bourgeois treason can be traced; what remains as a residue of this long history is a ghastly shadow of rural destitution, which, much like the pervasive corruption that has now been fully internalized into the fabric of institutional culture, symptomatically represents the metamorphosis of the nation's economic life.

An equally important indication of how the imperative to earn money bears down on Ali's already afflicted mind appears before us when the bereaved father unceremoniously returns from his son's grave without performing the *monajat,* the culminating part of the prayer where the devotee raises his palms to God in supplication. After returning home, Ali learns that his wife, too, has contacted diarrhea. Instead of staying back and attending to his grieving and ailing wife, upon the insistence of his father-in-law he quickly returns to his workplace—the graveyard—to recover the losses for his missed days of work. This moment productively captures the utter antipathy with which Muslim-Bengali families treat women. The complete silence—except at the moment when Ali's grief-stricken wife lets out a loud heart-wrenching shriek—that the story imposes on her, signifies her expulsion from her own family's decision-making process. Neither Ali nor his father-in-law seem to care much about what she feels about his return to the city. What is simultaneously brought to attention in this segment is how Ali prioritizes financial considerations over his wife's health and over his own grief and loss.

It is possible to read Ali's hasty departure from his native village as a symptom of his capitulation to material pursuit. Given Ali's obsessive pursuit of money, we may even feel tempted to perceive him as an economic being—*homo œconomicus*—albeit such quick inferences may land us on a faulty premise when we weigh in on his other thoughts and actions, especially his desperation to leave the city. It is clear that the stubborn persistence of money in Ali's unconscious has

"Kanna" and the Monetization of Affect **45**

less to do with his personal craving for wealth than it has with a culture that fetishizes money, indeed worships it. On the one hand, money's mediating capacity in capitalist society comes to light, and, on the other, the objective world in which the *de rigueur* fetishization of money attains ubiquity begins to come into view. If Ali is constantly pricked or singed by money, it is not enough to point toward the various appearances of money in his consciousness to show how money's forms—paper and metal—reveal themselves in his memory and actions. That Ali is literally tortured and tormented by money—that he bleeds and burns by the figurative touch of money—also speaks powerfully about the violence of money in a society that fetishizes it and worships it. Here, in this symbolic apprehension, the shape of the monetized culture in which a rural Madrasa educated *moulvi* is first pierced and then burned attains a different connotative visage, affording money vitality, and making it appear as the master who can brand and torture its subjects at will. It needs to be pointed out that Elias's story does not present Ali as an overtly avaricious person, which rules out the possibility of reading this moment as the poor *moulvi*'s eager subjection to the lordship of money. Indeed, his anxiety about being trapped in the graveyard suggests the opposite, making apparent that he does not see money as an end in itself. He accepts commodity-infested urban life only begrudgingly, hoping his son will free him from his condition one day. It is his discontent, and not his acquiescence to go back to the city a day after his son's death, that awakens us to the possibility of reading "Kanna" as a critique of monetization. If we pay careful attention to the story's closure, we notice that what initially appears as a subjective condition (his monetized consciousness) is indeed a commentary on the objective condition in which both emotions and affect get buried under the weight of a commoditized world in which money constantly silences positive feelings and bodily reactions. Only when the totality is taken into account—the complete social whole against whose backdrop exchange takes place and things attain abstract value—does the complexly intertwined thread of the story's critique begins to reveal itself. "Kanna," then, appears as a critique of money's power and mediation, an apprehension of Ali's helplessness in the brutal monetized culture where he not only loses his son but also the agency to mourn for his child. To explore this idea further, I will now turn to Marx's theories on money, for here money's mediation of social power—its fetishistic existence in our capitalist society—come in full view.

Money and Reification: "Kanna" as a Critique of the Objective Condition

The money that pierces Afaz Ali's neckline and singes his thin skin is also the same commodity that binds him in a relationship of debt to Abdul Quddus Howladar—Monu Mian's father and a distant relative who lives in the

46 "Kanna" and the Monetization of Affect

neighboring village. It is not only the want of money that forces Ali to suppress his grief for his son; it is also his debt—that the fruit of his future labor is given over to others and that others can make a claim on his future earnings—that silences him when he tries to talk to Monu Mian about his uncertain future after losing his son. Yet, when we look into the world that lies outside Ali's emotional and financial struggles, it looks extra-ordinarily prosperous. Right at the beginning of the story, we are introduced to the "ash-colored smoke and slightly sweet fragrance of Indian incense sticks" ("Kanna" 376) that heighten the effects of Ali's emotional *monajat*. We are also told that the graves in the graveyard Ali works in are "entirely gilded in marble," "mosaicked," or "built using red ceramic bricks." Many of these graves have "borders of red Chinese grasses," while others have decorations of local and imported flowers ("Kanna" 377). While performing his *namaz*, Ali hears "the sweet sound of opening and closing of car doors" ("Kanna" 382). The car that has arrived has brought in people who would select the burial space for a "young man" whose father is "a very big officer in a foreign corporation" and whose relatives are flying in from "the US, Germany and Japan" to join the burial prayer ("Kanna" 382). The narrator also informs us about Ali's clients, whose medical treatments take place in "Bangkok" and "America" ("Kanna" 384). When Ali is about to leave for Dhaka after visiting his son's grave, his father-in-law gives him "1000 taka," asking him to return it quickly because that money is not his own. "Money," he tells Ali, is "flowing in from England and America, for the infidels have come to understand that there they cannot do without Islam" ("Kanna" 388). This last sentence is remarkable for its strategic use of irony, which simultaneously takes aim at the rigidity of institutionalized religion as well as the NGO-led aid politics in Bangladesh, which reached its apogee in the 1990s. It is against this backdrop of heightened economic activities and the influx of foreign commodities that the story invites us to account for Ali's loss. Its titular reference to grief—that the story's title "Kanna" refers to Ali's struggle to give ritualistic form to his loss by mourning in public for his dead son—puts under the microscope the objectifying process that turns emotion into a subjugated experience that cannot be made public without the mediation of culture and money.

The observation that I make in the last sentence about subjugation of Ali's affect demands further justification. In the last part of Elias' story, we find Afaz Ali desperately soliciting the responsibility of conducting the *monajat* for the dead son of the "big officer" whose ostentatious presence offered Ali's hope for financial recovery. However, when he begins his prayer, his language attains emotive doubleness, simultaneously whipping up the grief of the young man's father and channeling his own angst and grumble. As the convention demands, he begins by asserting the greatness of the Supreme Being whose actions cannot be disputed: "Allah, you have brought back your dear servant to you and we have no objection, no one has any objection, I have no objection" ("Kanna" 390). While the repetition of the word "objection" affirms the superiority of Allah over his[10] subjects, who must accept his actions without any questions, what is also at play here is Ali's rhetorical prowess, which, through repetition, has attained musicality and is geared toward stirring up emotions. Yet, the use of the word "objection" also raises the possibility of reading the prayer as a grieving father's disinclination to accept his loss as fate, as a divine intervention. The moment of seeking comfort for another, thus, becomes the instance of injecting subjective remonstration, inscribing within the ritualistic and objective expression of grief the burden of the insufferable subjective loss. Thus, as the prayer progresses, Ali's language becomes more acrimonious, incriminating:

> Do you love him so much that you didn't think of his parents even once? Allah the Merciful, did the river of your mercy go dry after showering its mercy on Shatab Kabir? ... [G]rant him heaven Allah. But, holy creator, didn't you get time to notice his father? Will he rund around the graveyard for the rest of his life? ("Kanna" 390–91)

As Ali voices out his complaints, not only does he lose his composure, weeping profusely and bringing in public his long-held gripe against the supreme creator, but he also loses his balance, almost falling face down, saving himself by holding on to a bamboo stake. The overlap between Ali's emotional outburst and his corporeal response calls for a deeper analysis of the relationship between affect and loss. Denied a proper material condition for expressing his grief—Ali's son, it needs to be mentioned once again, is buried in a graveyard that resembles a slaughterhouse and is too dirty for a sacred rite—Ali has to defer what is required of him by convention and training. Held back and temporarily abandoned, his ritualistic prayer can only be expressed through something else, some other figure. It is this mediation of another figure and medium, that allows us to read Ali's affect as a subjugated affect—a reified affect—which expresses corporeal emotion through a body that is not the subject's own.

I am suggesting, therefore, that we read the closure of the story as a further exploration of the power of money in the capitalist society. It is only when we apprehend capitalist society as monetized society that we can apprehend the symbolic significance of Elias's ventriloquized affect. After all, only in a monetized society will affect remain subjugated, unable to express itself without the mediation of an object. Affect's ventriloquism also speaks powerfully about class power, suggesting those who possess money have the ability to mediate and suppress the affect/emotion of those who do not. This allows us to relate the agency of the money form—the note and the coin, not to mention creditmoney—to the agency of the class that possesses it and is its custodian. Marxist thinker Rosa Luxemburg, in her monumental work *The Accumulation of Capital: A Contribution to the Economic Thoery of Imperialism* (), has explained the process

48 "Kanna" and the Monetization of Affect

through which money is made to return to the capitalst class through commodity circulation. In her reckoning, the worker has only temporary access to money and is forced to return it to the true possessors of the coveted commodity through commodity consumption. While discussing Marx's elaboration of the process of simple reproduction, which has been captured, in its most succinct form, through the deceptively simple equation of M-C-M′, Luxemburg notes the following:

> Since the whole social process of circulation is set in motion by the capitalists, who are in possession of both the means of production and the money necessary for the mediation of circulation, everything must end up in their hands once again after each circuit of social capital, and more precisely it must revert to each group of capitalists and each individual capitalist in proportion to the investment made by them. Money is held by workers only temporarily while it mediates the exchange of variable capital between its money-form and its natural form; in the hands of the capitalists it is the appearance-form of a part of their capital, and as such it must always return to them. (Luxemburg, *Complete Works* II 59)

For Luxemberg, then, money is not meant to be in the possession of the worker, for the capitalist system is built around the process that requires money to be concentrated in the custody of the ruling class that must have easy access to it. It is important to remind ourselves here that money that is advanced by the capitalist class through the purchase of labor power is not the real locomotive of the valorization process; nor is the capitalist class the rightful owner of all social wealth because it is not their labor that goes into producing commodities. Indeed, neither Marx nor Luxemburg leaves us with any confusion about the fact that labor is the real engine behind commodity production and the true source of all social wealth, including money. The money that remains in circulation is advanced for productive or individual consumption and is neither withdrawn from circulation nor put aside by the workers whose labor goes into the production of commodities. Instead, surplus value comes back to the capitalist class in money form, only to be advanced once again as capital. The structure of capitalist relations of production, therefore, remains fundamentally opposed to the enrichment of the working class;[11] capitalism's *raison d'être*, instead, is the transfer of almost all social wealth into the possession of the capitalist class. Hence, Luxemburg's observation that capital returns to the capitalist class in the money form after commodity's value is realized.

Money embodies this systemic inequality, reflecting the class bias of a productive system which rides on money (and through it other commodities as well) to torment and trivialize those who do not have it. Ali's stalled ritualistic grieving and vicarious mourning attains their critical tenor only if we take the entire social

"Kanna" and the Monetization of Affect **49**

process that lurks at the backdrop like a spectre. The story's constant evocation of the moulvi's lack of agency is perhaps a reminder that the true object of its critique is not just the state and its inequality, but also the entire social system where money exists as a perennial tormentor, a symbol of class power. It is not the object as such that Ali's subjugated affect critiques, but rather the wall of social inequality that is symbolically attached to the object that his unarticulated emotions complain about. Does he have any response to his objectification and subjugation? What does Ali do when he becomes vaguely aware of his destitution? Why does not he rebel? The concluding section of this chapter will specualte on the possible answers to these questions.

Conclusion

Ali's channeling of his grief through another figure and medium, therefore, needs to be comprehended not simply as a moment of agency and subversion but also as an apprehension of his reified affect, which, having found no direct outlet has now chosen to express its emotion through another body—the body of a corporate executive. If the pricking and singing of Ali's neck by money represents his reification in the form of debt, his derivative grief embodies his lost subjecthood within the social structure. This loss of subjecthood, in turn, affirms his objectification within the social schema where he exists only to perform someone else's prayer, where he is a mere tool for meeting social need for parceling out private grief and mourning. In a sense, his labor is always given over to someone else—someone who is positioned higher in the social ranks and is able to pay the right price for his service[12]—but the nature of his labor is immaterial as no material object is produced by it. To be more precise here, the object of his production is emotion/affect, and the use value of his labor-power does not take the form of producing something tangible but instead in his ability to move people emotionally through his compelling prayers. Just as the worker puts his labor-power into commodities, thus producing something of value, so Ali produces an emotionally charged *monajat*, where his affective labor attains reified form, assuming increasingly commodified form even as the social function of delivering *monajat* persists, almost by definition, as non-commodified labor. As such, the product of his labor bears all the symptoms of his alienation, as do other commodities where the labor of the worker exists in reified forms. It is in the reification process that one needs to locate the source of Ali's inability to mourn for his son publicly. The vicarious weeping that releases Ali's pent-up frustrations, therefore, is not a moment of freedom, but rather a further confirmation of his imprisonment in a social system that has chained him twice: first, by binding him in a relation of debt and, secondly, by subjugating his feeling and emotion to the dictates of the capital-relation. It is, then, of little surprise that Ali's complaint is directed toward a transcendental subject—his creator. Having found no

50 "Kanna" and the Monetization of Affect

worldly solution to his worldly problems—the loss of his son due to the inadequate medical facilities existing in the rural area and the loss of his wealth to a socially brokered network of corruption—Ali chooses to blame the creator for his misfortune, thus transferring a worldly problem to the custody of a transcendental being. That the bereaved father, despite being tormented by material concerns, decides not to question the existing social relations that are responsible for his suffering but seeks justice from his creator, may appear to imply defeatism but that he takes issues with his creator for subjecting him to loss and poverty is indicative of his defiance as well. His complaint against his creator, therefore, should not be taken literally, as if having lost his belief in the transcendental being, he has willingly surrendered himself to the dictates of money. Rather, it should be seen as his total rejection of the monetized world that has failed and incarcerated him, binding him to the same distant graveyard he wishes to escape. But he has also come to realize that no supreme being will come to rescue him from his present predicament either. Ali's radicalism lies in his rejection of both: that he holds strongly to the idea the solution of this world's problems cannot be transferred to the norms and dictates of another world. It is here that his realism comes into full view—a realism that veers toward materialism but is also steeped in utopianism, seeking a respite from the tormenting world of money.

It is difficult to understand a complex figure like Afaz Ali by using a simplistic and totalizing concept like *homo œconomicus*—a subject whose sole purpose in life is to financialize the self by becoming "human capital" (*Undoing* 33). Ali, I have already pointed out in the previous chapter, cannot fit into such a category because he is at once inside and outside such norms: the rural *moulvi*'s subjectivity points toward his vague awareness of the necessity of earning money at all costs, while also faintly pointing toward his discontent against the processes of monetization and objectification. It is not like entrepreneuriality is unavailable to him. Indeed, the story presents a number of other characters who seem to have internalized the entrepreneurial culture that has begun to take hold on people of his profession. But the story does not tell us clearly why he chooses not to be like his father-in-law and fellow *moulvi* Haider Boksh—both of whom use their religious education to their advantage. One needs to look outside Ali's consciousness—the outside world whose culture is changing, where a precipitous consumerist culture has begun to germinate, and where the power of money has begun to torment those who do not possess it—and connect it to his complex subjecthood to apprehend what is transpiring in his world.

To conclude, let us remember that "Kanna" was among the last published works of Akhtaruzzaman Elias. Only two more fictional works were completed after this story—a short story titled "Jaal Shopno Shopner Jaal" and an epic novel titled *Khoabnama*, a novel that has been mentioned before, a novel that is considered by many including Mahasweta Devi as one of the greatest novels written in Bengali language. Published in 1996, a year before his death, this novel marks the summit

"Kanna" and the Monetization of Affect **51**

of Elias' substantive creative corpus. These three works, which were all written the 1990s, are notable for their pessimistic tenor and stylistic ingenuity. Although the early 1990s in Bangladeshi history was marked by the optimism of being able to break from the yoke of military dictatorship that had been the feature of Bangladeshi life for about fifteen years, no sign of that positive historical turn can be traced in Elias' late work. Instead, we encounter in them a somber glum about the return of the same putrid bourgeois politics that has plagued the Bangladeshi nation all through its history. "Jaal Shopno Shopner Jaal" engages with the collective heartbreak of having to witness the rise of the defeated Islamist collaborators who once aided Pakistani army's genocide in Bangladesh. *Koabnama,* on the other hand, digs deep into the history of Bengal to locate another moment of disappointment—The Tevaga Movement—which initially brought hope for rural farmworkers and sharecroppers but lost steam as the loud trumpet of the national independence movement of 1947 drowned out the muffled drumbeat of the peasant rebellion. The treason of the nationalist bourgeois remains the overlapping theme in both of these late works. It is only in "Kanna" that one finds no such overt political overtones; what the reader encounters in it, instead, is a façade of loss and mourning, a compelling exploration of subjective loss. But, as we have seen in the course of our earlier discussions, Afaz Ali's private grief is merely a gateway to a broader political reorganization of society and culture. Despite their differences, however, all three of these works are powerful repudiations of not only their own moment of origin, the epoch of neoliberal transformation, but also of the long capitalist century, which ushered in hope only to crush it afterwards.

Besides grief and loss, another important theme that "Kanna" touches upon is the theme of spatial unevenness—an element of the story that this chapter has only superficially gestured towards. Yet, the theme of ghettoization of both the rural and the urban, combined with an urban exodus, is perhaps the most pervasive image of neoliberal reorganization of space and geography and, as such, demands attentive examination, not least because the uneven relation between labor and capital—the foundational contradiction of capitalism—maps on to the surface of the production of space under capital. One can see an echo of such spatial inequality in the episode of Ali's return to his native village, where his ritualistic visit to his son's grave invokes in him a comparison between the hapless condition in which his son is laid to rest and the ordered graves of the upscale graveyard where he himself works. This moment of apprehension of spatial difference is extremely important because what has been evocatively explored through it is not simply uneven development as such but the very structure of production of space which is reflected in this spatial inequality. In the next chapter, we will examine how the uneven geographical map of neoliberal India has been satirized in Adiga's *The White Tiger* and how the novel's protagonist's cognitive mapping of space itself is informed by a neoliberal schematization of the relation between the urban and the rural.

Notes

1 A *monajat* is an imploration to Allah for forgiveness and blissful after-life in heaven. It is customary for Muslims to raise their hands after prayers and ask for forgiveness for themselves and others in the family and community.

2 In her study of the relation between sensory experiences and the economic relations in *A Political Economy of the Senses*, Anita Chari mentions that theories of radical democracy, the kind that has been advanced by Ernesto Laclau, Chantal Mouffe, and others, are unable to account for fetishism. I feel, the idea can be applied to the theories of governmentality and biopolitics as well. Too eager to explain the society and subjects through the lens of juridical formations and the social production and control of the body, such theories often fail to note that the juridical subject is also a subject of sensory experiences, affected by and affecting the material world that such subjects are surrounded by.

3 In Bangladesh, post-burial *monajat* is often emotional and elaborate. The *moulvi* who conducts a *monajat* is often praised for elaborate and ornamental use of language that evokes both empathy and pathos.

4 My translation. All the translations from Elias's story, henceforth, are my translations.

5 Muslims are instructed by the Quran to pray five times a day: at daybreak, at noon, in the afternoon, in the evening, and late in the evening. *Asar* is the afternoon prayer.

6 The actual sentence in Bengali is far more revealing than what I have been able to come up with in my translation. It clearly states that Ali's son is the vehicle for his future freedom; it is through his son that Ali is planning to escape his imprisonment in the graveyard where he is "buried alive." Such an emphasis clearly states that Ali's inclination is not to advance his career further but to retire from work and return to his rural domicile where his family is stationed. Here is the literal translation of what he actually says in Bengali: "Not suggesting that my son needs to have B.A. or M. A. degrees: even if he manages to get a small job somewhere after passing his I. A., I can free myself from this graveyard where I am buried alive." ("Kanna" 380).

7 In *Capital Vol. I*, Marx draws attention to the separation of town from the country as one of the pivotal moments in the historical development of capitalism. The importance attached to the division between town and the country is demonstrated by the use of the phrase "summed up," implying how this feature remains a fundamental condition not only under capitalism but also in the "economic history" of society in general. Marx writes: The foundation of every division of labor which has attained a certain degree of development, and has been brought about by the exchange of commodities, is the separation of town from country. One might well say that the whole economic history of society is summed up in the movement of this antithesis. (472)

8 Although Michael Hardt, following Spinoza, has described affect as "corporeal reason" (x), which involves both "the body and the mind" as well as "reason and passions" (ix), Fredric Jameson is more interested in positioning affect against language and "named emotions" (*The Antinomies of Realism* 29) suggesting that named emotions and affect are binary opposites (31). "[A]ffects," Jameson adds, "are bodily feelings, whereas emotions are ... conscious states" (32). In this essay, I use the word "affect" in the Jamesonian sense to refer to bodily feelings that elude language and nomenclature.

9 The allegorical value of the loss of the book of dreams to an entrepreneurial national bourgeoisie cannot be overstated, for to read the history of *Tevaga* as a lost opportunity to cease upon the reappearance of an event—to borrow Pothik Ghosh's concept from "Akhtaruzzaman Elias: Beyond the Lived Time of Nationhood"—which gets stolen by an opportunistic bourgeoisie is to set up a parallel between the past and the present in which the past is asked to bear the temporal/historical burden of the present. What *Khoabnama* simultaneously stages are the stories of capitalist system's sublation of rural

"Kanna" and the Monetization of Affect **53**

life and institutions into its capacious universe. The agrarian culture and economy which held back farmers and rural artisans now must set them free for absorption in the newly independent Pakistan state's burgeoning private enterprises. If *Khoabnama* is an allegory of the neoliberal present, it is not so because it enacts a relation between the past and the present; rather, what casts this novel in the mold of an allegory is the precise manner in which it gazes at the past, recreating a world that looks much like the one Bangladesh has experienced at various moments of its history.

10 In Muslim cultures, "Allah" stands as a proper name for the supreme creator who has no material form or gender. My use of the masculine form is a subjective imposition that has emerged out of the necessity to translate a non-gendered expression into a gendered one.

11 Indeed, one of the richest discussions about this topic comes in *Capital Volume I*, where Marx writes the following: What flows back to the worker in the shape of wages is a portion of the product he himself continually reproduces. The capitalist, it is true, pays him the value of the commodity in money, but this money is merely the transmuted form of the product of his labor. While he is converting a portion of the means of production into products, a portion of his former product is being turned into money. It is his labor of last week, or last year, that pays for his labor-power this week or this year. The illusion created by the money-form vanishes immediately if, instead of taking a single capitalist and a single worker, we take the whole capitalist class and the whole working class. The capitalist class is constantly giving to the working class drafts, in the form of money, on a portion of the product produced by the latter and appropriated by the former. The workers give back these drafts back just as constantly to the capitalist class, and thereby withdraw from the latter their allotted share of their own product. The transaction is veiled by the commodity form of the product and the money form of the commodity. Variable capital is therefore only a particular historical form of the appearance of the fund for providing the means of subsistence, or the labor fund, which the worker requires for his own maintenance and reproduction, and which, in all systems of social production, he must himself reproduce. If the labor-fund constantly flows to him in the form of money that pays for his labor, it is because his own product constantly moves away from him in the form of capital. But this form of appearance of the labor-fund makes no difference to the fact that it is the worker's own objectified labor which is advanced to him by the capitalist. (712–13)

12 It would be interesting to return to Marx once again to understand how the great German thinker saw the production of commodities and the production of the worker as an essentially connected process. In one of his most insightful passages in *Capital Volume I*, Marx writes that the capitalist production process itself "reproduces and perpetuates" the conditions that make the exploitation of the worker possible. Even before "the economic bondage" tosses the worker into the mix of commodities to be sold in the market, the social conditions turn his labor power into "a means by which another man can purchase him." It is because of this that capitalist production is not simply the production of commodities and the capitalist class; it is also simultaneously the production of the worker whose labor must be sold over and over to those who own capital (money). Here is how Marx puts it: Capitalist production therefore reproduces in the course of its own process the separation between labor-power and the conditions of labor. It thereby reproduces and perpetuates the conditions under which the worker is exploited. It incessantly forces him to sell his labor-power in order to live, and enables the capitalist purchase labor-power in order that he may enrich himself. It is no longer a mere accident that capitalist and worker confront each other on the market as buyer and seller. It is the alternating rhythm of the process itself which throws the worker back onto the market again and again as a seller of his

54 "Kanna" and the Monetization of Affect

labor-power and continually transforms his own product into a means by which another man can purchase him. In reality, the worker belongs to capital before he has sold himself to the capitalist. His economic bondage is at once mediated through, and concealed by the periodic renewal of the act by which he sells himself, his change of masters, and the oscillations in the market-price of his labor. The capitalist process of production, therefore, seen as a total connected process, i.e. a process of reproduction, produces not only commodities, not only surplus-value, but it also produces and reproduces the capital-relation itself; on the one hand the capitalist, on the other the wage laborer" (723–24).

3

THE WHITE TIGER AND THE SUBSUMPTION OF THE RURAL

Introduction

There is an intriguing passage in the penultimate chapter of Aravind Adiga's Booker winning novel *The White Tiger* (henceforth *TWT*)—a passage that conjures up the image not only of a divided city but also of a divided country (and as I will make clear in the course of this discussion, of a divided world market as well). Balram, the narrator of the novel, takes leave from his employer one Sunday morning to explore Delhi's G. B. Road, where the city's famous "red-light district" is located (*TWT* 215). Exasperated by the suggestive remark of a *paan*-seller who asks him to have a *paan* to overcome his sexual nervousness, Balram charges into him and is subsequently chased out of the premise by pimps and street-vendors. He starts aimlessly wandering around the streets of Old Delhi, where he observes a slew of objects and people who, to him, seem like things belonging to an old and lost world, oblivious to the changes taking place around them. He notices heaps of old books and practitioners of old trades and professions. With his characteristic sarcasm, Balram remarks that Delhi is the capital of not one but two different countries, severed from one another by a wealth gap. New Delhi, with its affluent suburbs and shiny shopping malls, belongs to the India of light, whereas Old Delhi, with its stone buildings and lugubrious inhabitants, belongs to the India of darkness. Here is how Balram unpacks his feelings about the divided cityscape:

> Delhi is the capital of not one but two countries—two Indias. The light and the Darkness both flow into Delhi. Gurgaon, where Mr. Ashok lived, is the bright modern end of the city, and this place, Old Delhi, is the other end. Full

DOI: 10.4324/9781003324768-3

56 *The White Tiger* and the Subsumption of the Rural

of things the modern world forgot all about—rickshaws, old stone buildings, the Muslims. (*TWT* 215)

The cataloguing of forgotten objects (and also people) in the passage is evocative but not entirely unexpected. What it conjures up is the image of the spatiotemporal distance between Old and New Delhi, made conspicuous by its juxtaposition of rickshaws and Muslims. Gurgaon, the suburb where the narrator's employer Ashok lives, is a place of "bright modern" buildings and global brands, whereas Old Delhi is a dumping yard where the objects and people that the "modern world" has forgotten about exist in anachronistic anomaly. The chasm between the two spaces is pronounced, marked by the presence and absence of modernity. This passage also alludes to an earlier observation by Balram in the very first chapter of the novel, where he proclaims that India is not a single country but "two countries in one" held together by the "India of Light" and the "India of Darkness" (*TWT* 12). In his remarks about Delhi, Balram re-invokes this spatial dichotomy not simply to assert the similitude between the city and the nation—both ruptured and irreparably divided—but also to register a difference existing within these divided spaces, a temporal lag taking the appearance of uneven geographical relation. Gurgaon, where Balram's employer Ashok lives, is new ("modern") and affluent ("bright"), whereas Old Delhi, from which he is chased out, is corruptible and anachronistic, reeking of poverty and outmodedness.

In "Neoliberalism and Allegory," Betty Joseph offers to read the novel's tropological evocation of the relation between "light" and "darkness" as a metonymic representation of the unequal relationship between the neoliberal cosmopolitan India and the nation's agrarian and semi-feudal rural. Adiga's novel, for her, is a satire that allegorizes the vicissitudes of India's neoliberal makeover. The narrative of "two Indias" that Adiga's protagonist gloats about is indeed a parody of the rhetoric of divided India advertised by multinational corporations and right-wing nationalist parties such as BJP (Joseph 74). Referring to a full-page advertisement run on the front page of *The Times of India*—a leading national daily—Joseph suggests that such narratives function by simultaneously undermining welfare state policies and by valorizing neoliberal economic reforms (Joseph 72). The anthem of suburban progress and rural/inner-city backwardness, she contends, is a rhetorical strategy of neoliberalism, which it deploys not simply to postulate the idea of the superiority of the suburban over the rural/inner but also to denigrate the less-commoditized locations existing in the nation. In Adiga's novel, then, the fractured map of "two Indias" is brought forth to satirize the neoliberal remapping of space where the rural (and the urban ghetto as well) is often slotted into the category of "undeveloped" and "feudal," and the gentrified suburban/urban is enshrined as "developed" and "postmodern."

The substance of Joseph's sympathetic reading of Adiga's representation of spatial relations in *TWT*, however, has been questioned and critiqued by a host of other Indian scholars, most notably by Amitava Kumar, Mrinalini Chakravorty, Snehal Shingavi, Amardeep Singh, and Swaralipi Nandi, who have expressed their reservations against the novel's representation of the rural. Kumar has accused the novel of misrepresenting Bihar, excoriating it for failing to note the linguistic and cultural nuances of the rural subaltern existence. In the third chapter of her book *In Stereotype: South Asia in the Global Literary Imaginary* (2014), Chakravorty, likewise, has questioned its representation of the urban underclass, calling it, following Munro, a "poverty porn" (Chakravorty 91). Shingavi, too, has echoed the same sentiment, critiquing *TWT* for "slumming" and playing "con-games" (Shingavi 3–4). Adiga's novel, he remarks, takes the attention away from the real issues surrounding caste and class by speaking through a narrator who is neither the worst victim of caste oppression nor a believer in radical class politics. Balram's "euphoria about having arrived at a post-casteist society," Shingavi tells us, "is a marker of reaction and not a call to radical redistribution of the social provision" (Shingavi 14).

In her thorough examination of *TWT* in "Narrative Ambiguity and The Neoliberal *Bildungsroman* in Aravind Adiga's *The White Tiger*," Nandi disputes Joseph's conclusion that the novel is a critique of neoliberalism. For the former, the critical overtone of the novel is underwritten by a less cynical optimism—one that can be exhumed only if we read it as a *bildungsroman*, a narrative of its protagonist's growth and education. One has to notice how Balram's voice "swings" between "self-parody" and "serious testimony" to fathom how his narrative is a rejection of his "oppressed, pre-capitalist" subjectivity and is an enthusiastic affirmation of "emerging neoliberal" subjectivity (Nandi 279). In the first part of the novel, before Balram kills Ashok, the former is filled with "filial sympathy" for the poor, expressing his scorn for the state that has failed them (Nandi 285), whereas in the latter part, once he has emerged as an entrepreneur, he seeks to replace the failed paternalistic welfare state by the paternality of the market, becoming an enthusiastic supporter of market-oriented education (Nandi 296–7). While the focus on paternalistic expectation permits Nandi to expose the gender norms that operate through political ideologies and institutions, demonstrating how, at its very core, *TWT*'s protagonist remains trapped in the fantasy of replacing one kind of paternalism by another, the insistence on prying into the narrator's utopia affords her a handle on the novel's concealed ideological anchorage in neoliberalism. However, since she reads the novel through the arc of subjective development, the conclusion that she draws from it remains narrow, only devoted to the figuration of the novel's protagonist's personal growth and his transition from one productive sytem to another. The real object of Nandi's critique is the novel (and its author), whereas the true target of Joseph's critique is the systemic inequality that is lampooned in Adiga's novel—an assumption that leads her to read it as a neoliberal allegory.

58 *The White Tiger* and the Subsumption of the Rural

It is imperative that we recognize the significance Nandi's proposition, taking note of her critique of the novel's tacit endorsement of paternalistic impositions, but it is also important that we bear in mind that by insisting on reading *TWT* as a *bildungsroman* she circumvents its unmistakably parodic and critical tenor, reducing the novel's schizoid movement between satire and pastiche. Although Adiga's novel has been taken to task[1] by some critics for its failure to represent the complexity of Indian reality, it still remains, till today, one of the most significant literary explorations of the nation in the new century, not because it is a parody of the new India but because, underneath its simplistic and synoptic retelling of Indian history, *TWT* carries a nuanced understanding of the nation's tanglement in global history. Some of the criticisms levelled against it, especially the ones advanced by Sarah Brouillette, Shingavi, and Nandi, are substantive and important because they help us understand how it fans the market demand for particular types of cultural stereotypes. However, it is also important to note that when read as an allegory, *TWT* is able to yield unexpected rewards—the kind that can be used to understand the processes of capital, to observe how caste and class operate in some of the most immiserated parts of India. One can also argue that it is also possible to draw similar lessons from other anglophone novels as well, specifically from Rohington Mistri's brilliant work *A Fine Balance* (1995), Arundhati Roy's compelling narratives *God of Small Things* (1999) and *The Ministry of Utmost Happiness* (2017), and Neel Mukherjee's relentless exploration of rural and urban poverty in *A State of Freedom* (2017). It would be difficult to dispute such claims. Indeed, the works mentioned above do a far better job at giving insight into the reality of India's caste-class double bind, at making the eviscerating experience of caste oppression and grueling poverty available to the global readership. However, what makes *TWT* truly challenging is that, unlike these other works that are unequivocal when it comes to their critique of caste and class oppression, it does not take up on those issues directly. Its parodic form and unconventional narration render any definitive commentary on caste-class relationship equivocal, subject to possibility but also potentially off-target.

Although it is still important to be attentive to the aforementioned critics' conjecture about *TWT*'s anchorage in neoliberal ideology and postmodern aesthetic values, this chapter will not lend itself to the task of forging similar critiques of it. Rather, this chapter will pivot on the presenation of the relation between the nation and the global capitalist system, hypothesizing how its narrativization of its narrator's entrepreneurial rise allegorizes the nation's annexation into an integrated world market. Given how the novel casts light on the divided nation, it will be productive to look into the existing debates about spatial relations to see how *TWT*'s cognitive mapping of the city and the country as divided spaces offer a glimpse into the pulsting heart of capitalism's production of space. This chapter will also take a detour through Marx's meditations on subsumption, partly to address the tendency among some postcolonial scholars to conjecture about coexisting modes of productions. In what follows, this chapter will first cast a close look into the debates about the production of space under capitalism and then discuss how the temporalization of space function fetishistically, undermining, on the one hand, utopian imaginations and embalming, on the other, the deeply inflected wounds of class exploitation.

A Primer into Uneven Spatial Relations

The idea that *TWT* is a critique of feudalism and socialism—the precise proviso of Nandi's argument about Adiga's work—owes its origin to the presupposition that India is a confusing coagulation of modernist and pre-modernist economic practices and cultural habits, and its internalization of modernity is incomplete and partial. In *Provincializing Europe (2000)*, historian Dipesh Chakrabarty has criticized the tendency to characterize India this way, as if its different historical moments exist in permanent contradiction, "telescoped into" a single temporal conjuncture (*Provincializing* 49). For the Subaltern historian, however, the real issue is not so much the homogenization of history but the failure of the British Marxist historian E. P. Thompson to account for historical difference in his seminal essay, "Time, Work-Discipline and Industrial Capitalism" where he hypothsizes that the worker belonging to advanced capitalist countries sheds pre-capitalist habits of work and internalize "work-discipline" as capitalism becomes dominant. "The same fate," Chakrabarty writes, "awaits the worker in the third world," because Thompson speculates that industrial work-discipline will arrive in the "developing world" too (*Provincializing* 48). It may appear, as though, Chakrabarty's ulterior motive is to draw attention to the limits of Thompson's broad observation about history which casts the worker from every part of the globe in the same teleological path. Yet, if one dives deep into the subaltern historian's main tenet, one will be able to locate that his real object of critique is not the British historian per se but the entire doctrine of Marxist thought that considers capitalism a "social whole," a totality with its own unique history. Already convinced that "histories posited by capital," are unable to totalize "histories that do not belong to capital's life process" (*Provincializing* 50), Chakrabarty emphatically claims that "[no] historical form of capital, however global its reach, can ever be a universal" (70). Its semantic erudition notwithstanding, his proposition that there is a difference between global reach and universal reach offers little substantive discussion about universality as such and fails to explain why a pervasive mode of production like capitalism needs to be seen as anything other than a social whole. If it is not, is there any other competing mode of production that is currently in existence and can offer astute resistance to capitalism? Paradoxical though it may appear, Chakrabarty's notion of historical difference shares a strange semblance with Nandi's assumption about co-existing modes of productions: they both reject the notion of totality and contest the idea of subsumption. Before an argument is

60 *The White Tiger* and the Subsumption of the Rural

advanced as to how the novel testifies to the subsumption of India's rural under the logic of capital, let us turn to Marx for an insight into his elaboration of the idea of subsumption.

Theorists of uneven development, thinkers such as Immanuel Wallerstein, Andre Gunder Frank, Samir Amin, and others, have long argued that capitalism annexes other modes of productions as it becomes dominant. From the perspective of world-systems theory, the thesis of coexisting productive systems appears flawed,[2] although different thinkers belonging to the trandition imagine the broader capitalist history differently. It is generally believed that the creation of a world market is established on the foundation of subsumption of pre-capitalist relations of production under the capitalist one, a proposition that Chakrabarty disputes in the second chapter of *Provincializing Europe*. As capitalism looks to expand globally, it is argued, it brings within its orbit all pre-existing relations of production that it encounters as barriers to be overcome. In *Grundrisse,* Marx observes that capital posits every limit—external as well as internal—as "a barrier" and tries to go "beyond" it (*Grundrisse* 410). In other words, capitalism expands by subsuming all that appears non-capitalist to it and by internalizing what exists outside its already expanding horizon. Elaborating how capitalism fundamentally alters "old ways of life" so as to construct the condition for "the development of the forces of production" (*Grundrisse* 410), Marx asserts that "the tendency to create the *world market* is directly given in the concept of capital itself" (*Grundrisse* 408). This idea of capital's tendency to totalize what exists outside its orbit can be noticed in the writings from his youth as well, especially in *The Communist Manifesto*, where, in a powerful passage, he asserts that capitalism "creates a world after its own image" by battering down the walls of resistance (*Manifesto* 11).

Marx, of course, does not imagine annexation of the preceding mode of productions to be a linear and transparent process, let alone as one without contestation. He sees capitalism as a complex historical unfolding that meets resistance everywhere as it expands and takes over institutions. He also notes how, by taking over feudal relations of production, capitalism subsumes labor under capital initially formally, without ideological and technological transformation, and then, materially, by developing institutions and technologies that are capitalist in their very constitution. In his *Economic Manuscripts of 1861–1863*, notes which later contributed to the creation of *Capital Volume I*, Marx writes that at the beginning of capital's formation it "takes under its control" existing labor processes without fundamentally altering them. He calls this process of taking hold of the feudal institutions the "formal subsumption of the labor process" (*MECW 30,* 93). In the course of its further development, however, capital "not only formally subsumes [sic] the labor process but transforms it," which gives the mode of production "a new shape" and creates a "mode of production peculiar to it" (*MECW* 92). The shaping of the labor process that is peculiar to capitalism

The White Tiger and the Subsumption of the Rural   61

alone is what the German thinker describes as the real subsumption of labor under capital. To be precise, the real subsumption of capitalism presupposes not only the subordination of labor under capital but also the reshaping of labor—the kind that reflects the vitality and essence of capital. Although the idea of subsumption is nebulous to a degree, it is not difficult to understand that formal subsumption relates to the processes of reshaping the relationship between labor and capital through the juridical, political, and cultural institutions inherited from the feudal era, whereas the real subsumption corresponds to capitalism's hegemonic stage, when it has already altered the foundation of social relations, exerting its power through its own institutions—the state, the judiciary, the education sector, the cultural institutions, and so on—mirroring labor's subjugation under capital.

In what is sometimes referred to as the "missing sixth chapter" of *Capital Volume I*,[3] the German revolutionary proceeds further, explaining how the real subsumption gradually unfurls with the metamorphosis of the merchant capitalist into "an industrial capitalist," and the transfer of feudal institutions into bourgeois hands. He notes:

> [The] real subsumption of labour under capital, i.e. capitalist production proper, begins only when capital sums of a certain magnitude have directly taken over control of production, either the merchant turns into an industrial capitalist, or because larger industrial capitalists have established themselves on the basis of formal subsumption. (*Capital I* 1027)

It is noteworthy that real subsumption is described here as the "capitalist production proper," the production system that is, in form and content, properly capitalist. Marx notices that it can happen in a number of ways, especially through the process of the metamorphosis of the capitalist class (which in turn means the metamorphosis of capital as well) and through the accumulation of political and juridical power—through the transformation of existing legal and political institutions (expressed here as the larger industrialists establishing themselves through formal subsumption). Although the general features of the formal subsumption remain throughout the history of the mode of production, "irrespective of its technological development" (*Capital Volume* 1034), real subsumption begins to emerge only when institutional and technological changes have solidified enough to fundamentally alter the labor process that existed in another form before (*Capital Volume* 1035). Formal subsumption, thus, exemplifies the more general condition of labor's subordination to capital, whereas real subsumption implies both technological and institutional conditioning, which accords capital the power to extract surplus value in all possible forms and modalities, specifically by extending beyond "absolute surplus-value." It is because of this reason that Marx attaches real subsumption to the extraction of relative surplus-value, suggesting capitalist extraction of surplus-value enters a more

62 *The White Tiger* and the Subsumption of the Rural

complex and pervasive phase with the emergence of real subsumption. For Marx, the change that is required for ushering in the real subsumption is nothing short of a revolution in the mode of production; the advent of real subsumption means capitalist production has established itself as the "*sui generis*" mode of production and its ascendency has been established beyond any doubt (*CapitalI* 1035).

It is important to note that, the transformation of the juridical laws and institutions, that some historians of the 18th-century, including Foucault, identify as the moment of emergence of the biopolitical state, is indeed inextricably linked to the bourgeoise takeover of the political institutions. In their typical fetishistic fashion, these historians attribute the transformation in the socio-economic to a political-juridical revolution, relegating a radical transformation in the production relations to an epiphenomenon corresponding to reorganizations of the legal and political institutions. If anything, the transformation in the laws and institutions work symptomatically, implying a deeper transformation in life and society. In many ways, Marx's discussions about formal and real subsumptions allow us to understand the gradual morphing of society, the contradictory processes through which the dominant production systems (along with relations of production) of the past come under the control of the hegemonic production system of the present moment, and how the new legal, political and cultural processes deflect the changes taking place in the production system.

Based, therefore, on Marx's discussions of capitalist subsumptions, is it possible to answer the question whether India's rural economy—the economic system in which Balram grows—is feudalist in character? If we take formal subsumption of labor under capital as the starting point of capitalist subsumption proper, then we must conclude that feudalism in India is history, for we do not encounter labor-capital relations in a feudal form in contemporary India; what we notice, instead, is how, even where the agricultural sector appears feudal, it has come under the norms of money and wage labor—both symptoms of the capitalist takeover of the rural economy. Indeed, the persistence of the pre-capitalist norms and practices resemble more to the existence of the "residual culture" than to a separate mode of production; if anything, the tenacious presence of the feudal practices in rural India is a manifestation of the neoliberal capitalist state's inability to harness the rampant uneven development, which is one of the most pervasive global phenomena at this moment of history.

The confusion among Indian scholars regarding surviving feudal practices, however, is not new. In the 1980s, long before Nandi and Want discussed the presence of feudal systems in contemporary India, Indian scholars were debating whether India's agriculture sector was semi-feudal (both feudal and capitalist) or entirely capitalist. In his response to N. Sen Gupta's characterization of India's agricultural economy as semi-feudal, Dipanker Gupta categorically reminds his interlocutor that a discussion of such nature must begin from an analysis of the mode of production itself. Modes of productions, Gupta insists, are identified on the basis

The White Tiger and the Subsumption of the Rural   **63**

of relations of production and, as long as relations of production are concerned, India's agriculture is subsumed within the capitalist relations of production because Indian state itself is capitalist (A98-A99). By drawing upon Marx's passages on formal and real subsumption, he also emphasized that by the time labor is formally subsumed under capital, "the destruction of feudal institutions" has already taken place, which makes the argument about the real subsumption redundant (A99). Gupta then goes on to debunk Sen Gupta's proposition that capitalism is "ultimately constrained by the presence of pre-capitalist remnants" by explaining that the pre-capitalist remnants that resist capitalism always get subsumed by it; the logic of capital eventually overcomes any barrier that is put up by pre-capitalist remnants.

Chakrabarty, we have noted earlier, is not swayed by the argument that capitalism hems in everything that puts up a barrier on its path. The second chapter of *Provincializing Europe,* we have noticed, is particularly notable for not only challenging the theory of a capitalist totality but also for dismissing the notion of subsumption on the grounds of historical difference. Citing how Marxist historians and Indian businessmen both see history as a singular instance comprised of contradictiory tendencies, he writes:

> [T]he relationship between the logic of capital and historical difference appear to sustain historicism in different ways. In Thompson's position, historical time is the waiting that the third world has to go through for capital's logic to be fulfilled. One can modify the Thompsonian position by the thesis of "uneven development" and make distinctions between "formal" and "real" subsumption of capital. But this still keeps in place the idea of empty and homogenous historical time, for it is over such time that the gap could ever close between the two kinds of subsumption. (*Provincializing* 50)

After our detour through Marx, perhaps it is not even necessary to point out where Chakrabarty's assumption has struck its aporia. The German revolutionary, for his part, makes it amply clear that there is no time lag between "formal" and "real" subsumption. One mode of production can ripen inside another, more dominant, mode of production, and while, from the standpoint of the emergent mode of production, the time that takes it to become dominant can be conceptualized as the waiting room of history, from the standpoint of the dominant one, that is history proper. Only those who are suspicious of dialectic would cast succession and antagonism in the mold of parallel existence and pure difference, as if to negate the historical dominant one must exist as pure other, somewhere else where the hegemonic inscription of the dominant is absent. Likewise, the supposition that somehow the neoliberal exists outside the mediation of capital is to risk propounding the discovery of a new mode of production within whose body both feudalism and socialism exist in annexed form. The implied undertone in both these formulations is not just that India's

64 *The White Tiger* and the Subsumption of the Rural

history is different but also that somehow the particular history of capitalist development in India is able to dodge its sublation within the global capitalist norms, fending off totalization.

The novel, however, shows little deference to historical difference. Although the idea of India's uniqueness is continuously posited, it is done so in a manner that instead of attesting to India's difference from other nations of the world, its likeness to other nations becomes more conspicuous. What is emphasized in the course of Balram's evolution is not India's annexation from the rest of the world but its role in the global division of labor. If one pays adequate attention to the commodities that Balram is surrounded by in Laxmangarh—like radio, tube well, coal, rickshaws, motorcars, and so on—one is immediately overcome by a sense of apprehension of the spectral presence of the world market, which has made its appearance even in such a remote part of the country. The frenzied clatter of production, circulation, and consumption of commodities (further amplified by the constant movements of workers and capital from the rural to the urban and the global markets), that *TWT* makes audible is a resounding rejection of the thesis about India's dodging of the capitalist subsumption of its rural. Perhaps, a deeper glance at the novel will allow us to see how the pulse of global capitalism (and capitalist modernity) continues to throb in the remotest villages in India, asserting the presence of neoliberal capital rather than the absence of it.

The White Tiger and Spatio-temporality

TWT's plot stands on the warp and woof of rural to urban movement. Balram describes his own story as an "autobiography of a Half-Baked Indian" (*TWT* 8), a story that begins at Laxmangarh, a rural village located in the north-eastern part of India, and ends in Bangalore, India's fast-growing IT capital. The son of a rickshaw-puller and his fragile wife slowly dying in the village, he remains unnamed until his first day at school. Noticing that he is simply called "Munna" or "Boy," his schoolteacher names him Balram after "the sidekick of the god Krishna" (*TWT* 11). Surprisingly, the narrator does not fault his family for not naming him; rather, he casts the blame of not naming squarely on the place he comes from. His anguished rhetorical question "what kind of place is it where people forget to name their children?" (*TWT* 11), implies how he resents being born in a place where people do not even have the interval to name their children. The "backwardness" of his village is further highlighted by the narrator's description of the four landlords who control its resources. Named after four animals by the people of Laxmangarh because of their habits of exploitation, the "Stork," the "Buffalo," the "Wild Boar," and the "Raven" own not only the arable and non-arable lands around the village but also the river that flows outside it (*TWT* 20–21). They live in "high-walled mansions" outside the village and control both the economic and the social life of its populace. The intensity of

The White Tiger and the Subsumption of the Rural **65**

their oppression is such that a large number of inhabitants are forced to seek out a livelihood elsewhere, far away from the village. The narrator compellingly narrates how "the Animals ... fed on the village, and everything that grew in it, until there was nothing left for anyone else to feed on" (*TWT* 21). It is in this life-emptying circumstances that the migration to the city takes place. Unable to make a life in Laxmangarh, the villagers scatter around the urban enclaves of India in search of food and a livable life, choosing the most difficult and labor-intensive work only under compulsion. This is how Balram describes the mass exodus of his fellow villagers, who flock to the cities in search of employment:

> Each year, all the men in the village waited in a big group outside the tea shop. When the bus came, they got on—packing the inside, hanging from the railings, climbing onto the roofs—and went to Gaya; there they went to the station and rushed into the trains—packing the inside, hanging from the railings, climbing onto the roofs—and went to Delhi, Calcutta, and Dhanbad to find work. (*TWT* 21–22)

Balram's vivid description of landlords' relentless oppression and the consequent mass exodus of rural people to the cities offers another way of grasping his antipathy toward his birthplace—not so much as an aversion to the geographical space itself, but rather as a resentment against the socio-economic conditions that render his native village, as well as the entire state, unlivable. The evocation of the metaphor of "Darkness," therefore, is not just an evocation of the essential difference between affluent coastal cities (India of Light) and less affluent rural hinterland (India of Darkness) but also a commentary on uneven distribution of wealth and privilege, and an acknowledgement of the social practices that stifle human potential and throttle the dream of a better condition.

Indeed, one of the main reasons why Balram writes to the Chinese Premier is because he feels compelled to leave behind a narrative of the gutting of his own potential. When Balram is at school, he shows promise as a student—potential that is noticed by the school inspector who compares him to a "white tiger" (*TWT* 30). Despite the signs of promise, however, he is taken out of school to work in a teashop so his family can pay back the loan they have taken. Balram's rickshaw-puller father's dream is to see at least one of his sons "live like a man" (*TWT* 26) thus comes to a premature end, as does Balram's own hope for escaping grueling poverty through education. He joins his brother Kishan and begins by breaking large chunks of coal into smaller pieces. Noticing that Balram is more interested in the conversations of the customers than in the work he has been employed to do, the owner of the teashop sends him back. After a failed attempt to find work in the neighboring coal mining city of Dhanbad, he, with financial help from his family, learns to drive cars. After weeks of fruitless

66 *The White Tiger* and the Subsumption of the Rural

door-to-door solicitations, Balram finally finds employment at Stork's house as the landlord's son's driver. The entire first chapter is thus redolent with descriptions of unemployment, extreme poverty, and exploitation in the agrarian northeastern part of India. The absolute power of the upper caste landlords and the daily struggles of the lower and middling caste villagers are all examples of the rural decrepitude that Balram evocatively makes visible in his discussion about the India of Darkness. However, it is not in Laxmangarh—Balram's rural home—but rather in Delhi, the nation's capital, where his corrupt intents begin to devolve into a monstrous desire for killing his employer.

In Delhi, Balram's transformation comes sweepingly fast. He distances himself from his family and stops sending them money. He also begins to siphon off his employer's petrol, and bill "him for work that was not necessary" (*TWT* 195–96). The more Balram steals from his master, the stronger grows his desire to get rid of him. He finally slashes his employer Ashok's throat and runs away with his cash. He conceals his identity, deliberately moves about different parts of the country, and finally settles down in Bangalore—the city "full of outsiders" (*TWT* 254)—where he uses the money acquired through violence to start a luxury transportation service that shuttles the city's IT workers to and from their workplaces. The expansion of this "start-up" (*TWT* 258) allows Balram to consolidate his position as an entrepreneur and claim at the end of the novel that he has "switched sides" and is "now one of those who cannot be caught in India" (*TWT* 275).

The relation between American capital and Indian labor comes to light each time the novel shifts its attention to the outsourcing companies of Bangalore whose late-night working shift is in sync with the working hours in the United States.[4] When Balram arrives in Bangalore, the first thing he notices is the city's obsession with information technology. So deep is its relationship with the hi-tech companies abroad that every other aspect of its urban environment and experience seems to flow from it. Balram's description is remarkably perceptive: "Everything in the city, it seemed, came down to one thing. Outsourcing. Which meant doing things in India for Americans over the phone. Everything flowed from it—real estate, wealth, power, sex" (*TWT* 255). This short passage is acutely suggestive because in it the generative capacity of global capitalism has been expressed unabashedly. International capital here is not only obliquely organizing the landscape of the city through "real estate" but also reorganizing the city's culture and social life by redistributing "wealth and power" in the hands of India's newly emerging IT elites. What needs more attention, however, is the process through which the city's wealth is generated. Bangalore, in reality, is the provider of labor power in the global IT industry and its relation to "America" mirrors the relationship of labor to capital in the capitalist system, i.e. the relationship of capital's domination and control of labor.

The White Tiger and the Subsumption of the Rural   **67**

In its typically fetishistic form, this relationship appears as labor's dependence on capital, as Indian IT workers' dependence on multinational hi-tech corporations—a phenomenon that Adiga captures in the expression "everything flowed from it." Yet, in its characteristic ambivalent way, the novel also shreds to pieces the same fetishistic veil that goes into papering over capital's dependence on labor—dead labor's dependence on living labor. While addressing the Chinese Premier at the beginning of the novel, Balram mentions that despite lack of "drinking water, electricity, sewage system, public transportation, sense of hygiene …" India edges out everyone else in the overabundance of "entrepreneurs" (*TWT* 2). These entrepreneurs have set up "outsourcing companies" that "virtually run America now" (*TWT* 3). It is clear that the object of Balram's sarcasm here is India's uneven development: the lack of infrastructure in the rural is overcompensated by the prolific production of "entrepreneurs," whose only ingenuity seems to reside in its capacity to provide labor power for America's information technology sector. The narrative strategy here is to undermine India's entrepreneurs by overestimating their capacity to influence things in America. On the one hand, this comment can be taken as an example of Balram's characteristic undercutting of the official drumming up of India's economic prowess; on the other, it can be also read as a nifty critique of India's designated role in the global division of labor, where it is merely a provider of technological labor power, a ghostly shadow of the core companies operating in the United States. However, if we press further and take Balram's words literally, we open up the possibility of another interpretation in which the claim about Indian "outsourcing companies" virtually running America appears to gesture toward the hidden vital force that keeps the world market functional. It is here—in the expression "virtually run"—that the creative energy of labor gets spelled out and the dependency of capital on labor gets revealed.

Capitalism's uneven global expansion has been eked out in Adiga's novel in another way as well: not through the movement of capital but through the movement of raw materials. Joseph claims that *TWT* is a representation of "continuing colonization of the rural" by India's urban cores (Joseph 85). She discusses how the novel emerges as a corrective to neoliberal discourse about rural India's dependence on urban and technologically advanced India, depicting not only the state's withdrawal from rural areas but also the process of continual "resource appropriation" that siphons money from India's rural areas to its urban locations, draining the rural resources and capital (Joseph 78).

What Adiga's novel productively puts on display is the process of emptying out of both labor and resources from rural India so as to put them at the service of international capital. The novel depicts how Stork's family benefits from exploiting Laxmangarh's waterways. A portion of the money that Stork extracts by squeezing the villagers is put into coal mining in Dhanbad—coal that ends up in China and is used in production. The rural that is imagined in the novel is not a space that exists in isolation: the brilliance of the novel lies in its continuous

68 *The White Tiger* and the Subsumption of the Rural

evocation of interconnectedness, which allows readers to schematize the role the rural plays in a world connected by capital and trade. Capital that flows from the multinational corporations from the United States and other parts of the globe to India does not directly contribute to the quality of life in its less privileged spaces like Laxmangarh. Rather it moves into an already receptive city like Bangalore, alters and reorganizes it after capital's own image, and then returns, multiplied, to the corporate headquarters located in the United States.

TWT thus imagines an interlinked world with fluid movements of capital on the one hand and "international division of labor" on the other. It also navigates, with ease and insight, the uneven map of India, depicting the extreme wealth gap between rural and urban India. The novel's dialectical vision glides easily between local and global scales, imagining, on the one hand, a world brought into contact by capital and, exploring, on the other, deep economic and social divisions that trouble India. It also sheds light on the extreme inequality that shapes the existence of India's mega cities, especially Delhi, whose suburbs exist as antitheses of its roadside slums. Particularly important is the novel's depiction of the rural as a steady supplier of cheap labor. Balram's village is not only a site of "primitive accumulation," where the four landlords have established their reign of terror, but also a steady supplier of cheap labor to adjacent mining towns and big cities where migrants from Laxmangarh swarm in great numbers to escape the grueling poverty of the village. The novel's description of this spatial accumulation process, in which capital that is affixed to a particular geographical place in the form of land and water are advanced to produce, on the one hand, more wealth and, on the other, poverty and migration, is both powerful and compelling. *TWT* vividly captures the desperation of the rural migrants who seek to travel to the cities for self-preservation. Yet, as it also shows, the fruit of such a painful journey is rarely ever commensurate to the trouble taken for such escapes. Balram's father, in the process of pursuing his desire to escape the landlords of the village, ends up becoming a rickshaw puller in a city, eventually dying from hard labor and poverty. On his way to Delhi, Balram notices trains of people leaving the rural areas of "darkness" and comments: "You'd think the whole world was migrating" (*TWT* 94). But when he reaches Delhi, he notices how the desperate migrant from the rural areas have been forced to embrace the same inhuman life they sought to escape. Of course, a significant portion of the migrant labor is not immediately absorbed into the city's formal economy; "[t]housands of people" who live under the "huge bridges and overpasses" (*TWT* 99) become the city's "surplus population," variously brought in and thrown out of the orbit of production according to the capitalist city's ability to absorb such labor.

One visible site of the absorption of the migrant labor is the city's cosmopolitan makeover and expansion, effected, predominantly, by global trade and establishment of "American Express," "Microsoft," and so on (*TWT* 101) and, also, by the neoliberal reorganization of the city's landscape. The expansion of

The White Tiger and the Subsumption of the Rural **69**

Delhi, as depicted in the novel, is motivated by two principles that are bound to each other—the separation of the wealthy and the affluent from the city's underclass through gentrification and creation of gated communities, and the production temporary dwellings and slums, so that the labor absorbed in construction remains cheap and constantly available. While visiting a slum populated mostly by rural migrants from "darkness," Balram caustically reflects on the ethical incongruity that lies at the core of the expansion process. Of course, Balram seeks to understand it simply as a local manifestation of injustice toward the laborer. He recalls a visit to a newly built slum populated by construction workers: "These people were building homes for the rich, but they lived in tents covered with blue tarpaulin sheets, and portioned into lanes by lines of sewage" (*TWT* 222). Although Balram is in no position to relate it to neoliberal/capitalist organization of society in general, his outcry draws attention to the sheer immorality of punishing those on whose back the shiny offices and malls are built.

Balram's sharp critique of Indian culture and traditional family through the figure of the servant has been read by Nandi as proof of his "aggressive neoliberal individualism." That, after becoming an "entrepreneur," Balram attempts to distance himself from his past employers—landlords from rural India—by not following their tracks is interpreted by Nandi as a symptom of his "anti-feudal attitude" and his rejection of "India's traditional feudal structures" (Nandi 295). Unlike Joseph, who applauds *TWT* for drawing attention to the continued concealment of "the impoverished rural" by India's political elite (Joseph 74), Nandi argues that Adiga's novel stages a rejection of the "pre-capitalist" rural by "absolving" capitalism and by not calling into question India's "structural inequality and social injustice" (Nandi 296–97). Fundamental to her argument, then, is the notion that the relationship between "Darkness" and "Light" is a temporal one: darkness embodies "pre-capitalist" India, whereas the "India of light" is a representation of India's "post-capitalist system" (Nandi 288). Her discussion about Balram's rejection of feudalist India concurs with Lily Want's observation that Balram breaks away from "feudal norms" to embrace "capitalist relations" (Want 74). Want and Nandi's conclusions put them at odds with the presuppositions of the major proponents of uneven development, who reject the hypothesis of simultaneous coexistence of feudalism and capitalism in the era of an integrated world market.

We have already discussed about the theoretical predicament of considering remnants of feudalism as a separate economic system, working outside the capitalist relations of production. The discussions offered by Marx and Gupta, help us understand why apparently backward agricultural sectors of both developed and underdeveloped nations are as much part of the global capitalist ecosystem as are the technologically advanced cities parading the regional headquarters of multinational corporations. As this chapter noted earlier, one of

70 *The White Tiger* and the Subsumption of the Rural

the most ingenious thematic arrangements of the novel rests on how the uneven relation between labor and capital, in its local and global manifestations, is made visible through the narrative of a person who has never traveled abroad—whose local experience is adequate enough to afford him an understanding of the dynamic of global capitalism—and whose relationship to capitalism is not antagonistic. Balram's rejection of feudal relations illustrates why it is important to consider not only the novel's thematic presentation of uneven geographical development but also the dialectical tension that exists between Balram's self-legitimation and his narrative presentation. So long as we treat this novel as a murdering entrepreneur's narrative of his becoming, the gap between his earlier self and the new one will appear much wider than it actually is. Balram does indeed posit the "India of darkness" as a pre-capitalist space, although his narrative presentation leaves us with sufficient evidence to cut beneath his fetishization "India of light" and discover how the relation between the two Indias mirrors the uneven national scale, dividing the rural, agrarian India from the technologically advanced urban. If too much importance is attached to the difference between the rural and the urban, between the India of light and the India of darkness, one may fail to notice how both are parts of a larger global system mediated by the uneven exchange between labor and capital, between those who produce and those who own capital. Just as the rural villages of darkness exist as a steady supplier of cheap labor for urban India, so, too, the affluent urban locations of India serve as the steady supplier of cheap labor for tech-firms located elsewhere, in the core capitalist countries of Europe and North America. In Balram's narrative, what is often present is the unequal relation between labor and capital, which projects onto all other social relations, and which we see played out over and over again not only in the village where four landlords reign undeterred and the tea stalls of Dhanbad where Balram and his brother Kishan work, but also on the roads of Delhi and Bangalore, where the urban poor huddle, and in the shopping malls of Delhi, where drivers like Balram cannot enter.

Conclusion

If Balram's narrative appears to be a rejection of the feudal relations that persist in some parts of rural India, it is because as an entrepreneur—an apostle of capitalism—he inherits the dominant temporal fetish of the productive system of which he is a part. Capitalism, Marx proclaims in *Capital Volume I*, posits its own violent past as pre-history. As capital marches toward the future, it seeks to erase all the traces of its violent past, so as to present itself as neat and clear, devoid of savagery. That capitalism's past is revelatory of its propensity for violence, leads its propagators to conceal its history either by papering over it or by inventing a fictitious narrative of its origin. It is this concealment that forms the basis of capital's temporal fetish.[5] Marx points out in *Capital* that the discourse of political

The White Tiger and the Subsumption of the Rural **71**

economy is culpable of attempting to conceal capitalism's violent history by mythologizing its past. Although "conquests, enslavement, robbery, [and] murder" have been the means through which accumulation of capital has been carried out, political economy has obfuscated this gruesome history by telling the tales of an "idyllic" past devoid of expropriation and violence. Such tales, according to Marx, are falsification of capitalism's true history because surplus extraction itself depends on the use of violence on most occasions. Yet, in the narratives of political economy, such moments never appear with clarity, as if violence remains external to capitalism's historical progression and must be accounted for in terms of its temporal and spatial outsidedness. Marx, cognizant of this mystification, takes the discipline to task by writing:

> In actual history, it is a notorious fact that conquest, enslavement, robbery, murder, in short force, play the greatest part. In the tender annals of political economy, the idyllic reigns from time immemorial. Right and 'labor' were from the beginning the sole means of enrichment, 'this year' of course always excepted. As a matter of fact, the methods of primitive accumulation are anything but idyllic. (*Capital I* 873–4)

Marx's sarcastic reference to political economy's "tender annals" that carefully leave out capitalism's history of violence is a clear indication as to how classical political economists tried to cleanse the violent history of capitalist accumulation by propagating, on the one hand, that capitalism's past is "idyllic" and, on the other, its present violence is an exception—"always excepted," in Marx's own parlance. Capitalism's reliance on violence features prominently in Rosa Luxemburg's works too, especially in her magisterial "Accumulation of Capital," where she draws upon Marx's notion of "primitive accumulation" to explain how capitalism constantly resorts to violence for surplus accumulation (*Complete Works II* 262, 329). Just as Marx ridicules political economy for secreting capitalism's ravages, so, too, Luxemburg takes political economists to task for propagating capitalism as "the only possible and eternal social order," thus foreclosing the possibility of change (*Complete Works I* 258).

Both revolutionary theorists thus draw attention to the fetishistic norms that conceal capitalism's systemic violence. The narrator of *TWT*, it seems, fetishistically pigeonholes violence into spatial categories by suggesting that the "India of light" is intrinsically less violent than the "India of darkness," ignoring the possibility that the differential allocation of violence may by a reflection of capitalism's systemic unevenness. Abdullah Al-Dagamseh has perceptively drawn attention to the connection between Balram's violence and the systemic violence of capitalism, although his essay erroneously categorizes *TWT* as "World-Bank literature"—an idea about the relation between economic institutions and culture that U.S. Marxist critic Bret Benjamin advances

72 *The White Tiger* and the Subsumption of the Rural

in *Invested Interests: Capital, Culture, and the World Bank* (2007). Balram, Al-Dagamseh notes, thrives only after participating in "the violent system by committing acts of violence" and justifies his action by suggesting that his violence is neither exceptional nor pathological (Al-Dagamseh 5); rather, it is an attribute of those who have become successful: "Kill enough people and they will put bronze statues of you near Parliament House in Delhi" (Adiga 273). Thus, as Al-Dagamseh accurately observes, Balram's violence is a reflection of the violence of the system itself, a mirroring of "the global economic system dominating Bangalore, New Delhi, and other parts of the world" (Al-Dagamseh 5). Yet, surprisingly, Balram is convinced that the singular moment of killing his employer and, consequently, endangering his own family has been an exceptionally violent moment, belonging to his past; his present, in which he has emerged as a spokesperson for his class (a self-described "entrepreneur"), never appears to him as a moment of integration into the system, which makes violence a precondition for success.

Although Balram singles out the culture of "Darkness" as the source of misery, his narrative leaves a trail of evidence of the presence of a broader reality, which mediates "subjective violence."[6] The rapacious women of his family who squeeze out every hard-earned penny from Balram's father (*TWT* 22), the youth of Darkness who lie watching photos of film actresses all day because they have no job (*TWT* 46), the urban workers of Delhi who build "homes for the rich" but they themselves live "tents covered with blue tarpaulin sheets" right next to sewage (*TWT* 222), and the "manual laborers" of Bangalore who have been "left behind" (*TWT* 259)—all are parts of the same cut-throat reality that disenfranchises the poor and unevenly distributes political and social power so the landlords of Darkness, corrupt politicians of Delhi, and the entrepreneurs of Bangalore can accumulate more wealth by using violence to their benefit. If Balram is scornful of the culture and not the economic system, it is because as a beneficiary of the corrupt and unjust system he is unable to impute the very process that has placed him in a position of domination. He is, after all, one of those "who cannot be caught in India" (*TWT* 275). A member of "India's secessionist global elite," he feels that neoliberalism has brought into being a "post-race, post-class, post-revolutionary society" (Adkins 183), where class solidarity has become obsolete, and where "[e]very man must make his own Benaras" (*TWT* 261).

Since Balram takes no note of systemic inequality, his utopian dream only reaches as far as educational reform. His solution to systemic oppression is the establishment of an educational institution, which is in sync with the market, euphemistically termed as "reality" by the novel's narrator. In a candid confession to Jiabao, his audience of one, Balram divulges that he plans to sell his start-up business and move to real estate, which, he deems, is the future of Bangalore's business. "After three or four years in real estate," he writes:

The White Tiger and the Subsumption of the Rural   **73**

I think I might sell everything, take the money, and start a school—an English language school—for poor children in Bangalore. A school where you won't be allowed to corrupt anyone's head with prayers and stories about God or Gandhi—nothing but the facts of life for these kids. A school full of White Tigers, unleashed on Bangalore! (*TWT* 275)

What this passage ridicules are not merely the utter disconnect between India's education system and its socio-political reality, but also neoliberal utilitarianism, which wishes to purge any trace of idealism fearing that such ideals may not be useful for India's burgeoning business community. It also exposes the limit of neoliberal utopianism, whose solution to the world's woes seems to reside in further expansion of capitalism by bringing every institution into the service of capital. Hence, the necessity of institutionally manufactured "White Tigers" who will reign in Bangalore.

Balram's knee-jerk rejection of any form of solidarity exemplifies to what extent he has internalized a neoliberal vision of the world. A representative of "the new managerial-entrepreneurial class" (Adkins 183), Balram treats state welfare system with scorn and sarcasm. On a number of occasions, Balram mentions India's Naxalites in passing, not allowing the ghastly presence of resistant Naxalites come to the fore. He also depicts India's poor in a negative light, essentially framing them as passive and "bereft of class solidarity" (Adkins 183). Such a conviction about the culture of passivity has led him to believe that ordinary Indians are like roosters trapped inside a rooster coop, unable to muster enough courage to rise up against their oppressors (*TWT* 147, 166). Balram's rejection of collective resistance is evocative of the symbolism of the title as well. As a white tiger—a rare animal of unmatched cunning and agility—he finds no essential value in forging collective bonds. After all, how can there be a bond between a tiger and the encaged roosters? Indeed, his entire narrative continuously undermines all kinds of affinities, making collective affiliations look ridiculous. It is through his rejection of solidarity that Balram's cynical realism expresses itself most articulately, without pretension.

Yet, it is important that one draws a line between Balram-the-entrepreneur's worldviews and desires, and that of the novel, which seems to maintain a critical and ironic distance from the object that it parodies. While one can always question the novel's protagonist's predilection for a neoliberal world shaped by utilitarian and practical education, which, without doubt, only affirms his internalization of neoliberal ideology, the novel itself can hardly be charged for corroborating the same visions of the world, for the underlying motivation behind Adiga's work's relentless exposé of neoliberal India cannot be a return to neoliberalism itself. It is because of this that we need to factor in the question of genre when we approach *TWT*, especially when our claim is that this novel is a neoliberal bildungsroman whose underlying motive is to critique feudalism and

74 *The White Tiger* and the Subsumption of the Rural

socialism. Only when we allow it to dawn on us that Adiga's first novel is a parody, that it mocks the entire social reality its protagonist is a part of, do we begin to notice how, instead of merely critiquing feudalism and socialism, it undermines the social whole sustained by the fortresses of capital. Perhaps, this is not how the authors intended the novel to be read. The possibility, however, to read a novel in an unintended way always remains.

Notes

1 A large number of reviews and articles by Indian scholars on *The White Tiger* have been antagonistic, if not outright dismissive. For instance, Amitava Kumar's "Bad News" in the *Boston Review* and Sanjay Subrahmanyam's "Diary" in the *London Review of Books* are both extremely critical of *TWT,* both taking the novel to task on the issue of verisimilitude. Snehal Shingavi, as has been pointed out, has taken the novel to task for misrepresenting India's caste system. Himansu S. Mohapatra's "Babu Fiction in Disguise," Mrinalini Chakravorty's chapter "Slumdog or White Tiger?," and Swaralipi Nandi's "Narrative Ambiguity and The Neoliberal *Bildungsroman* in Aravind Adiga's *The White Tiger*" are also overtly critical of the novel's thematic presentation of Indian life.
2 Most of the important theorists of uneven development are critical of the tendency to separate the urban from the rural (and also local from the global). Andre Gunder Frank, in particular, is wary of the predisposition to characterize certain spaces and sectors as "modern and relatively developed" and other sectors as "feudal and pre-capitalist," (Frank 4). Although Argentine political philosopher Ernesto Laclau has upbraided Frank for conflating a number of political economic categories, including the distinction between modes of production and economic systems, he nevertheless agrees with Frank on one major point: it is development itself that generates underdevelopment (Laclau 31). Laclau, specifically, insists on the necessity to "confront the system as a whole" to "show the indissoluble unity that exists between the maintenance of feudal backwardness at one extreme and the apparent progress of a bourgeois dynamism at the other" (Laclau 31).
3 Printed as an Appendix in the Fowkes translation.
4 The peculiarity of Bangalore's schedule and its dependence on U.S. time has been captured well in a passage where Balram expresses the following: "See, men and women in Bangalore live like the animals in a forest do. Sleep in the day and then work all night, until two, three, four, five o'clock, depending, because their masters are on the other side of the world, in America" (255).
5 In *Representing Capital*, Fredric Jameson has shed light on Marx's discussion on capitalism's temporality. Drawing materials from Marx, Jameson has explained how, on the one hand, capitalism itself is built up on the continually renewed exchange between labor and capital or, in Marx's parlance, capitalism's "eternal virginity," and, on the other, capitalism operates by eliminating its past, by extinguishing remnants and practices of other modes of productions. See Jameson's chapter titled "Capital in its Time" for further discussion on the topic.
6 I borrow my idea of subjective violence being conditioned by something more objective and systemic from Slavoj Žižek. The Slovenian philosopher gives an account of the fetish character of subjective violence in *Violence*, where he claims that we often get so caught up in the horror of subjective violence that we become oblivious of less visible but equally, if not more, penetrating "symbolic" and "systemic" violence (1–2).

4

HOME BOY, THE RELUCTANT FUNDAMENTALIST, AND "THE RESERVE ARMY OF CAPITAL"

Introduction

Mohsin Hamid's *The Reluctant Fundamentalist* (henceforth *TRF*) and H. M. Naqvi's *Home Boy* (*HB* from hereon) are both novels of departure. In that sense, they are also allegories of return, standing in contrast to earlier postcolonial novels chronicling the protagonist's fortuitous arrival to the metropolis. V. S. Naipaul's *The Mystic Masseur* (1957) and *Mimic Men* (1967), Monica Ali's *Brick Lane* (2004), Jhumpa Lahiri's *The Namesake* (2004) and *The Lowland* (2013), Zia Haider Rahman's *In the Light of What We Know* (2014)—all these novels are allegories of arrival, telling the tales of the immigrant's struggles to cut a place for themselves in the metropolitan West. Both of Naipaul's comic novels chronicle the mêlées of their narrators with their own countries. Ganesh Ramsumair and Ralph Sing, the protagonists of *The Mystic Masseur* and *Mimic Men* respectively, overcome initial poverty and challenges in Trinidad but eventually leave their island home to settle down in the United Kingdom. Nazneen, the central character of Ali's debut novel, arrives in London through her marriage to a man much older than her and, after hardship, finally finds her independence from men who seek to define the contours of her walls and worlds. Lahiri's two novels, likewise, thematize first-generation immigrants' gradual assimilation into the socio-cultural tissues of the United States. Both these novels examine the trauma of exile, depicting how settling down in the West, which appears to offer a relatively convenient life in comparison, is also underwritten by anxiety and loneliness. But, at least on first look, all the above-mentioned novels have positive impressions about migration, considering it rewarding, albeit not without precarity or peril.

DOI: 10.4324/9781003324768-4

76 *Home Boy, Reluctant Fundamentalist,* & Reserve Army of Capital

The two Pakistani writers' works, by contrast, are not the already familiar tales of successful migration, let alone of happy affiliation; they are, rather, stories of difficulties and disappointments, of sad departure and sullen retrenchment. They narrate how, at the wake of the terror attacks of September 11, Changez and Shehzad, the narrators of *TRF* and *HB*, find themselves in changed circumstances, profiled as enemies. Their precarious state of being—marked by joblessness, religious marginality, and racial antipathy—lead them to understand that they have become pariahs in their own cities, where their very existence provokes anxiety and antipathy among fellow New Yorkers. Traumatized by racialization and haunted by material struggles, they decide to depart NYC—the city that they once called home. *TRF* and *HB* thus reveal the perils of nestling in the cozy cosmopolitan capital of the world, narrating how the metropolitan west's racial and religious antipathy remain veiled under the shiny veneer of its discourse of inclusivity and tolerance.

Thematically, these novels deal with similar issues, almost identical when it comes to exploring the trauma of the agonizing departures of their protagonists. In terms of narrative presentation and style, however, they differ immensely, one adopting dramatic monologue as narrative technique, while the other appearing like a postmodern picaresque, almost veering toward a *bildungsroman*. The likeness between the novels predominantly reside in the optimistic arrival and the traumatic departure of their protagonists. Changez, the protagonist of Hamid's novel *TRF*, enjoys relative success as a young executive of a small but elite asset valuation firm named Underwood Samson until his travels to the Philippines and Chile, and failed relationship with a young American woman named Erika, begins to have their effect on his ambition to settle down in the United States. As he travels to Manila and Chile, the mask of the empire begins to fall off, making him vaguely conscious of his complicit role in the global imperial structure. However, when, after 9/11, his otherwise convenient life in the metropole falls apart, he begins to unravel, eventually losing his job and means of subsistence. As the promise of a convenient and prosperous life in NYC draws to an abrupt end, he leaves global megacity, returning to his city of birth, Lahore.

Similar disappointment works in Shehzad's life as well. Unlike Changez, whose trauma ensues from his disappointments in the United States, Shehzad carries the trauma of losing his father at an early age—a loss inflicted by his father's suicide—to NYC, seeking refuge in the company of his friends, comprised of a "dandy" named Ali Chowdhury (AC) and an aspiring musician named Jamshed Khan (Jimbo). His ulterior motive is to settle into a good job, attain a green card, and bring his mother to the same city, where he feels like a homeboy. 9/11 shatters that promise, forcing him to encounter the reality that the promise of happiness has been withdrawn from the likes of him. With Chowdhury in prison and Jamshed abandoning his dream of pursuing his career in music, Shehzad, unable to withstand the trauma of having to live in a city that resents

Muslims like him, decides to forgo of his American dream, choosing to return to the city of his birth, Karachi, instead.

It comes as no surprise, then, that these novels have been read as narratives of precariousness and resistant Muslim identity, for religious marginalization and racial antipathy are the most conspicuous themes dealt in these works. Joseph Darda, for appropriate reasons, has described *TRF* as the story of Changez's apprehension of his own precariousness—"the story of one man's awakening to the frames of recognizability" (Darda 111). The young man's empathy for the other victims of the U.S. empire, Dadra suggests, is the outcome of the novel's protagonist's ability to extend the arc of empathy, using his subjective precariousness to apprehend the precariousness of the other (Darda 121). Brite Heidemann has similarly drawn attention to Naqvi's *Home Boy*'s resilience, suggesting that as a novel, it is anti-essentialist, positioned against the systematic production of cultural stereotypes. It is, in her reckoning, a "counter-Orientalist" novel—one which intends to fend off the neo-Orientalist essentialization of "brown-skinned people," debunking the "underhandedness" imparted by "normative labels" like terrorism and so on (Heidemann 290–1). Both these critics consider *TRF* and *HB* politically conscious, resisting the racial and religious zealotry that spilled into the U.S. political imaginary after the 9/11 attacks, while also pointing toward Changez and Shehzad's awareness of their own precariousness brought into being by the changed circumstances after the 9/11 attacks. Both Darda and Heidemann consider these two protagonists' return as their rebellions against racial and religious antipathy and the processes of essentialization.

Much like the essays cited above, this chapter too will focus on the issue of precariousness, but not the kind that Darda and Heidemann have expressed their interest in. Instead of pirouetting around the subjective apprehension of precariousness, which is how precariousness is often understood today, this chapter will focus on the systemic production of precarity, demonstrating how these novels blurt out, almost half-consciously, their critiques of capitalism's production of misery. The premise of this chapter is the presentation of economic crisis and unemployment in these works—the "other" precariousness that remains buried under the dominant discussions about identity and marginality, although the production of such forms of immiseration is the most pervasive feature of contemporary neoliberal capitalism.

Popular as a literary critical concept, precariousness saturates contemporary debates about class, race, gender, sexuality, and ecology. In *Precarious Life* (2004) and *Frames of War* (2009), U.S. feminist theorist and philosopher Judith Butler approaches the phenomenafrom the standpoint of Levinasian moral philosophy, seeking to understand it as an ontological condition related to one's apprehension by the other. Finitude and vulnerability, that our lives can be lost at any given time, render all lives precarious. What make them livable, however, is the condition of

78 *Home Boy, Reluctant Fundamentalist, & Reserve Army of Capital*

grievability, that is to say, the possibility that if they are injured or lost they will be grieved for (*Precarious* 29–31). Her positing of precariousness as a general expression of our existential vulnerability—a broad ontological observation—is later accounted for by a narrower reflection—one that is political—which states that there is a differential allocation of precariousness in society, an allocation that runs along the racial, class, gender, sexual, and religious line. "A hierarchy of grief," she writes, "could no doubt be enumerated," prompting us to rethink how we tend to ignore the normative distribution of precariousness (*Precarious* 32). In *Frames*, she pushes the boundary of her argument further, contending that socially acquired frames often mediate the unequal distribution of precariousness, engendering more violence and trauma (*Frames* 3). Butler thus posits the question of precariousness from the standpoint of existence, using her broad existential observation about precariousness to bear upon the contexts such asthe wars in Iraq and Afghanistan, that have produced myriads of vulnerable people around the world. Her moral philosophical interpretation of precariousness is thus counterpoised by her political application of it, whose dominant impulse is motivated by an admirable moral philosophical call for a politics of non-violence.

In other postmodernist-left discussions, however, the same idea of precariousness is advanced differently, not only to imply economic marginalization but also to presage the emergence of a new political subject. In *Empire* (2000), Michael Hardt and Antonio Negri celebrate the arrival of this new political subject—the nomadic and aterritorial "multitude"—who will push the old capitalist regime from its orbit, replacing it with a more egalitarian "republic" (Hardt and Negri 403–5). Guy Standing, following the same path, has described the new revolutionaries "lacking a cohesive alternative agenda" as "the precariat" (Standing 1–2)—"the incipient political monster" that has been created by the "neo-liberal" policies undertaken by governments around the world (Standing 1). Unlike Butler, whose description of the phenomenapertains to the general condition of vulnerability, Standing's and Hardt and Negri's elaboration of it leans toward a political-economic anatomy, exposing the nexus between labor, migration, and marginality, optimistically presaging the radical transformation that will soon be a reality.

In recent years, however, "precarity" and "precariousness" have come to signify more than just what Pierre Bourdieu once called "subjective insecurity"—the existential precariousness caused by migration, dependency, and state withdrawal from social well-being (Bourdieu 83). Emily J. Hogg points out how precariousness has come to denote a number of existential and material conditions, from "temporary work contracts to imminent environmental catastrophe, from state violence to pervasive anxiety" (Hogg 1). Although these concepts are useful in understanding Changez and Shahzad's racial and economic marginality and their rebellion against the processes of marginalization, they fall short of pointing toward a systemic production of misery and vagrancy in the era of neoliberal capitalism.

What is also elided in the above-mentioned theoretical discussions is the role that imperial wars and neoliberal financial crises play in generating masses of precariats all over the world—both inside the bowel of the empire and outside it. This chapter will draw attention to this relationship by navigating the Marxist discussions on imperialism on the one hand and by looking into Marx's concept of "surplus population" on the other. The objective is to demonstrate how *TRF* and *HB* allegorize such conjunction, making visible the relation between finance, imperialism, and immiseration. The abandonment of NYC by the young protagonists of the two novels, symbolically represents the abandonment of the Muslim middle-class' utopian vision of permanently inhabiting the cosmopolitan city space. *HB* offers a window into the interlaced world of race and class, exposing not only the paradigms of systemic racism but also the processes through which workers from around the world are brought into the cosmopolitan urban centers, creating a "reserve army of capital" to be taken advantage of when necessary. *TRF*, on the other hand, offers a cartography of the U.S. empire by unmasking its equally violent financial exploitation in distant territories. Although it may appear as though the production of racial marginalization and the domination of the financial empire correspond to two different sets of ideas, this chapter will argue otherwise, claiming that they are bound by the same processes of capital whose objective is to harness financial crises through the systemic production of a vulnerable populace. In what follows, this chapter will first dwell on the theoretical elaborations provided in the Marxist tradition about the relation between capital and production of misery, and then closely read *HB* and *TRF* to understand how the contemporary productions of misery have been rendered visible in these two novels. Its concluding section will bring back the earlier discussions about utopian visions to note how these novels deal with the question of alternatives.

The Empire of Finance

It is no secret that Marxists in general have emphasized the necessity to treat imperialism primarily as an expression of the contradictions of capital at the scale of the world market, as opposed to the liberal models that posit it as a cultural and civilizational issue. Although the ideas of expansion and domination are built into the fabric of Marx's discussions on capitalism, he did not develop a separate theory of imperialism when he was alive. The expansive corpus of Marxist theories of imperialism are developed on the foundations provided by V. I. Lenin, Rudolph Hilferding, and Nicolai Bukharin, who are generally referred to as the founders of "classical Marxist theories of imperialism" (Brewer 79). These revolutionary figures saw imperialism as a stage in the history of capitalism—a stage that is marked on the one hand by intense competitions among the most powerful capitalist nations and on the other by increased financialization and cooperation among capitalist institutions. The works of the world systems theorists such as Gunder Frank, Samir Amin, and Wallerstein develop a different model for schematizing imperialism, where they see imperialism embedded in the capitalist accumulation strategy itself, which accords unequal advantage to a few core capitalist nations that draw capital and resources from peripheral nations and agglomerate them in their own national spaces. What is distinctive about the World Systems theorists' conceptualization of imperial relations is that they see underdevelopment as an inevitable outcome of a peripheral nation's inclusion within the capitalist totality (Brewer 161).

In more recent times, especially after the publication Michael Hardt and Antonio Negri's millennial manifesto *Empire*, which argues that the old forms of imperial competition and outright domination have been replaced by the formation of a new biopolitical "Empire" that operates on the basis of cooperation among the powerful institutions (*Empire* xii), and at the wake of United States' invasion of Afghanistan, Iraq, and Syria, a rich body of Marxian prognosis of imperial formations began to emerge. These works, instead of relying entirely on the Leninist definition of imperialism as intra-capitalist competition, offer more varied descriptions of imperialism, delineating how the occupation of these aforementioned sovereign countries by the U.S. mark the arrival of a new historical juncture, one that is characterized by the desire of the unipolar world to harness capitalist crises. In the introduction to his book *Naked Imperialism* (2006), John Bellamy Foster contends that there is nothing uncharacteristic about the U.S. occupation of Iraq because territorial aggression is woven into its very being. Since its inception, the United States has always been an "expansionist power"; what has changed, however, is that its expansionist logic, "the nakedness" of its imperial aggression, which often remains hidden behind its covert financial domination, has become the object of scrutiny because of the wars in the Middle East and South-central Asia (Foster 11). Foster's contention, it seems, is premised on the observations made by David Harvey, who, at the wake of United States' Iraq invasion, described the U.S. imperialism as "new imperialism," marking a definitive stage within the capitalist system (*The New Imperialism* 1). The latter's conjecture derives its materials from the history of United States' gradual move away from production since the 1970s, and its increased dependence on finance in the decades afterward (*New Imperialism* 62). The aggressive move to occupy Iraq was a way for overcoming the economic contraction the United States has been facing since the end of the 1990s. One of the most important observations advanced by both Harvey and Foster has been the conjunction between imperial aggression and finance. Although both refer to the increased influence of financial and multinational corporations in state affairs, neither of them, at least at this point, make their claims about the corporate takeover of the state explicit. It is only in their later works that both Harvey and Foster begin to claim that U.S. imperialism in the new century has been driven primarily by the necessity to overcome the crisis of financialization.[1]

The connection between imperialism, financialization, and the production of surplus population has been more categorically explored by Utsa Patnaik and Prabhat Patnaik, who, in an essay published in *The Monthly Review*, argue that the necessity to stabilize the value of money drives the core capitalist nations to forcefully impose underdevelopment on peripheral nations. Much of the wealth today, they write, is held either as money or in "money denominated assets," i.e. financial assets. It is, therefore, imperative that capitalism does not allow the value of money to sink in relation to commodities because that will lead toward crisis. In order to keep the value of money stable and to ward off depreciation, the capitalist class of the core nations constantly resorts to two means: first, the production of a large reserve population at home and in the periphery, and, secondly, the draining of surplus from the peripheral nations either through corporate investment or through imports of petty commodities "from the capitalist metropolis" ("Imperialism in the Era of Globalization"). Neither the production of the reserve army of capital, nor the imports of petty commodities from the metropolis can happen without coercion. The vexing problem of "diminishing returns" of capital, which is one of the primary causes of stagnation, can only be averted if the diminished sum is socially dumped on the shoulders of the peripheral reserve army of workers, and on the metropole's own surplus population ("Imperialism in the Era of Globalization").

What is noteworthy in their discussion is how capitalism's internal urge to stabilize the value of money, the medium of all values and commodities, leads it to shift the economic cost of diminishing returns on an ever-expanding surplus population. But such an action requires the threat of violence and coercion as well. Hence, the increased significance of imperialism in today's world. The imperialist wars of the last two decades certainly give validity to this observation. But what is equally demonstrative of this argument's cogency is the exponential growth in the world's reserve working-class population. As Forster has noted, the "global active labor" army was almost half the size of the "global reserve army" population in 2011, which means most of the world's population at that time did not have stable jobs ("The New Imperialism of Globalized Monopoly-Finance Capital"). But how is this phenomenon connected to the processes of capitalist accumulation? What relation does it have with capitalism in general? In order to understand systemicity of the relationship, we need to return to grand-old Marx, who, in *Capital Vol. I* spells out as to why it is important for the survival of capitalism to produce "surplus population" (*Capital I* 782)—part-time workers who are ready to take up any job, who are also referred elsewhere as the "industrial reserve army" (*Capital I* 784).

The capitalist accumulation process, Marx notes, constantly produces a relatively "redundant working population" whose labor power is intermittently employed during the production process. As the productivity of labor increases and technology improves, the capitalist system's drive for relative

82 *Home Boy, Reluctant Fundamentalist, & Reserve Army of Capital*

surplus value propels it to let go of workers at an increased rate (*Capital I* 783). But when social production expands, these workers or others are re-employed, only to be "repelled" again when competition tightens, or crisis shows up (*Capital I* 785). Since the capitalist system goes through constant transformations—"periods of average activity, production at high pressure, crisis, and stagnation" (*Capital I* 785), to quote Marx—and labor's demands for better wages and fewer working hours mount, capitalism's survival depends on the production of surplus population to maintain pressure on fully employed workers, who are forever threatened by the part-time workers who may take their place. It is because of this that Marx refers to the production of the surplus population as "a condition for the existence of the capitalist mode of production" (*Capital I* 784). It is worth quoting a lengthy passage from *Capital I* here, because in it Marx details how the surplus working population is taken advantage of by the capitalist system of production. He writes:

> ... [T]his surplus population also becomes, conversely, the lever of capitalist accumulation, Indeed it becomes a condition for the existence of the capitalist mode of production. It forms a disposable industrial reserve army, which belongs to capital just as absolutely as if the latter had bred it at its own cost. Independently of the limits of the actual increase of population, it creates a mass of human material always ready for the exploitation by capital in the interests of capitals own changing valorization requirements. With accumulation, and the development of the productivity of labor that accompanies it, capital's power of sudden expansion also grows; it grows not merely because the elasticity of the capital already functioning increases, not merely because credit, under every special stimulus, at once places an unusual part of this wealth at the disposal of production in the form of additional capital; it grows also because the technical conditions of the production process—machinery, means of transport, etc.—themselves now make possible a very rapid transformation of masses of surplus product into additional means of production. The mass of social wealth, overflowing with the advance of accumulation and capable of being transformed into additional capital, thrusts itself frantically into old branches of production, whose market suddenly expands, or into newly formed branches such as railways, etc., which now become necessary as a result of the further development of the old branches. In all such cases, there must be the possibility of suddenly throwing great masses of men into the decisive areas without doing any damage to the scale of production in other spheres. The surplus population supplies these masses. The path characteristically described by modern industry, which takes the form of a decennial cycle (interrupted by smaller oscillations) of periods of average activity, production at high pressure, crisis, and stagnation, depends on the constant

formation, the greater or less absorption, and the re-formation of the industrial reserve army or surplus population. In their turn, the varying phases of the industrial cycle recruit the surplus population and become one of the most energetic agencies for its reproduction. (*Capital I* 784–5)

Marx's calibration of the systemic production of the "surplus population" as the lever of capitalism's continuity allows us to schematize the relation between reproduction and violence, the systemic necessity for the production of misery as a potenial precondition for continued existence. How else can poverty and misery be reproduced except through war, genocide, racial oppression, gender violence, and other forms of normative allocations of vulnerability?

The production of precarious worker, let us bear in mind, is the production of misery and wretchedness, destitution of the kind discussed above, cannot be produced in peaceful means, without manipulating and deploying state apparatuses.[2] Marx, at least in this passage, shows little interest in anchoring his analysis of the system in particular modes of oppressions, although the contour of his prognosis of specific forms of violences is present in the last chapter of *Capital Vol I*, where he catalogues numerous instances of legal and social violence. The relation between race, gender, and capital, thus, remains implied and not fully developed. Nevertheless, it is in the works of Alexandra Collantai, Rosa Luxemburg, M. N. Roy, C. L. R. James, Frantz Fanon, to name a few, that the nexus between capitalist structure and different forms of oppressions appear with clarity.

The German theorist's discussion on the systemic production of precariousness, however, goes a long way in revealing the propinquity between economic crises and the production of a class of people who may be thrown in and out of work according to the necessity of the capitalist system. While it is true that the production of poverty and misery in this era has taken more complex and organized form, Marx's anatomy of the systemicity of the process cannot be brushed aside, specifically because of his insistence on seeing the differential allocation of precariousness as a systemic and orchestrated effort rather than a colletaral and dispersed effect of capitalism. Indeed, the profoundness of the observation is illustrated by its very usefulness today—almost 150 years later. Yet, it is also important to note that one has to stretch Marx beyond Marx to realize the full potential of the statement quoted above. Other than economic crises, the two major processes of production of precarity are (imperial) wars and racial/ethnic/sexual/gender/caste/religious violence. Naqvi's *HB* makes visible the transaction between racial/ethnic marginality and economic crises, whereas Hamid's *TRF* allows us to see the thread that binds religious antipathy, imperial aggression, and economic crisis in a relationship together. How they do so will be the focus of the next two sections of this chapter.

84 *Home Boy, Reluctant Fundamentalist,* & Reserve Army of Capital

Home Boy and Racial Antipathy

Naqvi's novel's beginning introduces its three protagonists—AC (Ali), Jimbo (Jamshed), and Chuck (Shehzad)—as "self-invented and self-made" urban youth, eclectic in culture and taste. They are familiar with the city's secret corridors and have knowledge of its more dangerous corners. The narrator describes his and his friends' inclusivity in the following manner:

> [we] slummed in secret cantons of Central Park, avoided the meatpacking district, often dined in Jackson Heights; weren't rich but weren't poor (possessing, for instance, extravagant footware but no real estate); weren't frum but avoided pork ... and drank everywhere, some more than others ... (*HB* 1–2)

Ali, the eldest among the three, is a schoolteacher who has been in and out of the PhD program and depends on his more stable and successful sister for additional support. He is described by the narrator as a "charming rogue, an intellectual dandy, a man of theatrical presence" who is both confrontational and compassionate. Jamshed, on the other hand, is quiet and thoughtful, with a steady girlfriend who lives in "a swank corner apartment" on Broadway (*HB* 17). Shehzad, in contrast to his friends, is neither an immigrant nor a citizen, but a student who thinks he had "claimed the city and the city had claimed" him (*HB* 3), but as we discover in the latter part of the novel, his claim on the city is met with a hostile rejection. Part of the reason why *Home Boy* reads like a bildungsroman is because the city's attitude toward these three Pakistani men abruptly reverses, leading its protagonist to learn from his traumatic experiences that he is an outsider. "I was growing up but thought I was grown-up" (*HB* 3) is how the narrator sums up this maturation process.

Shehzad's awareness of his outsideness begins to form a few days after the September 11 attacks, when he first comes out of his house after lying low for a while. He and his friends meet at Jake's, a local bar, to discuss the disappearance of one of their friends, Mohammed Shah, or "Shaman," whom he describes as "an American success story, a Pakistani Gatsby," who drives a "scarlet Mercedes 500 SEL" and lives in an affluent neighborhood in Westbrook, Connecticut (*HB* 21). As AC gets visibly upset about not being able to trace Shaman and starts venting his frustration at the 9/11 attackers, saying, "they've fucked up *my city*," two burley "brawlers" approach them, asking: "Whatchugonnafuckup?" (*HB* 23). As the two men keep harassing Shehzad and his friends, calling them "A-rabs," "Moslems," and finally physically assaulting Shehzad, a brawl breaks out between them. Jake, the owner of the pub, comes running down, screaming at them "GETATAHERE! ALLAYOUS! ... NO ROOM FOR YOUS!" (*HB* 24). It is at that point that they begin to understand that "[t]hings were changing"

(*HB* 25). The idea that there is no room for the three young men in the neighborhood pub can be seen as a metonymic exploration of the change in New York City's dominant culture, where Muslim men begin to register as dangerous, unworthy of being allowed in. The undertone of white privilege that mediates the normative determination of who belongs and who does not is embodied in the figure of the burley brawlers whose violent interruption of Ali's narrative can be construed as a narrative apprehension of the power of whiteness in New York City's, and through it the nation's, cultural imaginary. This episode stands in stark contrast to the one discussed earlier, where Shehzad makes his claim about being an insider. This episode, along with the one that follows later in the novel where the three friends get arrested, echoes the novel's ironic title, which essentially dismisses the possibility of belonging to New York City as a Muslim migrant.

The back-and-forth movement of *HB* takes us to another set of antinomies in the next few chapters after the bar incident, initially revealing Shehzad's relative success as a bank employee, only to take us to the next phase when he finds himself jobless, becoming a New York City "cabbie," living day to day. An English department graduate from one of the city's best universities, he easily lands a job in an investment bank during the boom, when the economy is thriving. He begins to plan for the future so he can become formally integrated into the lifeworld of the city. He imagines an affluent future ahead of him, with his bank sponsoring his green card in the near future and then, a few years down the line, him sponsoring his mother (*HB* 28). It is during these more prosperous days that Shehzad feels happy to be a "part of the secret, intricate, if procrustean machinery that made Capitalism tick." Although he is not entirely convinced by its modes of working, he comforts himself by questioning, "who ain't a slave?" (*HB* 29). Despite working "fourteen, fifteen-hour days, including most week-ends," he gets terminated when the "bull-run" ends, bringing the boom to a stall (*HB* 29). However, once he loses his job and his boss tries to comfort him saying he is taking "one for the team," the vague awareness that makes him see the procrustean machinery that made capitalism tick also accords him the insight into its class character, making him realize it has to "do with the bottom line" (*HB* 30). He tries to keep afloat by investing in "stocks with high price-to-equity ratio," but as the market plunges further, he finds his investment "reduced to a few cents on the dollar," leaving him with little to survive on. He drastically reduces his expenses and tries to survive by investing in lottery tickets, but nothing works in his favor. He finally accepts his fate, blurting out his utter helplessness by stating the following: "There wasn't much more I could do. The market had soured. I found myself in profound funk" (*HB* 31).

It is this extreme poverty and helplessness that shoves him toward becoming a cab driver. He fortuitously meets a fellow Pakistani cabbie who agrees to allow him to drive the only cab he owns. For his license, he needed to complete an

86 *Home Boy, Reluctant Fundamentalist,* & *Reserve Army of Capital*

80-hour requisite course. For two weeks, Shehzad wakes up "at the crack of the dawn" and takes two different trains to go to the NYS Federation of Taxi Drivers Academy so he can attend his 8:30 class, which goes on until 5:30 (*HB* 36). It is here that he notices the other 18 people who are there for the course, most coming from Asia and Africa:

> There were nineteen of us, none of whom was Pakistani … A bony Indian from Patna, a wide-eyed Bangladeshi, a square-faced Egyptian, and a small, intense Xingjiangi fellow sat up front, taking abundant notes, while the self-designated backbenchers—an Albanian, a Haitian, and a Sikh—mostly glowered … The rest hailed from the Dark Continent: there was a Kenyan nightwatchman, a Beninese busboy, and a convivial Congolese tribesman named Kojo with whom I became lunch buddies. Over sandwiches and soda, he regaled me with riveting tales of his barefoot and bloody escape from the copper-rich province of Kivu during a routine spasm of violence. (*HB* 37)

This passage allows us to peer into the city's working-class immigrant life. By tying into its description of migrant workers from different nations and places the narrative of Kojo's escape from the copper-rich province of the Republic of Congo, this passage offers us a fragmented view of the violence and corruption that make the peripheral nations unsafe—a key reason why people leave those places to work in cities like New York.

The processes of concentration of labor on the one hand and capital on the other for capitalism's metabolic necessity has been discussed not only by Marx but also by Engels. The latter in his precocious urban ethnography in *The Condition of the Working Class in England* comments that England's biggest cities were the consequences of capitalism's necessity to have at its disposal both excess labor power and excess capital. Written when Engels was only 24, *The Condition* thus identifies the features that became paradigmatic for cities created by capital: the concentration of capital on the one hand and of workers on the other (*Condition* 66). In *Capital Volume I*, Marx further explores the processes of expropriation, explaining how forceful eviction and immiseration are necessary for the production of workers. Joblessness, however, creates a labor population of a different kind, what Marx calls the "reserve army of capital." These partially employed or wholly unemployed workers—the group that is described as "floating surplus population" in *Capital I*—keeps growing as capital looks for a cheaper and younger labor force (*Capital I* 794). Although most of the workers described by Shehzad in this passage fall within the category of the "floating surplus population," Kojo, it seems, is a victim of a more violent process—a process, if approached theoretically, will resemble what Marx calls "primitive accumulation." The tale of mineral-rich Africa, whose violence comes as much from its comprador military and corrupt civilian leadership as it does from multinational corporations who require staged anarchy to quietly siphon off surplus, is too familiar to detail here. Just as South Asia, with its history of violence, oppressive rulers, and restrictive social norms—to which Michael Ondaatje's *Anil's Ghost* (2001), Neel Mukherjee's *Lives of Others* (2014), Kamila Shamsie's *Home Fire* (2017), Mohsin Hamid's *Exit West* (2017), and Arundhati Roy's *The Ministry of Utmost Happiness* (2017) bear witness—has been a steady source of migrant workers, so Africa with its ethnic wars and inherited exploitative system has been a copious supplier of cheap labor (long after the chattel slave trade ended). Violence thus ensures not only the supply of labor power to core capitalist nations but also the production of the lumpen population, whose presence keeps the workers of the metropolis on the edge, afraid. It is important to notice how the passage on migrant workers leaves us with a vague silhouette of some of the most gruesome practices of the global capitalist system, whose uneven world and imperialist practices collect people from all around and bring them to cosmopolitan cities to exploit their cheap labor.[3]

The effect of the imperial coercion through which capital and labor are concentrated in core urban locations is suffered in insular local communities as well, where the relation between the empire and the periphery on a global scale is played out in its miniature form, leading toward joblessness and despair on the part of the worker and enrichment on the part of the capitalist class. Contrary to what is conjectured by some of the novel's critics, the objective of Shehzad's narrative, then, is not to posit a differential understanding of the center and the periphery but to expose the similitude of the two spaces by zooming in on internal maps of core capitalist nations. The day after the barfight, the narrator accompanies Jamshed to Jersey City, where the latter's family lives. On his way to their house, where Jamshed's father "Old Man Khan" and sister Amna live, Shehzad takes a good look at the city. Once prosperous and busy, the city has lost its population, becoming a run-down place inhabited mainly by immigrants. A city where "Caucasians are a minority," outnumbered by African Americans, Hispanics, Arabs, and Muslims, Jersey's history is replete with antecedents of racial violence. The parallel between the "routine violence" of the extractive wars that Kojo runs away from, and the "the murderous Dotbusters" who "stalked and killed Asians with clubs and boots and pipes" well into the 1980s (*HB* 45) is a reminder of the likeness between the United States and the Republic of Congo, not an evocation of their essential difference. The veneer of racial tension, it seems, is underwritten by collective destitution of the entire working-class population of Jersey City. Loss of jobs and economic activities work as subtexts in this narrative of racial antipathy, pitting one community against another, creating a rift within the body politic. This

88 *Home Boy, Reluctant Fundamentalist,* & Reserve Army of Capital

is how the city's desolate small businesses and communities have been described by the narrator:

> You could feel it walking down some streets: people didn't avert their eyes or nod when you walked past but often stared, either tacitly claiming you as their own or dismissing you as the Other. Jersey City has been defined by a decided troubled bustle ... The skyscrapers downtown were erected in the seventies and looked it: you didn't see any stucco or stonework, only steel and darkened windows. At night, the buildings seemed to brood. And despite the gentrification of Jersey City through the Great Bull Run, there were boarded-up strorefronts in the side streets, closed movie theaters, bodegas with iron grills. (*HB* 45)

The description of boarded-up storefronts and closed movie theaters bears an eerie resemblance to David Harvey's account of Baltimore city with its abandoned houses and impoverished working-class neighborhoods (*Spaces of Hope* 133–135). This short description also forces us to notice how the contours of Shehzad's narrative are not only shaped by September 11 but also by the Great Bull Run, whose end in the mid-1990s marked the beginning of a prolonged era of crisis. Jersey city's destitution is a reminder of the failures of the neoliberal experimentation of the Regan-Thatcher era, which, instead of enriching the working-class, impoverished them even further. Since this idea of the race-class conjuncture and its relationship with the financial crisis will be further developed in the latter part of this chapter, let us now turn to the novel's closure, which takes us back to the issue of racial oppression.

HB's unusual narrative closure, where the narrator's departure from the city and his first arrival are relayed in succession, makes it difficult to arrive at any definitive conclusion about its thematic development. Those two moments are preceded by the events leading to their arrest and detention on suspicion of wrongdoing. After Shehzad and Jamshed return form their monthly visit to Old Man Khan, the three men take Abdul Karim's cab to go to Westbrook, where the Shaman lives. When they reach his house, they find it uninhabited, with no sign of their friend. As they loiter around Shaman's house, his suspicious neighbors call the cops on them, a report that escalates in the immediate post 9/11 hysteria from a local police incident to a federal terrorist investigation. When the FBI comes and the intoxicated friends, unable to understand what is going on, attack the intruders not knowing who they were, they get arrested. After days of torture and inquiry, both Shehzad and Jamshed are released without any charges. AC, however, faces the prospect of 15 years of life for possession of cocaine, the penalty for which is "the same for second degree murder" (*HB* 193), a critique of the Rockefeller drug laws that have contributed to the racial disparities of mass U.S. incarceration.

Home Boy, Reluctant Fundamentalist, & Reserve Army of Capital   **89**

Traumatized and broke, Shehzad decides to go back to Karachi, despite a job offer and the prospect of settling down with Amna.

There is no after-story in Naqvi's *HB*—no follow-up of what happens after Shehzad (Shehzad) leaves the city. A crestfallen, dejected Shehzad departs from New York City, leaving AC in the detention center. Before his departure, he meets Amna, who asks him to stay. The last few days of Shehzad's New York City life are very economically described, with little clue as to what his thoughts are. Since Shehzad's is a deeply personal story, it ends in a personal note too, with a reminiscence of his first arrival to the city. However, the penultimate chapter of the novel gives the reader a clue about the trauma the FBI investigations and AC's incarceration leaves in Shehzad's unconscious, showing how the fear and puzzlement makes him collapse in terror near Central Park after seeing what he believed to be a police officer hailing him, and even prompts him to attempt suicide. Indeed, Shehzad's traumatic breakdown demands that, following Freud, we consider his abandonment of NYC and the United States as a melancholic subject's desperate attempt to preserve his ego by withdrawing from the lost object (Eng and Kazanjian 3) and by sadistically trying to destroy himself for failing to retain the object of love (Freud 252). Both NYC and his friend AC appear to be the objects/ persons on whom the narrator dotes. But the penultimate chapter offers another prism, allowing us to construe the narrator's trauma as a symptom of his rejection of anonymity, racial and cultural erasure. Before leaving his apartment for good, Shehzad discovers in a newspaper an obituary for his missing friend Shaman (Mohammed Shah), who died while attending a conference in the World Trade Center. The obituary describes Shaman as an unusual Muslim, one who was more like "us": "Everybody thinks all Muslims are fundamentalists ... Mohammed wasn't like that. He was like us ... He worked hard, played hard" (*HB* 170). Shehzad accurately notices that there is no mention of the likes of him and his friends in the Manichean post-9/11 narrative; the young, carefree, cosmopolitan, immigrant community of which he is a part has suddenly become unrepresentable:

> It was the oddest obituary. Perhaps all obituaries are fundamentally odd. There was no mention of the ship jumping, gas pumping, porn watching, cigarette running—*de mortuis nil nisi bonum*—and there was no mention of us. The story was simple, black and white: the man was a Muslim, not a terrorist. (*HB* 170)

What Shehzad wants is the recognition of his identity, the acknowledgement of his and his kind's existence. Although this demand may appear incommensurate to the damage he experiences and the loss he suffers, behind the narrator's anguished desire for recognition exists his harrowing memory of being cast as a member of a community he and his friends carefully chose not to belong to. The normative understanding of Muslim identity in the United States, notes Aparajita De, "functions to demonize" them in dominant narratives in such ways that "their experiences and articulations become disposable, dismembered, and dysfunctional" (De xii). It seems as if Shehzad is battling against the processes of such demonization, which, after obliterating his and his friends' narrative, has chosen to replace it with their juvenile ideas about good and evil, "us" and "them," the same juvenile Manicheism that President Bush articulated in his State of the Union address in the lead-up to the invasion of Iraq and Afghanistan (a speech Shezad and his friends hear on the night before their arrest).

HB's closing chapters make it imperative that we take note of the post-9/11 U.S. cultural polity, which disperaged and otherized the entire Muslim, Arab, and South Asian population living inside the borders of the nation. But the novel does not do so by drowning out the economic fallouts of institutionalized racism, nor does it propagate a belief that race relations in the United States are merely subjective paranoia, flowing from the white man and moving toward the South Asian Muslim object. Indeed, one of the subtle thematic moves of the novel is to place multiple moments of empathy and compassion in its narrative, showing how, despite systemic production of racism in culture, human beings treat each other with kindness. These subjective and particular forms, however, are set against the backdrop of the broader frames of socio-economic generality. As we have discussed earlier, the novel's depiction of race relations is channeled through the city's—also the nation's—economic reality, their deep history.

In *Racism and Cultural Studies* (2002), E. San Juan Jr. contends that ethnic identities in the United States cannot be understood "apart from the historical trajectories, the workings of the state, and the contingencies of political economy" (*Racism* 99). In order to understand the race relation in the United States, he maintains, it is essential that we look into the nation's long imperial history, and its relationship with other nations. Naqvi's novel forces us to notice how the perimeters of race relations are conditioned by class relations and vice versa, but it also tells us how destitution itself generates its own divisions, demanding loyalties, pitting one community against another. Although his novel addresses some of the most pressing issues emerging out of the events of 9/11, what remains distant and not fully comprehended or articulated in its narrative are the contours of the U.S. imperial relations, which, by engaging with distant worlds of nations and impinging upon other people's lives, draws people in only to exploit them even further. The cab drivers who arrive in the city barefoot, the frightened migrants who leave America to find a safe abode somewhere else, the terrified citizens of South Asia who wait to see the consequences of the destruction of the Twin Towers—all point toward an imperial presence and its uneven human consequences. *Home Boy* deftly narrates the story of a fractured city and national space, while only gesturing toward the distant imperial relations. The novel that addresses the issue of the United States' global/imperial presence even more boldly and explicitly is Mohsin Hamid's *TRF*—a monologue in which a Muslim man is the speaker and an American agent is his audience of one.

The Reluctant Fundamentalist and U.S. Imperialism

Published in 2007 and shortlisted for the Man Booker Prize, *TRF* is Pakistani-born British writer Mohsin Hamid's second novel—the novel that established his pre-eminence among the writers of his generation. His first novel, *Moth Smoke,* was published in 2000, using Lahore as its setting and thematizing Pakistan's internal strife, especially addiction and economic despair. Like this first novel, *TRF* is set in the same city of Lahore, Pakistan's second largest city, but its actions mostly take place in the United States. The novel begins in a marketplace in Lahore, where Changez, a university lecturer at a local university, engages an American in a conversation. Although the narrator's interlocutor is not given a voice in the narrative, it is possible to conjecture what the content of the conversation can be by following the threads of the narrator's discourse. In her elegant discussion of Mohsin Hamid's *TRF,* Rajini Srikanth mentions that Changez's monologue is a counter-discourse aimed at ending the monopoly of the United States on the topic of terrorism. She reads the silence of the American agent as a deliberate narrative strategy, geared toward reducing the vociferous locution of the privileged imperial subject into mere listening. In the opening scene of the novel, we see the loquacious narrator trying to strike up a conversation with an American who, he thinks, is "on a mission," suggesting he is an American agent. Claiming he is a "native" of the city and can speak English fluently, Changez offers to assist the visitor, in case he needs it (*TRF* 1). He reassures the alarmed agent by saying that he has lived in America for four and a half years and has worked in New York City. A graduate from Princeton, he has also spent a substantial amount of those four and a half years in New Jersey, where the university is located (*TRF* 3). As the narrative progresses, the readers get to know how his Princeton days were marked by financial and academic strife, and how he had to juggle between odd jobs to keep afloat, while also maintaining a high grade-point average to retain his scholarship. When, after graduation, he is hired by Underwood Samson, a savvy evaluation firm that researches the financial prospects of companies for potential investors, he feels elated, thinking his hard days are over. The money that Changez receives as a sign-on bonus allows him to holiday in Greece—his first one to Europe. This is where he first meets Erica, a fellow Princetonian, whom he befriends and later falls in love with. While he enjoys the company of wealthy Princetonians, he is put off by the brashness of their attitude, especially by their irreverent attitudes toward people much older than them (*TRF* 21). The impudence with which Americans treat others, which the narrator identifies as an expression of their imperial power, is contributed to by their relative ignorance about the rest of the globe. The narrator's distaste for American impudence testifies to his own ambivalence as well: on the one hand, he sees it as a culture devoid of sensitivity and empathy and, on the other, he is drawn toward it, so much so that his

92 *Home Boy, Reluctant Fundamentalist,* & Reserve Army of Capital

narrative is redolent with positive experiences, especially his memories of being in the city of New York, which he compares with being at home.

Although the differences between Shehzad's and Changez's New York are pronounced, there is also likeness in the manner in which they embrace and celebrate the city. For Shehzad, the city is the place of his mental and intellectual growth, the very fabric of his cultural sensibility, whereas for Changez, it is a sanctuary, a place imbued with warmth and familiarity. For the latter, the city is a place where he will not stick out among the crowd; there are many more like him in that city. It is symptomatic that New York City enters the narrator's discussion as a point of comparison. Lahore, we are told, is the second largest city of Pakistan, and is "home to nearly as many people as New York" (*TRF* 7). It is in the third chapter of the novel that the narrator makes specific references to NYC, claiming moving to this city was like going home (*TRF* 32). He also explains why the city feels homey to him. It is a city where he hears his first language, Urdu, being spoken by cab drivers. There is also a Pakistani restaurant just two blocks from his apartment. All these details make him feel comfortable, so comfortable that he claims: "I was, in four and a half years, never an American; I was *immediately* a New Yorker" (*TRF* 33). The evocation of the idea of belonging to the city allows us to see the parallel between the two narrators' fondness for the place. Yet, unlike Shehzad and his friends, who are traumatized by the attacks on the WTC building, Changez is pleased to see the towers go down. Although he later tries to complicate his initial reaction by claiming that it was accompanied by a "profound sense of perplexity" (*TRF* 73), that his initial reaction was not of horror but of satisfaction allows the complexity of his relation to the city to emerge on the surface. It is difficult to conjecture whether Changez belongs to NYC in the same way that Shehzad does. But the former's ambivalence toward the city makes apparent how in his consciousness the city exists as a place mediated by the nation and its imperial ambition. It is perhaps because of this that when the Twin Towers go down, he likens it to the American empire being brought to its knees; the traumatic event is, in his reckoning, an attack on the empire and not the city. After confessing to his interlocutor how he was initially "remarkably pleased" to see the Twin Towers go down, he tries to clarify his response using the following reasoning: "But at that moment, my thoughts were not with the *victims* of the attack … no, I was caught up in the *symbolism* of it all, the fact that someone had so visibly brought America to her knees" (*TRF* 73).

The symbolism of seeing America on her knees thus informs his initial response to the tragedy of loss of life in the Twin Towers attacks. Belonging to the city does not deter him from deriving pleasure at its destruction because in his mental space; America and New York exist as separate entities. It is here that Changez is different from Shehzad. Whereas Shehzad is able to expand his arc of empathy and extend it to others who face tragedy, Changez faces perplexity and a dilemma, and is consequently unable to empathize with those whose lives are lost. What further complicates his representation of his relation to the city is the symbolism of being a lover of America. Erica, it has been suggested, is a metonymic representation of America. In the symbolic sense, loving Erica is loving America. Yet, what complicates the whole concept of loving Erica/America is the trauma of losing her. While the narrator of *The Reluctant Fundamentalist* mourns the loss of Erica, the best he can do at the city's loss is to conceal his real feelings in front of his colleagues (*TRF* 74).

One explanation for Changez's responses to the city's tragedy can be this: unlike Shehzad, who feels that he has a stake in the city's cosmopolitan culture, Changez feels no such obligation toward the city. His outsideness, for instance, has been pointed out to him by his boss, Jim, who credits his watchfulness to him being "out of place" (*TRF* 43). What is also probable is that his gradual understanding of America's imperialist history and an acquaintance with its victims (in Manila and in Chile) condition his unconscious response to its tragedy. Albert Braz, in his insightful essay titled "9/11, 9/11: Chile and Mohsin Hamid's *The Reluctant Fundamentalist*" gestures toward this second possibility by suggesting that Changez's antipathy toward America is due to the nation's long history of disrupting lives elsewhere, thus creating a common experiential frame where America features as an imperialist power bent on destroying democracies and buttressing authoritarian regimes who suppress people (Braz 241–3). The three trips that he takes to evaluate companies for his value firm, all unpack for him the way the imperial state treats not only people from other nations but also its own working-class population. Srikanth's characterization of Changez's discontent as "deliberate dissatisfaction" valorizes the idea that his is a conscious disengagement with America. Yet, the trajectory from voluntary servitude to intentional distancing is not a linear development. Erica, whose love Changez seeks and who symbolically represents America, both disrupts and hastens Changez's antipathy toward the American empire. Srikanth traces the beginning of Changez's transformation way back in his first business trip to Manila. Sitting in a limousine with his colleagues in Manila's thick traffic, Changez feels the heat of the "undisguised hostility" of a jeepney driver's gaze, wondering what might have induced such resentment. Although Changez is unable to understand the rationale behind the driver's "obvious, intimate" dislike (*TRF* 67), he gradually mounts up enough understanding of the capitalist accumulation process and American imperialism to critically look into his own contribution to both. Changez reveals that he has "always resented the manner in which America conducted itself in the world" (*TRF* 156), but his awareness about his own complicity does not fully emerge until he is confronted by the Chilean book publisher Juan-Bautista. Already troubled by America's indiscriminate bombing of Afghanistan and arm twisting of Pakistan, Changez starts neglecting work when he is sent to Chile to evaluate a book publishing company. Juan-Bautista,

94 *Home Boy, Reluctant Fundamentalist, & Reserve Army of Capital*

the chief of the company whose understanding of books runs much deeper than those evaluating his business, is both irate and troubled because of the intrusion of the valuation firm. Convinced that Changez is different from the rest in his firm, the old book publisher takes him out for lunch. "Does it trouble you," he asks Changez, "to make your living by disrupting the lives of others?" (*TRF* 151). Unconvinced by his young companion's answer that Underwood Samson is only an evaluation firm, Juan-Bautista asks if Changez has heard of the janissaries. In response to Changez's baffled "no," the veteran publisher says: "They were Christian boys ... captured by the Ottomans and trained to be soldiers in a Muslim army, at that time was the greatest in the world. They were ferocious and utterly loyal: they had fought to erase their own civilizations, so they had nothing else to turn to" (*TRF* 151).

Changez later recounts how Juan-Bautista's historical chronicle "plunges" him into "a deep bout of introspection," inducing in him the awareness that he was "a servant of the American empire" (*TRF* 152). The essential irony of the situation lies not so much in Changez's realization that he is working against the interest of his own nation but, rather, that his cosmopolitan life in Princeton and New York City accords him no insight into his own reality. It is the outside—the spaces that have already experienced the brunt of the brutality of U.S. imperialism—that make him aware that he is indeed the empire's mercenary.

However, how is it possible that a person who is no soldier is lumped so carelessly in the category of the janissaries? At the moment when Juan-Bautista chastises him for being on the wrong side, he is merely an employee in a valuation firm. What, then, is the real import of this statement? In order to understand the stakes of this implied culpability as a financial analyst, we need to look into the way finance has been depicted in this novel, and how the novel figures the coordination and cooperation between corporeal violence and the financial empire. In a fascinating paragraph where Changez tells his American interlocutor that his country's "constant interference in the affairs of others was insufferable," he also asserts that "finance is [sic] the primary means by which the American empire exercised its power" (*TRF* 156). Changez's conjecture about the nexus between imperialism and finance demands that we carefully scrutinize how violence has been used to open up new markets for capitalist usurpation and how, by forcefully imposing neoliberal economic policies on another nation and by enforcing austerity measures, the U.S. empire has amassed huge wealth in its cities. It also solicits us to notice how the American "interference" in other parts of the world has allowed its ruling elites to have a reserve army of workers at its disposal.

Conclusion

Changez describes his departure from New York succinctly, revealing that his final days were passed in a state of incoherence and confusion. The thought of

Home Boy, Reluctant Fundamentalist, & Reserve Army of Capital **95**

leaving the city redolent with memories of Erica drives him into a state of frenzy and depression. He narrates how he went out and tried to provoke people by flaunting his beard and Islamic attire, only to return to his room to watch the media and well-respected journalists lapse into the kind of rhetoric that reflects hubris and righteousness (167–68). On his way back to Pakistan, he looks out through the window of his plane to locate the place from which Erica went missing after jumping off a cliff into the Hudson river. As he returns to Pakistan, he obsesses over Erica, fantasizing about her and imagining what might transpire if she was with him in Lahore. The trails of trauma that Changez leaves behind in the last few chapters of the novel are too numerous to address here, but it suffices to mention that his time in American leaves a permanent void in his life, and his struggles to overcome it partially defines his deep emotional investment in Imperial America.

The penultimate chapter of *Home Boy,* on the other hand, where the narrator's departure from the city is described, alternates between first person and second person narratives, describing first Shehzad's lunch with Amna and then the moment of his discovery of Shaman's obituary in a newspaper. Before he leaves the city, she drops by unexpectedly with a dish of sweets—"gulab jamuns" (210)—which prompts him to take her out for dinner. As they have dinner and chit-chat about her family, Amna asks him: "why're you leaving?" Although he tells her he does not know exactly why, deep inside his head he relays why he is leaving, thinking:

> If I had a couple of drinks in me I might have told her about the fear, the paranoia, the profound loneliness that had become routine features of life in the city, about my undistinguished career as a banker and a cabbie. If I had a couple of drinks in me, I just might have spilled my guts. (211)

It is, then, not only his fear of being alone in the city he collectively experienced with his friends that drives him out; it is also the paranoia that has become the characteristic feature of the city that repels him. The thought is vague enough to suggest that, even to the narrator himself the reasons for abandoning the city are not transparent. Although the city's antipathy is hinted at, his reasons for leaving the city remain deeply personal, suggesting a nebulous indeterminacy that mediates his action. Before leaving his apartment, he notices Shaman's obituary in the newspaper with which he is about to wrap Amna's gulab jamuns. After reading the "odd obituary," he offers a prayer for his dead friend—a Muslim custom—and then, "when it was time to go," he departs (*HB* 216).

As has been mentioned earlier, there is no after-story in *HB*. There is no discussion about what happens in Shehzad's life he departs. The final chapter recounts Shehzad's first arrival, how he says "'[h]aya doin'" at the immigration, and how from his cab he notices "blurred images framed by graffiti and rubbish"

(*HB* 215). Despite his initial disappointment from observing a homeless man with "the contents of his life spilling from a shopping cart," he feels upbeat and optimistic when he arrives. This return to the moment of beginning can be aesthetically and formally schematized as a circular closure: the story ends where it begins. Symbolically, however, this formal circularity can be read as Shehzad's entrapment in his NYC memory, which enacts its own totality by denying any other beginning in its space. As a traumatized subject, he must return to the object of trauma again and again to realize the meaning of his existence. The circular temporal logic enacted by the last chapter of the novel leaves us at the doorstep of two different figurations: following the footsteps of Lauren Berlant, we can interpret Chuck's return to the source of his trauma—New York City—as a moment of "cruel optimism" (Berlant 94); and, toeing the line of Marxist hermeneutics, we can also see it as a moment of imposing on the stylistic form of the novel the neoliberal logic an eternal capitalist future—the end of history, as Francis Fukuyama phrased it as. The first figuration's limit is that it fails to convincingly explain Shehzad's desertion of the city. Why, having invested in the object of love, does he withdraw from it only to return to it time and again? The second interpretation allows us to understand why there is no after-story. Unlike Changez, whose apprehension of the United States as an imperial power allows him to look for solidarity, Shehzad's atomized self sees no usefulness in extending his community beyond his friends. The departure itself is his ultimate resistance. Devoid of any means of extending his community beyond his friends, all he can think of is leaving the site of trauma behind and returning to his national space, where he must re-live the memory of friendship and petty-bourgeois migrant life. Simply put, NYC's cosmopolitan life remains his utopian moment to which he must return time and again. It is this element of his subjectivity that, despite his many similarities with Changez, also separates him from the latter. Shehzad caves in and re-immerses himself in a phantasmic return to the site of trauma, while Changez expands his arc of vision and engages in an anti-imperial politics. What informs the former's resistance, therefore, is a kind of "cynical reason" (Jameson, *Valences of the Dialectic* 413), which parlays the reality for Shehzad in such a way that he is unable to dig himself out of his deep pessimism about any other possible future.

In his elegant discussion of *Capital Vol. I* in *Representing Capital* (2011), Jameson hypothesizes that Marx's magisterial critique of capitalism posits two definitive features of capitalism's response to its own history. The first deals with erasure: capitalism seeks to erase its present violent history by positing it as its past. The second feature deals with the occlusion of a non-capitalist future: by constantly postulating itself as futuristic, capitalism tries to block the arrival of a post-capitalist future (*Representing* 104). By hiding the traces of its violence, and also by suppressing the imagination of a future utopia, capitalism offers itself as the only possible alternative. Cynical reason marks the occasion of our acceptance of capitalism's narrative about itself. Despite knowing "everything that is wrong with late capitalism, all the structural toxicities of the system," cynical reason declines indignation in "a kind of impotent lucidity" (*Valences* 413), rejecting the possibility of a different kind of future. The kind of post-colonial rage that makes Shehzad identify the "procrustean machine," but stops him from rebelling against it can be slotted as the kind of cynical reason that Jameson addresses in *The Valences*. In his pragmatism, one notices the internal-ization of one of the grand fetishisms of the neoliberal era—the idea of the eternal capitalist future. In this sense, Shehzad's desertion of NYC reflects his utopian desire to abandon a neoliberally conditioned racially divided city, whereas the absence of an after-story marks the playing out of a cynical reason.

Like Shehzad, whose narrative leaves the reader in an indeterminate space, Changez too offers the reader similar enigmas. It is very difficult to assume what his narrative's purpose is. There are moments when it seems as if his narrative is merely a subterfuge for holding the agent back until the evening so he can be stalked and ambushed. There are other moments when his narrative appears like a genuine tête-à-tête, aimed at unpacking a trauma. The indeterminacy of the closure, typical of postmodern fictions, resists definitive conclusions, thus obscuring not only the content of what is explored but also the politics of its representation as such. Nevertheless, the story of Changez's return to Lahore marks a rather successful filiation.[4] After mourning for Erica, and amidst the fear and anticipation of Pakistan's impending war with India, Changez joins the local university and becomes a very popular lecturer of finance—the subject he studied in the United States. Now convinced that U.S. imperialism is deeply detrimental to Pakistan's independence, he professes "disengagement" from the United States for "greater independence in Pakistan's domestic and international affairs" (179). Although his students mostly include "bright, idealistic scholars" whom he ad-dresses as "comrades," implying his left-leaning politics, the alternative that he suggests involves demonstrations against the bully of the United States. The book's final paragraph, however, renders Changez's entire narrative unreliable, and it is possible to read his narrative as a fictitious story constructed to allure the American agent into the dragnet. Since the last passage also blurs the distinction between Changez as a left-leaning university professor and him being an assassin possibly involved with right-wing religious groups, no determinate answer as to what constitutes Changez's resistance is possible. What is indeed possible is an account of whether or not Changez's return looks into an alternative outside capitalism. Having identified finance capital as the fundamental impetus behind American imperialism, the narrator of Hamid's novel has no other alternative but to recede back to the nationalist quasi-religious struggle.[5] It is not that Changez does not know what he is fighting against; it is, rather, having understood it all, he must channel his resistance through the nation/religion space because the existing reality conceals the other alternatives. The returns that close both novels

98 *Home Boy, Reluctant Fundamentalist, & Reserve Army of Capital*

embody hopes for an alternative mode of existence but the novels, having failed to find traces of that possibility in existing reality, remain trapped in what exists and what is dominant: the capital relation as expressed under neoliberalism.

It is difficult to definitively know what the narrators' return to their national space means. *HB* does not even embark on the task of narrating what happens once Shehzad returns. *TRF*'s narrativization of the return, on the other hand, leaves us in limbo because no conclusion can be reached on the basis of the closure that is attempted in the work. Irrespective of the confusion created by open closures, however, what can be surmised about them is that they stage powerful critiques of the world their narrators leave behind. It is here, in the desire of these works to critique not only cosmopolitan (neoliberally re-organized) New York City but also U.S. imperialism, that one needs to locate their utopia. Written in the aftermath of United States' war on terror, these novels could only collect the broken shards of the popular discontent against those imperialist wars. As is further explored in the next chapter, collective rage against neoliberalism was not voiced at that moment because the effects of neoliberal policies had not begun to come into full view. The war itself further obfuscated any clarity about the neoliberal policies that became ubiquitous after the financial crisis of 2008. The absence of a utopian collective practice is a mere reflection of the zeitgeist of the condition in which the novels are set. It is impossible to ignore the vague presence of radical utopian visions in Changez's attempt to instill anti-imperial values in his students, but perhaps the actions of the two narrators—that they decline the comfort of the cosmo-politan liberal utopia and return home—are equally powerful illustrations of a utopian zeitgeist as well, one that seeks to wrench itself free from old (neo) liberal dreams of settling down at the heart of the metropole and embark on a new beginning at home.

Notes

1 Long before Harvey and Foster, Lenin too noticed this important juncture between empire and finance. In his classic work "Imperialism, the Highest Stage of Capitalism," Lenin writes:

> Imperialism is capitalism in that stage of development in which the domination of monopolies and finance capital has established itself; in which the export of capital has acquired pronounced importance; in which the division of the world among the international trust has begun; in which the partition of all the territories of the globe among the great capitalist powers has been completed. (Lenin 237)

As is clear from Lenin's discussion, financialization plays an important role in imperialism in capitalism's monopolistic stage. What is significantly different about Harvey's deliberations on this topic is, he sees it as a process of producing surplus population as well.

2 Marx's discussion on the production of immiseration is both rich and compelling. He writes:

Accumulation of wealth at one pole is, therefore, at the same time accumulation of misery, the torment of labor, slavery, ignorance, brutalization and moral degradation at the opposite pole, i.e. on the side of the class that produces its own product as capital. (Capital 798–99)

3 Vivek Chibber has explained this uneven historical development by claiming that in the colonial world, "the reliance of producing absolute surplus value rendered capitalism highly coercive and violent ... in the advanced world, it was the production of relative surplus value that caused a switch to less personalized, more formal regimes of profit making" (Chibber 133).

4 A cornerstone of Edward Said's theorization of the intellectual in "Secular Criticism," the idea of filiation refers to seamlessly fitting into the environment one is born into or the conditions one belongs to, i.e. "birth, nationality, profession" etc. ("Criticism" 25). Said contrasts filiations with affiliative associations, such as social and political convictions and so on. In his later works, however, Said associates filiation with nationalist tendencies and affiliations with voluntary associations of an exile.

5 Matthew Hart and Jim Hansen foreground the idea that Changez's is a secular nationalism. They write:

> If it is neither religious nor ethnopoetic, how then to describe Changez's nationalism? The short answer is that it is political—political because it is predicated on an agonistic relation between two states, the U.S. and Pakistan, and on the judgement that the American response to 9/11 has only worsened Pakistani underdevelopment and insecurity. (Hart and Hansen 510)

However, the novel leaves us with no certainty about Changez's political pedigree and the symbolic import of Hamid's novel's beard points toward a quasi-religious form of nationalism.

5

CONCLUSION

In the Ruins of Neoliberalism

Introduction: The Loss of Utopian Dreams

In the last three chapters, we have noticed how contemporary South Asian novels and short stories aesthetically represent various local manifestations of neoliberalism, while simultaneously navigating its global structure—the feature that remains unmistakably present in all social contexts. No matter how we envision neoliberalism, whether considering it as a new logic of organizing society or perceiving it as a new modality of subject production, what remains constant in neoliberalism's very fiber is the concentration of wealth and political power in the hands of the capitalist class—the power with which it disciplines and suppresses labor and produces subjugated beings who see their existences tied to the existence of capitalism. The underlying system that silences Afaz and subjugates his grief is the money relation, which, in essence is but another manifestation of the relation between capital and labor. Similarly, the unequal geographical relations that Balram sees as rural/feudal India's leash on progressive/urban India is a fetish that obfuscates capitalism's systemic production of uneven space. Instead of mitigating the distance between the margin and center, capitalist globalization has made ubiquitous the unequal relation between center and margin, inner city and suburb, urban and rural, and core and periphery.[1] The inequality that bends the back of the rural poor is the same inequality that immiserates the lives of the urban underclass. The relation between the owners of capital and the owners of labor power is conditioned by the same fundamental inequality that underlies the production of uneven geographical space, especially the production of rural-urban relations. It is because of this that Changez and Shehzad's desertions of New York City appear as symbolic acts, signifying their

DOI: 10.4324/9781003324768-5

resistance against the racializing norms of the neoliberal city. NYC registers in their consciousness as a shattered dream, an unfulfilled promise. That their memories of the city are so redolent with a sense of loss emanating from their personal encounters with antipathy—antipathy that is underwritten by race and class relations—symptomatically represents the trauma of having to encounter xenophobic racial profiling. In a city whose demographic history is marked by the vectors of exclusion, it is only expected that Pakistani Muslim youth will, in the aftermath of the September 11 attacks, find themselves racially and ethnically profiled, harassed, and even imprisoned without any viable cause. What remains well-hidden from these Muslim youth is the unequal distribution of precariousness, the class logic of which only becomes visible to them when they themselves are subjected to cultural exclusion and economic disenfranchisement.

None of these works, it needs to be emphasized, explicitly critiques neoliberalism. Their thematization of certain elements of neoliberalism makes it possible to read them as neoliberal allegories, the presentations of which allows for a recuperation of the narrative traces of neoliberalism's adverse effect on lives. Yet, if there is one thing that all these narratives consistently point toward, it is the process of masking the systemic production of inequality. In the case of Afaz, the reality of the monetization of society remains concealed to him. What is blocked from Balram's consciousness is the gruesome reality of the neoliberal city built on the labor of the homeless urban migrants, who, like his father, have been driven out of their rural homes by poverty and oppressive landlords. Similarly, Changez and Shezad do not see their complicity in the financial system that comprises the heart of global imperialist structure. It is only at the moment of crisis that we begin to see neoliberalism's forms of appearance for what they truly are.

There is another important homology among the novels I discuss in my work: the absence of utopia. It is deeply symptomatic that none of the novels and stories discussed here represents any entrenched collective utopian project. Even if some of them allude to such visions—*The White Tiger*, for instance, vaguely refers to the Naxalites, only to expose the pettiness of their politics—it is done in an ironic tone, only to ridicule the futility of such dreams and projects. Just as neoliberalism itself forestalls potential utopian visions by propagating the idea that there is no alternative, so too do allegories of neoliberalism thematize absence of collective resistance by re-rehearsing idiosyncratic acts of defiance. Shehzad does not show any inclination to voice his discontent against the capitalist-imperialist structure he vaguely recognizes as the source of his suffering, whereas what Changez aims to achieve remains veiled under the indeterminacy of the novel's open closure. Faced with no other alternative, Afaz's only choice is to quietly return to the service of the wealthy and the powerful. Balram, true to his entrepreneurial spirit, can only think of a secular and utilitarian education as a viable alternative to state-sponsored corruption, rather than envisioning a systemic change.

102 Conclusion

Zafar—the mercurial protagonist of Zia Haider Rahman's brilliant first novel *In the Light of What We Know,* which also figures a critique of neoliberalism—turns into an eternal exile, moving from one place to another, trying to find a place where he can fit in. Disappointed by the elite liberal universe that abandons him after deceiving him and ashamed by his own "unspeakable" act, Zafar embraces displacement as his permanent condition, leaving behind the world of speculation and finance. His deliberate departure from speculative banking needs to be read as a critical presentation of the neoliberal financialized world. But, like other allegories of neoliberalism, *In the Light,* too, gets trapped in the singularity of existence, producing no solidarity, presenting no schema for the collective dream of transcending the ubiquitous capitalist norm. Despite being educated in some of the most prestigious institutions of the world, despite his familiarity with heavyweight philosophers and thinkers, and despite his working-class pedigree, Zafar is unable to see through the fetish of capitalism's eternal present, which produces him as a lonely, singular entity with no potential for collective overcoming.

The atomized individual is also the object of exploration in Amitav Ghosh's *tour de force,* the *Ibis Trilogy.* The three novels that comprise the trilogy—*Sea of Poppies, River of Smoke,* and *Flood of Fire*—despite their differences in stylistics and themes, culminate in the metamorphosis of Zachary Reid, who, from being a carpenter in the docks of Baltimore, rises to become an opium trader—a true-blue capitalist—in the final segment of *Flood of Fire, the final novel of the trilogy.* The constant evocation of the correspondence between past and present, the homology between the liberal and the neoliberal moment, is what casts this trilogy into the mold of an allegory. Ghosh's trilogy brilliantly zooms in on the past to expand our understanding of the present—imperialist war, self-congratulatory attitudes of venture capitalists, the corruption of political leadership, exile and displacement, ecological crisis ushered in by industrial production and cut-throat competitiveness to overcome poverty. In the *Ibis* trilogy, we find a historical depth absent from the other neoliberal allegories, providing greater analytical purchase on the structural dynamics of capital and empire. However, despite these novels' panoramic reconstruction of 19th-century's globalized world, they perform the same notable omission that marks each of the texts examined thus far: an inability to figure collective utopian practices.[2]

Why are these allegories of neoliberalism, which are surely invested in the project of critiquing finance and inequality, so uninterested in representing collective utopian projects? Perhaps there are both historical and economic answers to this question. Historically, neoliberalism's triumphant march was accompanied by the implosion of socialist states in Africa, Asia, and Europe. The triumphant march of neoliberalism across the planet was made possible by the collapse of the socialist block in Europe between 1989 and 1991, the dismantling of Keynesian welfare states in Africa and Asia in the 1980s and 1990s, and the large-scale economic reforms in communist China and social-democratic India in

Conclusion **103**

the 1970s and 1980s. As communist regimes in Poland, East Germany, Romania, Hungary, Czechoslovakia, The Soviet Union, and Yugoslavia fell one by one between 1989 and 1991, the narrative of communism's failure gained ground, turning into a conviction about socialism/communism's inherent inability to organize society around its utopian ideology. The narrative of capitalism's victory over communism and socialism allowed neoliberalism to gain ground not only in politics and economic strategies but also in educational institutions where the idea of market economy nestled so strongly that it became difficult to question capitalism in any meaningful way.

If the political defeat of communism/socialism was one element that allowed neoliberalism to expand globally, the other aspect that made it difficult to dream dangerously about revolution was cultural retreat. Aided by the post-structuralist fetishization of difference, which made it difficult to assert one's solidarity with a grand project without risking ridicule, neoliberal culture universalized the notion of the atomized subject entirely engaged in the process of achieving personal goals. The dwindling production of utopian narratives is an inevitable outcome of the internalization of a neoliberal postmodernist culture that rejects the notion of the collective pursuit of political and cultural goals. The strange correlation between the advent of neoliberal capitalism and the departure of utopian dreams has been cautiously noted by Jameson. In his perceptive essay "An American Utopia," he observes that the production of utopias has decreased remarkably in the last few decades ("An American Utopia" 1). Although it has become customary to present dystopian descriptions full of fantabulous moments of the destruction of the earth, imagining the end of capitalism and the beginning of a new era marked by equality remain outside the frame of imagination of contemporary writers.[3] The overproduction of dystopias on the one hand and the obliteration of utopian visions and politics from recent cultural memory on the other has contributed to the creation of a defeatist culture where "capitalist realism" (Fisher 2) appears to be the only condition of possibility.[4]

The absence of utopian politics in the allegories of neoliberalism, then, is an expression of a world where the supremacy of the neoliberal market appears uncontestable. Written before neoliberalism's widespread destruction of the planet began to appear clearly, before the time when even the core capitalist countries started displaying symptoms of widespread disenchantment about the mantra of freedom and equality doled out by the market, these novels predominantly represent the moments of neoliberalism's temporary social and political victory, depicting the struggles of people in a society administered by neoliberal cultural parameters. The significance of these novels' presentation lies in the manner in which they point toward the failures of neoliberalism and its concomitant culture.

One can always read their inability to communicate the collective utopia as a symptom of their formal and thematic complicity: being the products of the

104 Conclusion

culture of neoliberalism, how could these works remain immune to its ideological inscriptions? Yet, as I try to suggest through my readings of some contemporary South Asian novels and short stories, such easy conclusions should be avoided. If these works fail to articulate, clearly, a utopian vision, it is because an articulation of such a vision during the high neoliberal era would appear affected, artificial. The reason why Shezad, Ali, Balram, and Zafar do not form any collective space is because, as atomized neoliberal subjects, they have internalized neoliberalism's habitual suspicion of collective utopian dreams and, consequently, are unable to find any redemptive value in collective actions. Written when neoliberalism's crisis began to show up but before a widespread understanding of its climacteric effects, these works seem more invested in depicting the limits of neoliberalism than locating collective utopian practices. Hence, my observation that we need to locate the significance of their representation in their critical presentation of neoliberalism.

This observation is fortified by the reappearance,[5] albeit in limited scope, of utopian collective practices in more recent South Asian fiction pieces. As neoliberalism's blazing trail of destruction appears more clearly before our eyes and as crises become intensified, the neoliberal states' response to these crises become more desperate and draconian. It is no coincidence that the terrible environmental crisis and extreme inequality have been accompanied by the rise of fascism and a far-right extremism that not only denies climate crisis but also blames the growing inequality on immigrants and the poor working-class population. It seems, as if, instead of dismantling the veils of fetishism, late neoliberal crisis has further expanded fetishism's hold.

Perhaps our collective anxiety about the topsy-turvy world of the late-neoliberal era has been best captured by two recently published novels that depict not only the adverse impact of capitalism on climate but also the poisonous effects of fascism on society. The first of these two, Arundhati Roy's *The Ministry of Utmost Happiness* (2017), explores the raw wounds of the Indian nation through the experiences of two remarkable characters—Anjum, a hermaphrodite born and brought up in Old Delhi, and Tilottama, a rebellious woman whose unmarried teenage mother first abandons and then adopts her. It is through their experiences that the traumatic history of contemporary India becomes available to the reader. The second novel, *The Gun Island* (2019; henceforth *GI*) by Ghosh, engages with global issues, most notably global ecological crisis, planetary displacement, and capitalist greed. By reworking an old Bengali myth—the tale of Manasa and Chand Shadagar—this novel sets in motion an adventure that works like a meta-narrative capacious enough to touch upon vast swaths of history and experience, asking vexing questions about the relation between nature and commerce, humans and non-humans, myth and reality, to subtly suggest that the unfettered power of commerce that we observe today is the root of our agony.

Conclusion **105**

These works are somewhat different from the ones I have discussed earlier in another sense as well: standing amidst the ruins of neoliberalism, these two novels also point toward a possible collective future. They have their differences, of course. Roy's work is firmly rooted in India's internal injuries, whereas Ghosh's cli-fi takes the whole world as its setting, navigating the past to creatively zoom in on the present moment. Yet, they do look into the conditions of possibilities in their own ways: *The Ministry* does so by imagining the possibility of creating a counter-space inhabited by the traumatized, the damaged, the oppressed, and the abandoned, while *The Gun Island* does the same by stitching into its narrative the possibility of collective awakening, by narrativizing the possibility of a post-humanist future. In this concluding chapter, I will read these allegories of late-neoliberalism not only in terms of their presentations of capitalism's crises but also in relation to their utopian visions, so as to argue that these two novels hint toward a new structure of feeling, a feeling that has grown out of the ruins of neoliberalism and is looking toward a post-neoliberal future.

Utopian Visions in *The Gun Island and The Ministry of Utmost Happiness*

"[T]he world of today presents all the symptoms of demonic possession," is how Professoressa Giacinta Schiavon or Cinta—a character from Ghosh's latest novel, *The Gun Island*—verbalizes her anxiety about humanity's inability to properly assess the danger that looms large over our heads. In a sense, Cinta's description of human beings' incognizance about the impending danger points toward the operative fetishisms that distort our apprehension of reality, hazing us into believing that the crisis threatening our existence is unexceptional, mundane. It is no coincidence, then, that the novel's plot is organized around its protagonist Dinanath Dutta's awakening from the demonic possession that stymies his ability to understand how human-induced environmental crisis is threating life on this planet. As Dutta, a dealer in rare books and antiquities, visits Kolkata to recover from heartbreak, he is prodded by one of his old acquaintances to find out more about the "Bonduki Sadagar" (the Gun Merchant) who, according to that acquaintance, is a mythological figure like "Chand Sadagar," who is said to have escaped overseas to flee from the punishment from Manasa Devi, the goddess of snakes and poisonous beings (*GI* 5). Pursuit of the legend of the "Gun Merchant" sets Dutta on a long and harrowing journey that takes him to different parts of the planet—the Sundarbans, New York, Los Angeles, and finally to Venice—where he observes not only a trail of ecological destruction but also of human trafficking, war, and migration.

Thematically, the novel deals with three of the most familiar tropes of late capitalism—environmental crisis, migration, and commerce—yet ones that are rarely brought together on the same narrative canvas. The myth that exists at the center of the novel's thematic structure itself is a tropological exploration of

106 Conclusion

the antagonistic relation between nature and capital, capturing not only the stubbornness of the merchant class but also their hubris and insolence for which they become the targets of nature. This foundational myth, which comes from the ancient Indian epic *The Mahavarata,* has been locally appropriated in many different forms of Bengali and Asamese folklore, all narrating the stubbornness of Chand Sadagar—a merchant—who declines to treat the goddess of the snake with due deference. This myth has appeared and reappeared in many different forms in the Bengal delta in different historical junctures, especially during the times of crises (Haq 42). What is even more important about the complicated relationship between Manasa Devi and Chand Sadagar is that the former is seen as the subaltern class's deity, protecting the poor from the adversity of nature. In other words, the relation between Manasa and the Merchant is one that is already underwritten by the logic of class, where the merchant's insult of the subaltern goddess sets her on the path of revenge. In the novel, this antagonism is re-worked into a much broader one embracing the whole planet, figuring the metabolic rift between nature and capital.[6]

That the myth of Banduki Sadagar is a site of struggle between nature and commerce is clearly gestured to right at the beginning of *GI* when Kanai, the novel's narrator and Dinanath's distant relative, introduces him to the myth, saying:

> [E]very merchant who's ever sailed out of Bengal has had to pass through the Sundarbans—there's no other way to reach the sea. The Sundarbans are the frontier where commerce and the wilderness look each other directly in the eye; that's exactly where the war between profit and Nature is fought. (*GI* 8)

The idea of a "war" between nature and profit conjures up the image of the world in which capital is positioned against nature, a world in which their relationship is antagonistic. The evocation of this theme very clearly situates Ghosh's novel as a neoliberal allegory. In the latter part of the novel, when the pursuit of the legend of the Gun Merchant finally takes Deen to Venice, where the historical figure on whom the myth is based also took shelter in the 16th century, the same idea of the war between nature and profit is relayed once again, this time more compellingly. Sitting on a bench near the Piazza San Marco, the narrator gets lost in a dream that gives him a clue to the mystery of the merchant. He understands that Manasa Devi was not "a goddess" in the conventional sense of the term; rather, she was an arbiter between humans and non-humans whose job was to maintain a balance between the two. The merchant's refusal to submit to her dominion was a clear indication of his unwillingness to submit to the rules by which the balance of life was maintained. If, propelled by greed and hubris, the Gun Merchant and his like disavowed the goddess, the age-old boundary between the human and the non-human would

Conclusion **107**

collapse, and the balance of life would tilt. Hence, the significance of the pursuit and persecution of the Gun Merchant in the distant foreign land. In the narrator's words: "if he, and others like him, were to disavow her authority, all those unseen boundaries would vanish, and humans—driven as was the Merchant, by the quest for profit—would recognize no restraint" (*GI* 153).

The emphasis placed on profit in both these passages leaves little confusion as to what is implied by the idea of war between nature and capital. On the one hand, it points toward what Marx described as the irreparable "metabolic rift" between society and nature and, on the other, toward the antagonistic relationship between nature and capital. What is anticipated by those passages is the devastating effect of profiteering in a society ruled by merchants and their allies. It is not that the author himself is greatly convinced by Marxist discussions about the relation between nature and capital. Indeed, Ghosh's own position (in this novel, at least) can be best described as a kind of anti-imperialist post-humanism, the kind that is committed to identifying the entire human species as a hostile entity, complicit in the creation of the current crises. What these passages symbolically capture, therefore, are the hostile and confrontational relationships between human beings and nature. Their engagement with the history of capital remains cursory. Yet, in forgrounding the idea that a society driven by the logic of profit is inherenetly anti-nature, it lends a critical voice against the current mode of production. It is here that *The Gun Island* emerges as an allegory of neoliberalism.

If gesturing toward the metabolic rift is one of the novel's strategies for depicting the ruins of neoliberalism, the other strategy of doing so is cataloguing some of the most destructive and inexplicable catastrophes unleashed by nature. Taking an inventory of nature's destructiveness is one of the most interesting narrative features of Ghosh's work. While the depiction of natural calamities, such as cyclones, tornadoes, draughts, forest fires, and so on, allows the novel to illustrate the ravages of nature, such a narrative strategy also provides an outlet for channeling collective empathy by imagining shared victimhood. *Gun Island*'s narrative closure, which depicts pro-immigrant and anti-immigrant vessels facing off south of Venice in the.Adriatic seas, either to welcome or to chase away refugees, illustrates not only the antipathy that migration can trigger but also the empathy and shared victimhood that can powerfully nullify the threats of xenophobia. However, the novel's articulation of a utopian vision is not limited to this liberal optimism about the human capacity for goodness. What underwrites this utopian moment of welcoming a refugee boat full of migrants from all the troubled regions of the world is a broader post-humanist desire for a world of harmonious coexistence between humans and non-humans. The moment in which the refugee boat makes its entrance, with a storm of circling birds above and waves of bioluminescence underneath, with a robed woman commanding all the living entities—"*bhutas*"—to enact a miracle, is described in the novel as a

108 Conclusion

long expected *"miracolo,"* which will wake people up and make them see what is "happening in the world." "[T]his could be the moment," says Palash, a Bangladeshi immigrant, "when everything changes" (*GI* 284).

The stubborn hope for a miraculous change, thus, enacts its own counter-logic against the neoliberal message of hopelessness and despair. The obscene image of the Darwinian world that neoliberalism so effectively whips up to compartmentalize and alienate people, meets its utopian counterpart in Palash and Deen, who, standing amidst the ruins of capitalism, courageously hope for a hospitable world where humans and non-humans can harmoniously coexist. It is this utopian vision of a world of coexistence, the world as an ark giving refuge to all beings and things, that allows *The Gun Merchant* to be interpreted as a novel guided by a utopian impulse. If "utopia" is indeed a non-place as well as a "good place" (Ameel 786), the refugee vessel surrounded by birds and animals and steered by a Moses-like Ethiopian woman does create the optical illusion of a utopian space. But this is a moment that cannot on its own generate utopian transformation. What it offers, instead, is a catalyst-like mediation: a moment that exists to mediate the transformations of other moments. Utopia, here, arrives in the form of time, not space. Its potentiality depends on how other successive moments seize upon it. The novel thus leaves us at the threshold of miracle, with the feeling that something good may happen. It is here that the novel escapes the limits of its dystopian backdrop and flings itself into the realm of optimism. Unlike *The Ministry*, whose utopian impulse comes from the trauma of being rendered spaceless, prompting its protagonists to organize and produce a material space, *GI* seems to rely on the symbolic import of a moment to communicate utopian possibility that emerges in the radical disruption of capitalist temporality. Devoid of particularity—we do not know where the new awakening will take place and when or whether that new moment will summon into existence its own miraculous event—the utopian impulse of Ghosh's closure leaves us hanging in its globalist moment whose potential for collective catharsis remains limited.

Such a description cannot be applied to Roy's second novel, *The Ministry of Utmost Happiness* (*TMOUH* afterward). Writing about the difference between the Indian writer's two novels, Joan Acocella mentions that *God of Small Things* is about private and personal grief, while *The Ministry*, by contrast, is about national grief, about India's polity and public sorrows (n. pag.). Acocella's portrayal of Roy's recent novel as a mourning for India's national loss seems accurate when we look at it from the vantage point of national literature. It is, after all, a novel about trauma—the trauma that has risen out of the Indian nation's communal riots, genocide, domestic war, patriarchal oppression, and casteism. Roy's fragmented narrative, which is an assemblage of stories, obituaries, poetry, news items, legal documents, and music criticism, formally corresponds to these multiple national losses, gathering together every shard of pain that has come to haunt the nation's collective memory. Such an estimation also gestures toward the possibility of reading this novel as a tragedy, as a narrative exploration of trauma and loss. The moments in which characters recount losses are too many to ignore—whether of individualized acts of discrimination, or of communal pogroms in Gujarat, the sustained violence of Kashmir's military occupation, upper caste violence against Dalits, or the structural discrimination of the BJP—producing the novel's somber and traumatized tenor. What problematizes such a characterization, however, is the novel's closure, which, by exuding a serene feeling of hope and happiness, stubbornly resists the pessimistic overtone of the work. It is due to this utopian closure that Ana Christina Mendes and Lisa Lau have described it as the "celebration of the creative agency of the precariat" (Mendes and Lau 70).

The precariat—the vulnerable group of people without permanent employment, broadly synonymous with Marx's "surplus population"—occupy a prominent position in the novel. Both the protagonists of *The Ministry* are indeed economically and socially marginalized, although their economic marginalization has come, in part, from the conscious choices they have made (raising, again, the neoliberal fetish of choice independent of structural determinates). Other major characters, because of their religion, caste, gender, sexuality, and class position, are also marginal, although this marginality is not complicit, nor is it docile, because it empowers them to envision a parallel world that is more humane and empathetic than the one that lies outside the reach of their creative reimagination. What binds all these people together is trauma—the trauma and horror of being spared from death.

Anjum, who grows up as a boy in a Muslim family in Old Delhi, remains confused about her transsexual identity until one day she meets another of her own gender in the market. Later she runs away from her parents' house to join other "hijras" in "Khawabgah." Although her body remains a constant source of anxiety and agony, her most traumatic experience comes when she goes to visit Ahmedabad, where she is unwittingly caught up in the 2002 mass murders of Muslims passively, if not actively, overseen by Narendra Modi, then Chief Minister of Gujarat, now Prime Minister of India. Anjum's companion, a 70-year-old flower seller, is killed by Hindu extremists. She, ironically, is spared because of the religious belief that killing a "hijra" brings bad luck to Hindus (*TMOUH* 62–63). Unable to tackle the trauma of witnessing the communal riot of Ahmedabad, where Muslim men were killed with tridents and knives and women raped and burned, Anjum takes shelter in a graveyard, trying to piece together her life that has been shattered by the trauma of being spared.

The novel's intricate story also introduces us to S. Tilottoma, or Tilo in *medias res*. Born into a Catholic Christian family to an unmarried teenager, Tilo grows into a free-spirited[7] woman whose university life brings her close to three men of completely different dispositions and professions, who all find her attractive and

110 Conclusion

fascinating. Tilo, however, falls in love with Musa, a Kashmiri Muslim who later turns into a militant after his wife and daughter are killed by the Indian military in a random shootout. Through Musa, Tilo is introduced to the complex reality of Kashmir, an occupied territory whose struggle for freedom makes its people the target of the Indian state's ferocity and brutal violence. During her clandestine romance with Musa, who has by then become a legendary freedom fighter and a fugitive, she gets arrested, as she witnesses the brutal murder of a teenage boy who stayed with them and cooked—a boy who Musa doted upon. In police custody, Tilo is brutally tortured and is later saved because her two other friends—Biplab Dasgupta, who now serves in the army intelligence, and Nagraj Hariharan or Naga, who is now a famous journalist—use their influence to pull her out of the situation. She later marries Naga, in part to cover up her ongoing active participation in the Kashmiri independence struggle, but is so traumatized by her memories that she is unable to settle down in life. Like Anjum, she too leaves her apartment to settle down in the corner of the graveyard, where the former has established a funeral service and a shelter home named the Jannat Guest House.

In order to understand the utopian impulse of the novel, we need to understand how Jannat Guest House operates as a counter-site where the hierarchical relations of society are either suspended or turned on their head. Anjum herself tells a visitor that she is "Anjuman"—a gathering place, a many. "I am a *mehfil*," she announces, "I'm a gathering. Of everybody and nobody, of everything and nothing" (*TMOUH* 4). This reference to herself as a *mehfil* is, of course, a reference to her body: as a *hijra* she contains multitudes. Yet, it is also possible to read this spatialization of the self as a collectivizing practice. Instead of seeing the self as an atomic individual only invested in advancement of self-interest, which Anjum does up until the moment she experiences the trauma, she is able to posit the self as connected to, and constituted by, the presence of the many. The creation of Jannat, therefore, is an extension of the collective body in the realm of space, where she produces a space according to the logic of the utopian understanding of the body.[8]

As the Jannat Guest House becomes a sanctuary not only for human beings—most of whom were traumatized, if not abandoned and forgotten—but also for non-humans and the non-living, its difference from "Duniya," the outside world, also begins to grow. Zainab, an orphan whom Anjum discovered and raised at Khwabgah with the other transgendered residents of that place, and Saddam, a lower-caste Hindu whose father was killed by an upper-caste Hindu mob, turn the graveyard into a sanctuary for injured animals—"A Noah's Ark" of sorts (*TMOUH* 399). The residents of Jannat begin growing vegetables, although nobody is particularly keen on eating them. Tilo, after settling down in Jannat, begins giving lessons to poor people's children, where they come to learn "arithmetic, drawing, computer graphics ... a bit of basic science, English and eccentricity" (*TMOUH* 397). A pool with no water in it is built to compete with the ones that are in place in rich people's house. With "a People's Pool, a People's Zoo and a People's School" the life in the old graveyard begins to thrive (*TMOUH* 400). This distinction is maintained in the nomenclature as well. "Jannat," in Urdu, means heaven, while "Duniya," means the earth. The desire to turn Jannat Guest House into a heaven for those who are traumatized/marginalized by Duniya is visible in the manner in which Anjum reorganizes the abandoned graveyard. The outside world ravaged by the marauding army of right-wing zealots led by "Gujrat ka Lalla" stands in stark contrast with the world inside the graveyard, where the hierarchies of the outside world cease to operate.

The difference between the dystopian outside and utopian inside is maintained in another way: through the redistributive logic of happiness. One of most fascinating features of *The Ministry* is that it turns one of foundational myths of capitalism, the myth of the pursuit of happiness, on its head. The characters of *The Ministry*, especially those who live in Duniya, seem acutely unhappy and aggressive. Amrik Singh, the Indian army officer who used to call himself the *"lund"* or the phallus "of the Indian Government" (*TMOUH* 336) and reveled in torturing and killing Kashmiris, shoots his family members before shooting himself while living in the United States as an asylum seeker. It seems his excessively violent life pushes him toward the brink of self-destruction. Biplab Dasgupta, the patriotic intelligence officer who was Tilo and Musa's friend during their university days, turns to alcohol for comfort, losing his job, his wife, and his two daughters in the process. His service in Kashmir finally comes back to leave a haunting trail in his life. The madness of money and success, it appears, not only shatters other, less fortunate people's lives; it also seems to destroy the life of those who immerse themselves in the pursuit of success in the conventional sense of the term.

Anjum, too, whose experience of horror in the outside world leaves her traumatized, unable to sleep, only regains her composure when she founds her new universe in the graveyard. After spending numerous sleepless nights in Duniya, Tilo finally begins to sleep peacefully at night. The novel describes her transformed life in the following manner: "She worked a long day and, for the first time in her life, slept a full night" (*TMOUH* 397). By emptying the Duniya—the outside world of war, religious fanaticism, conspiracy, occupation, consumption, and comfort—of happiness, Roy's novel not only exposes the vacuousness of the monetized society but also questions the fundamental purpose behind the creation of such a world. It is not surprising, then, that the concluding passage of *The Ministry* is acutely optimistic and peaceful, evocative of a harmonious Elysium,

By the time they got back, the lights were all out and everybody was asleep. Everybody, that is, except for Guih Kyom the dung beetle. He was wide

112 Conclusion

awake and on duty, lying on his back with his legs in the air to save the world in case the heavens fell. But even he knew that things would turn out all right in the end. They would, because they had to.

Because Miss Jabeen, Miss Udaya Jabeen, was come. (*TMOUH* 438)

The novel's response to the threats of "saffron" fascism, military occupation, and mindless corporate destruction of India's ecology is serene optimism, as though Jebeen's urination and return to her room with her foster mother Anjum is a sign of utopian prospect in itself. But Guih Kyom's wait for the sky to fall and Jabeen's return home also operate on a tropological level, where the dung beetle points toward a harmonious post-anthropocentric future, and the presence of Udaya Jabeen—whose mother was a Maoist militant who left her in the mix of urban people so she could go back to her forest to reclaim her lost land—gestures to a radical, revolutionary future. Anjum, Tilo, and Revaty's daughter, Udaya Jabeen, function as a symbol of hope for the world. Through the convergence of three radical women vesting their hope in a single child, Roy offers the possibility of a utopian future about to arrive through the next generation.

Both novels leave us at the threshold of hope, and in their optimism the utopian tenor of these novels makes itself heard. But it also needs to be taken into consideration that these novels dream of a better future by standing amidst the climacteric destruction of ecology and the fabric of social life. The toxic erosion of the Sundarbans, the succession of massive hurricanes and storm surges in the Bengal Delta, the infestations and wildfires in California, and the sea-level rise in the beautiful city of Venice, which is destined to be submerged in the near future—all these moments that appear in *The Gun Island* are a reminder of the ecological reality we live in. *The Ministry,* similarly, begins by bringing into purview the problem of species extinction by telling the compelling story of the extinction of the "white-backed vultures" (*TMOUH* 1), who drop dead one by one after eating the flesh of cows that have been injected with diclofenac. Simultaneously, the narrative of expropriation of the indigenous people from the forests that have been their home for thousands of years presents a narrative of neoliberalism's "accumulation by dispossession" (*Imperialism* 148–49), geared on the one hand toward the production of cheap nature (Moore 112, 117) and on the other toward the creation of the immiserated reserve army of capital discussed in detail in the last chapter. The inventory of the processes of dispossession and violence that are brought to the surface by both these novels allow us to grasp the magnitude of the crisis we live in today. Still, as I will explore further at the end of this chapter, the hope that is corroborated by the closures of both the novels that I have discussed here, point toward the utopian possibility of collectivization from the ground up. It is here, in the collective waking up from "the demonic possession" and rebuilding the world laid to waste by neoliberalism, that our human potential lies.

Conclusion: In the Ruins of Neoliberalism

What appeared three decades ago as a vague structure of feeling about an ascending neoliberal world order has now catapulted into an undeniable conviction about neoliberalism's devastating effects on human societies and the planet. The two novels discussed above creatively explore some of these effects, making available the trauma that arises from ecological destruction, displacement, state and communal violence, and xenophobic nationalism. They also depict how, despite stubborn resistances from the hegemonic structure, ordinary people try to rebuild society from below, making meaningful lives in a place reserved for the dead. As the capitalist drive for surplus sucks the life out of the planet, these novels show oppressed and disenfranchised people trying to turn abandoned spaces into sanctuaries for all beings, creating interspecies bonds in the process. The utopian impulse of these novels, therefore, needs to be schematized as a reaction against the process of turning the planet into a massive necropolis governed by the logic of capital. Interestingly, these fictional representations correspond to a broader sense of apocalyptic future echoed by a number of theoretical propositions in circulation today.

Wendy Brown, in a number of works published in the last five years, has repeatedly sounded the alarm bell to suggest that western democratic institutions may not survive the assaults from neoliberal economic and cultural transformations. In *Undoing the Demos* (2015), a book that attracted both applause and criticism from the left, she draws upon Foucault's lectures on neoliberalism in *The Birth of Biopolitics* to suggest that neoliberalism needs to be understood not simply as a set of economic policies, as is often done, but also as "a peculiar form of reason" that is "quietly undoing the basic elements of democracy" (*Undoing* 17). Although her core argument is centered around the production of *homo œconomicus* [economic human] or "human capital," (*Undoing* 32) what she persistently maintains throughout is the idea that "liberal democratic institutions, practices, and habits" may not survive the neoliberal "economization" process (*Undoing* 17). This conjunction between the forces of neoliberalization and the destruction of democratic politics is also maintained in a recently published essay where she claims that neoliberalism "flourishes where politics, and especially government, are absent" ("Neoliberalism's Frankenstein" 13). One of the key components of her most recent discussions of neoliberalism is the notion that the "the catastrophic present" was not an intended outcome but an accidental "Frankensteinian creation" of neoliberal thought (*In the Ruins of Neoliberalism* 9–10). The conjunction between market freedom and traditional moral values that figureheads of neoliberalism like Hayek promulgated through their writings, later spawned into the kind of hysteric white working class "*ressentiment*" that led to the political rise of fascist right-wing leaders who are ruling the world today. To understand the rise of xenophobic right-wing fascism, she maintains, we need

114 Conclusion

to be able to track how the ideas of thinkers like Hayek unintentionally contributed to the corrosion of the pillars of democracy. It is, therefore, important that we apprehend the moral underpinnings of neoliberalism as solidly as we understand its economic and political rationality.

This is how Brown puts it in *The Ruins*:

> If neoliberalism is conceived only as a political rationality featuring the ubiquity of markets and *homo oeconomicus* (my claim in *Undoing the Demos*), we cannot grasp the affective investments in privileges of whiteness and First World existence in the nation and national culture or in traditional morality. We also cannot grasp the ways that the hierarchies and exclusions of "tradition" legitimately challenged democratic equality in the name of both family values and freedom. This means that we cannot grasp the new formations of subjectivity and politics that are, in good part, neoliberal effects. (*Ruins* 182)

Brown's critique marks a definitive departure from her own earlier prognosis of neoliberalism as a totalizing economic logic corroding the foundations of democracy. Additionally, it also shows how she struggles to account for the rise of Donald Trump and the fascist right—a historical event that made it difficult to see neoliberalism simply as an economic logic. By arguing that neoliberalism is not simply a political and economic issue but also as a moral one (*Ruins* 20–21), she tries to address her earlier oversight about neoliberalism's moral correlative. Her late realization about neoliberalism's moral logic also allows us to see the fundamental weakness of Foucauldian interpretation of neoliberalism, which seeks to understand neoliberalism through the lens of governmentality. Neoliberalism does not advance a new governmental logic but operates through the state and other institutions that are already in place, which they use to redistribute social wealth so as to concentrate it into the hands of the capitalist class. Had Brown looked not merely into the rhetorical charlatanism of Trump and other fascist leaders but into the content of their actions, she would have noticed that these totalitarian right-wing leaders and their conservative quasi-religious parties have been the staunchest defenders of capital. Beginning from Trump's trillion-dollar gift to the corporate oligarchy in the form of tax cut to Modi's extremely corporation-friendly economic policies, the actions of these totalitarian rulers leave ample proof that the protection of corporate capital is their first priority. Brown fails to notice how what appears like a restoration of lost white male privilege is often a vulnerable posture to defend the last remnants of what is left of the promises of collective prosperity—a piece of land, a low-paid job, a tattering small business whose existence is threatened, an old habit that is seen as lost, a community scavenged by desertion, and a lost culture that exists more in memory than in an actual space or body.

Conclusion **115**

Neoliberalism's turn toward what Williams aptly describes as "the residual"[9]; therefore, is no coincidence, because a turn toward what is lost and bygone is an effective way of draping over what is emergent and utopian. What Brown sees as neoliberalism's accidental unleashing of the weapons of family values and traditions is indeed its well-thought-out strategy of suppressing utopian politics by bringing within its orbit those who themselves are the victims of neoliberalism's economic policies. Its limits notwithstanding, Brown's observations in *In the Ruins* allow us to track how the history and trajectory of neoliberalism have taken a sharp turn in the last four years. What, even two decades ago, seemed like an economic policy of a few bankers and world leaders, now appears to be a global culture and ideology whose ubiquity cannot be questioned. Even those whose moral universe and religious beliefs seem antagonistic to the Mammonist dictates of neoliberalism now revel in the possibility of queuing up behind billionaires and corrupt politicians who offer lip service to religious piety and national unity. The coalescing of the working class around nationalist and religious politics does indeed point toward a new alignment in the struggle against global capitalism, where we see the subjects oppressed by the unequal exchange between labor and capital standing in solidarity with the forces of capital.

Anybody who has taken a close look at the history of neoliberalism around the globe should have no confusion about its pedigree, its conservative and totalitarian make-up. In Chile, the laboratory where neoliberal policies were first tested, the military dictator Auguste Pinochet's government's cultural inclinations leaned hard toward the right. Pinochet himself believed that he was engaged in a "holy war," which gave him the license to persecute and murder opposition members with impunity (Rector 189). In Pakistan and Bangladesh, I have discussed earlier, the rehabilitation of military leaders ushered in not only economic conservatism (neoliberalism) but also cultural conservatism marked on the one hand by jingoistic nationalism and on the other by of Islamic fundamentalism. In India, the emergence of neoliberalism was accompanied by the fortification of the ideologies of *Hindutva*, thus suggesting a connection between the forces of the market and the forces of religion. In Pakistan, too, the radicalization of culture was accompanied by the neoliberalization of the economy, both taking place under the aegis of military dictatorship. As early as 1996, noticing the conjunction between the liberalization process and the rise of BJP, Aijaz Ahmad wrote that the "liberalization" that the Indian state was leaning toward was not a social democratic liberalization but "the pristine, dog-eat-dog, nineteenth-century variety" of liberalism which had been "resurrected" "by the likes of Hayek and Friedman" (*Lineages* 213). This liberalization, he noted, was carried out by the same dominant structures that supported the kind of communal politics the right wing parties in India were engaged in. Neoliberalization was always conservative in terms of politics and practice; what was new about the neoliberalism of 1990s and 2000s was how, by seizing on the ideology of *there is*

116 Conclusion

no alternative, it was able to rope in the old political left that saw redemptive values in democratic practices. The contemporary fascist turn of neoliberalism, therefore, is a retreat to neoliberalism's elemental core, to its xenophobic rhetoric of piety and racial purity. Unable to tackle its recurring crises, which has most explicitly expressed itself in ecological devastations and unprecedented inequality, the forces of a market economy have now turned to disenfranchised workers and destitute rural population to delay the birth of any new project that seeks to build a future outside the guarded premises of capitalism.

The superfluity of fascist tendencies that Brown identifies as a threat to democracy is but one of the twin crises that plague the world today. Capitalism's expansion on a global scale has been accompanied by ecological crises of an unforeseen scale. In his "Foreword" to *Global Ecologies and the Environmental Humanities*, Dipesh Chakrabarty warns us about the fate of humanity in an era of climate crisis:

> The idea that we may be living through the beginnings of a series of overlapping and major environmental crises for humans all over the planet gains ground every day. The climate of the planet is changing with global warming, the rising seas are getting more acidic, the rate of species extinction is approaching a danger mark, the incidence of extreme weather events appears to be on the rise, and there are discussions—serious and alarming—of water and food security. (*Global Ecologies* xv)

Chakrabarty's proviso echoes his earlier concerns about the fate of humanity in the era of the Anthropocene—the age of human extinction. In his much-discussed essay "Climate of History: Four Theses," which was published in 2009 in *Critical Inquiry*, he foregrounded the idea that the scientific conclusions about climate change challenge not only the writing of history, but also "the ideas about the human," forcing on us the burden of rethinking both humanities and historiography ("Climate" 198). Not only does the Anthropocene collapse the boundary between human history and natural history ("Climate" 201), but it also requires us to put the "global histories of capital" in conversation with "the species history of the humans" ("Climate" 212). Our limited understanding of history, according to Chakrabarty, can be addressed only if we are willing to inject, in the veins of traditional historiography, species-capital history ("Climate" 220). In a follow-up essay published five years after his "Climate of History" article, Chakrabarty again urges us to consider the interlacing between planetary history, human history, and capital, suggesting the climate crisis has brought these separate objects on a collision course ("Climate and Capital" 1, 23).

The idea of the abstract human that allows Chakrabarty to hold the entire human species culpable for today's climate crisis, as well as equivocality about the role capitalism has historically played in ushering in global warming, has led many left-leaning environmental critics to question the position held by the apostles of the idea of the Anthropocene. Jason Moore, for instance, has argued that the Anthropocene argument "embodies the *consequentialist bias* of Green Thought" (Moore 171). One of his main objections against the enthusiasts of the Anthropocene emerges out of the observation that the idea of the Anthropocene not only posits the human as an abstract category, but it also obliterates the history of capitalist development as the key contributing factor behind our environmental crisis. In his own parlance, "the Anthropocene argument is not only philosophically and theoretically problematic ... it also offers an unduly narrow conceptualization of historical time" (Moore 175). Like Moore, Slovenian Marxist philosopher Slavoj Žižek also responded to Chakrabarty's climate hypothesis in *Living in the End Times* (2011), claiming "the dynamic of global capitalism" did not get enough importance in the latter's discussion of the Anthropocene, where he blames the whole human species for climate crisis. Explaining how Chakrabarty missed out on the "properly dialectical relationship" between the planet and the human, Žižek writes:

> Chakrabarty seems to miss here the full scope of the properly dialectical relationship between the basic geological parameters of life on earth and the socio-economic dynamic of human development. Of course, the natural parameters of our environment are "independent of capitalism or socialism"— they harbor a potential threat to all of us, independently of economic development, political system, etc. However, the fact that their stability has been threatened by the dynamic of global capitalism nonetheless has a stronger implication than the one allowed by Chakrabarty: in a way, we have to admit that the Whole is contained by its Part, that the fate of the Whole (life on earth) hinges on what goes on in what was formerly one its parts (the socio-economic mode of production of one of the species on earth). (*End Times* 333)

This is perhaps the reason why Moore calls the current environmental crisis the Capitalocene, or the era of the capitalist crisis. For Moore, this concept appropriately describes not only the cause of the climate crisis but also the process through which nature and human beings both become the object of capitalism's production of cheap nature.

Both the crises that have come to define neoliberalism today point toward one conjuncture: the crises of the capitalist system. Whether this crisis is a terminal one or not, history will decide, but what is available to us in the form of discussions by some of the most important thinkers of our era is the idea that human society is faced with a global crisis today—a crisis that threatens the existence of the whole species. It was Jameson who once quipped that it is easier to imagine the end of the world today than thinking of the end of capitalism. In a sense, this

118 Conclusion

idea speaks powerfully about the fetishism that exists in the neoliberal era, where thinking of a post-capitalist future appears as terrible as imagining death. Perhaps, our analysis of what is at stake today needs to begin from this premise.

Let me end my discussion of neoliberal allegories by referring once again to Jameson, who broadened the scope for allegoresis by writing the following: "everything is allegorical ... and all allegory is Utopian" (*Allegory and Ideology* 215). Jameson's unequivocal generalization of the allegorical form is, in one sense, a metacommentary on an essay he published many years ago to suggest that all third-world literary works can be read as national allegories. After all, it was that essay that earned him the long searing critique from Ahmad, who took him to task for persisting with a differential hypothesis that slotted the first and the third world in separate categories. One may see Jameson's sweeping hypothesis in *Allegory* as his response to his critics who chastised him for failing to notice that he was allowing a sweeping binarism to dictate his hypothesis. After all, how can a refined and erudite dialectician of his caliber fall such an easy prey to dualism! As has been pointed out by the likes of Prasad, Lazarus, and Joseph, Jameson's observation about national literatures of the Third World was not off point at all. Quite the opposite, his hypothesis accurately posited the problem of representation within a three-world-system.[10] Jameson's new hypothesis also needs to be seen as a historically informed proposition about world literature which, in a globalized, neoliberal world, has shaken off the old boundaries of the three-world system. In an era when no corner can claim its independence from capitalist relations, literary works, when read allegorically, can only be read as allegories of neoliberal, global capitalism. Hence, the fetishistic concealments that we notice in so many contemporary South Asian fictions.

If we look carefully into Afaz Ali's struggles with monetization, we will notice that what remains concealed behind his desire to escape his displacement in the city is a utopian dream of a system that does not drag people out of their communities to turn them into surrogate mourners for the wealthy and the affluent. His struggles to escape the dragnet of debt and monetization is underwritten by the silhouette of a distant utopian dream that is free from these tormenting objects' domination. Plainly put, his desire anticipates a world without money, thus imagining a post-capitalist future. Likewise, Balram's desire to escape the grip of the landlord is underwritten by the desire to live in a world where one's growth does not get suppressed under the weight of caste and class relations. His escape from the old world and his re-invention of himself as an entrepreneur, ironically, fall easy victim to neoliberal ideologies that promise individual freedom but fail to deliver a system that is just to the majority of the people, especially to those who are systemically left out of the orbit of good life. Shehzad dreams of a city that is not discriminatory, that does not stifle personal freedom. This aspect of his desire perhaps lumps him in the category of liberal reformist. However, once we look into the phenomenon of

Conclusion **119**

his declassment and the content of his desire for economic justice, we can easily trace the elements of a utopian dream of a world without the dictates of capitalism in his desire. The problem, it needs to be stressed, lies with giving a collective form to these different articulations of distress and desire for transcending such distresses. None of the protagonists are able to find a viable channel for collectivization. It is here that *The Gun Island* and *The Ministry* spark a new line of utopian neoliberal allegory. The protagonists of these two novels do not undermine the value of collectivization, nor do they see any redemptive quality in atomized individuality. That these novels do not look at collective efforts to create an alternate universe with scorn, is perhaps an articulation of a different structure of feeling, informed by the urgent need to create a better world than the one we inhabit today.

Notes

1 A detailed discussion of expansion of inequality around the world can be found in Neil Smith's afterword to the third edition of *Uneven Development: Nature, Capital, and the Production of Space*, where he argues that uneven development on a global scale has been matched by geographical unevenness within "national economies" (Smith 262). The entire chapter contains valuable discussions about how neoliberalization of economy has led toward a flat world of inequality abuzz with decrease of real wages for most people and increase in income for the uber wealthy. See Smith's "Afterword to the Third Edition" for further exploration of this topic.

2 There are moments in *Sea of Poppies* and *Flood of Fire* that depict different kinds of collectivization and cooperation. In *Sea of Poppies*, for instance, the women in the hull of the ship create a community where they become a part of each other's life by sharing stories and experiences. A world built upon empathy and shared experience, this community constructed by women is evocative of a powerful sisterhood built upon shared misery and insubordination. The rebellious Chinese peasants whose anarchic presence is registered in *Flood of Fire*, on the other hand, point toward the possibility of collective resistance outside national control and coordination. Despite these significant moments, however, the Trilogy remains deeply invested in the deep history of the imperial war that it thematizes—a war that is marked by the cooperation among the opium traders of different nationalities.

3 Both Fredric Jameson and Slavoj Žižek have commented on the difficulty of imagining a post-capitalist future today. Lamenting the absence of utopian projects in contemporary culture and politics, Jameson has commented that it is easier to imagine the end of the world than to think of the end of capitalism. Žižek, likewise, has discussed how it has become characteristic of today's culture to deny the apocalyptic possibilities, although evidence of such a possibility is strongly present before us. See his *Living in the End Times* (2010) for further understanding of this topic.

4 The same defeatist tendency has been noticed by Smith as well, who in his foreword compellingly argues that even the left has been infected by the idea of no alternative (*Uneven Development* 240–41).

5 In this respect, Fredric Jameson's observation in "An American Utopia" can be reiterated here to explain how the utopian has re-entered the political imaginary. Noticing the re-emergence of utopia in left politics, Jameson, who lamented the absence of it in the post-1970s era, writes the following: But in the last years, utopia

120 Conclusion

has again changed its meaning and has become the rallying cry for left and progressive forces and a virtual synonym for socialism or communism, now for the moment tainted words or programs. It needs to be said that this a generational change and that is seems to reflect a wholesale transformation in the social, political and economic attitudes of those who came to maturity during the 1990s, when the collapse of the traditional left movements made it possible to see just how predatory capitalism was when left to its own devices ("Utopia" 42).

6 The idea of metabolic rift remains one of the central areas of intervention for Marxist theorists of environment. Influenced as he was by the works of James Anderson, Justus von Liebig, and Henry Carey, Marx began to seriously investigate the capitalist production's effect on soil fertility and sustainable economy in the 1860s (Foster, *Ecology Against Capitalism* 156–161). The culmination of these investigations was the concept of the metabolic rift which Marx very briefly summarized in *Capital Volume III* as "the irreparable rift in the process of social metabolism" (*Capital III* 949). This later reflection on the rift between human beings and nature was also explored in *Capital Volume I* where Marx discussed how the concentration of workers in towns disrupts the metabolic relationship between human beings and nature (*Capital I* 637). Written as early as they were, there is, of course, some opacity in the manner in which the German revolutionary looks into the relation between humans and nature, but because of recent works in Marxist environmentalism we see more sustained efforts to develop upon the foundation Marx built. See Bellamy Foster and Paul Burkett's detailed discussion of the topic in the introduction of *Marx and the Earth* for further elaboration of the topic.

7 Her friend Biplab (Garson Hobert) describes her in the following way: "She gave the impression that she had somehow slipped off her leash. As though she was taking herself for a walk while the rest of us were being walked—like pets" (*TMOUH* 154).

8 To understand the relation between body and collective utopian practices, we can perhaps turn to Mikhail Bakhtin, who explains how the "material bodily principle" of "grotesque realism" operates differently from the logic of the individual body produced by the bourgeois culture. In Rabelais' grotesque realism, the bodily element is deeply positive. It is presented not in a private, egotistic form, served from the other spheres of life, but as something universal, representing all the people. As such it is opposed to severance from the material and bodily roots of the world ... the body and bodily life have here a cosmic and at the same time an all-people's character; this is not the body and its physiology in the modern sense of these words, because it is not individualized. The material bodily principle is contained not in the biological individual, not in the bourgeois ego, but in the people, a people who are continually growing and renewed (Bakhtin 19). Bakhtin's reading of the grotesque body, which is derived from his examination of Rabelais' two novels Gargantua and Pantagruel—both written in the 16th Century in the late Renaissance era—allow us to understand how the body in the collective and popular sense is fundamentally opposed to the bourgeois concept of the body that exists in its singularity, alienated from both other human beings and the planet, the "cosmic" world. The body that Bakhtin is drawing toward is the body of the ordinary or, what he calls, the "popular," whose singularity itself is multiple and is grounded in the material life itself. Despite historical difference between the contexts from which Bakhtin pulls out the grotesque body—early modernity and the advent of capitalism—and in which Anjum stands—the context of late capitalism—there seems to exist a homology as well, a semblance that emerges out of the utopian desire for collectivization and reclamation of space. Bakhtin's carnivals where fools feast (Bakhtin 5) is a place marked by its own codes of freedom; it is a place where "hierarchic distinctions and barriers among men" are temporarily suspended" (Bakhtin 15). Although unconscious of its conditions of

Conclusion **121**

possibility, this collective body, simply by being present, is able to overwrite the codes that exists outside.

9 According to Raymond Williams, residuals are those "experiences, meanings and values" that cannot be expressed in terms of the dominant culture. Although certain religious values are incorporated into the dominant culture, there other experiences that cannot be productively incorporated within in "because at certain points a dominant culture cannot allow too much of this kind of practice and experience" because it becomes risky for it ("Base and Superstructure" 170-171). For Williams, residuals represent those practices and habits that are often rural in nature and are struggling to become hegemonic. See Williams' chapter on base and superstructure for further understanding of the term.

10 See Aijaz Ahmad's "Jameson's Rhetoric of Otherness," Madhava Prasad's "On the Question of A Theory of (Third World) Literature," Neil Lazarus' "Fredric Jameson on 'Third-World Literature': A Defence," and Betty Joseph's "Neoliberal Allegories" for further information on the debate on the question of third-world literature.

WORKS CITED

Acocella, Joan. "Arundhati Roy Returns to Fiction, In Fury." *The New Yorker*, 29 May 2017, newyorker.com/magazine/2017/06/05/Arundhati-roy-returns-to-fiction-in-fury, accessed 26 Feb. 2020.

Adiga, Aravind. *The White Tiger: A Novel*. Free Press, 2008.

Adkins, Alexander. "Neoliberal Disgust in Aravind Adiga's *The White Tiger*." *Journal of Modern Literature*, Vol. 42, No. 3, Spring 2019, pp. 169–188. *Project Muse*, DOI: 10.2979/jmodelite.42.3.10

Ahmad, Aijaz. "Jameson's Rhetoric of Otherness and the National Allegory." In *Theory: Classes, Nations, Literatures*, Oxford UP, 1992, pp. 95–122.

Ahmad, Aijaz. *Lineages of the Present: Ideology and Politics in Contemporary South Asia*. Verso, 2000.

Akhtaruzzaman Elias Smarak Grantha [In Memory of Akhtaruzzaman Elias]. edited by Samiran Mazumder. Kolkata: Amritolok, 1997.

Al-Dagamseh, Abdullah. "Adiga's *The White Tiger* as World Bank Literature." *CLCWeb: Comparative Literature and Culture*, Vol. 15, No. 6, 2013, pp. 1–9.

Ali, Monica. *Brick Lane: A Novel*. Scribner, 2004.

Althusser, Louis. *On Ideology*. Verso, 2008.

Ameel, Lieven. "Cities Utopian, Dystopian, and Apocalyptic." *The Palgrave Handbook of Literature and the City*, edited by Jeremy Tambling, Palgrave, 2016, pp. 785–800.

Anjaria, Ulka. "Realist Hieroglyphics: Aravind Adiga and the New Social Novel." *MFS Modern Fiction Studies*, Vol. 61, No. 1, Spring 2015, pp. 114–137. *Project Muse*, DOI: 10.1353/mfs.2015.0005

Anwer, Megha. "Resisting the Event: Aesthetics of the Non-Event in the Contemporary South Asian Novel." *ARIEL: A Review of International English Literature*, Vol. 45, No. 4, 2014. pp. 1–30. *Project Muse*. DOI: 10.1353/ari.2014.0034

Arrighi, Giovanni. *The Long Twentieth Century: Money, Power, and the Origins of Our Times*. Verso, 1994.

Arrighi, Giovanni. *Adam Smith in Beijing: Lineages of the Twenty-First Century*. Verso, 2008.

Bakhtin, M. M. *Rabelais and His World*. Indiana UP, 1984.

Batra, Kanika. "City Botany: Reading Urban Ecologies in China through Amitav Ghosh's *River of Smoke*." *Narrative*, Vol. 21, No. 3, 2013, pp. 322–332. *JSTOR*, http://www.jstor.org/stable/24615400. Accessed 17 Oct. 2019.

Benjamin, Bret. *Invested Interests: Capital, Culture, and the World Bank*. University of Minnesota Press, 2007.

Berlant, Lauren. "Cruel Optimism." *The Affect Theory Reader*, edited by Melissa Gregg and Gregory J. Seigworth, Duke UP, 2010, pp. 93–117.

Bourdieu, Pierre. *Acts of Resistance: Against the New Myths of Our Time*. Translated by Richard Nice, Polity, 1998.

Braz, Albert. "9/11, 9/11: Chile and Mohsin Hamid's *The Reluctant Fundamentalist*." *Canadian Review of Contemporary Literature*, Vol. 42, No. 3, September 2015, pp. 241–256, *Project Muse*, DOI: 10.1353/crc.2015.0024

Brewer, Anthony. *Marxist Theories of Imperialism: A Critical Survey*. Routledge, 1989.

Brouillette, Sarah. *Literature and Creative Economy*. Stanford University Press, 2014.

Brown, Geoff. "Pakistan: Failing State or Neoliberalism in Crisis." *International Socialism: A Quarterly Review of Socialist Theory*, No. 150, 2016, www.isj.org.uk/pakistan-failing-state-or-neoliberalism-in-crisis. Accessed 18 Apr. 2020.

Brown, Wendy. *Undoing the Demos: Neoliberalism's Stealth Revolution*. Zone books, 2015.

Brown, Wendy. "Neoliberalism's Frankenstein." *Authoritarianism: Three Inquiries in Critical Theory*. University of Chicago Press, 2018, pp. 7–44.

Brown, Wendy. *In the Ruins of Neoliberalism: The Rise of Antidemocratic Politics in the West*. Columbia UP, 2019.

Brunhoff, Suzanne de. *Marx on Money*. Translated by Mauric J. Goldbloom. Urizen Books, 1976.

Butler, Judith. *Precarious Life: The Powers of Mourning and Violence*. Verso, 2004.

Butler, Judith. *Frames of War: When is Life Grievable?* Verso, 2009.

Caldwell, Bruce. "Introduction." *The Road to Serfdom: Texts and Documents*, U Chicago P, 2007, pp. 1–33.

Callinicos, Alex. *Imperialism and Global Political Economy*. Polity, 2009.

Chakrabarty, Dipesh. *Provincializing Europe: Postcolonial Thought and Historical Difference*. 2000. Princeton UP, 2008.

Chakrabarty, Dipesh. "The Climate of History: Four Theses." *Critical Inquiry* Vol. 35, No. 2, Winter 2009, pp. 197–222. *JSTOR*. www.jstor.org/stable/10.1086/596640

Chakrabarty, Dipesh. "Climate and Capital: On Conjoined Histories." *Critical Inquiry*, Vol. 41, No. 1, Autumn 2014, pp. 1–23. JSTOR, www.jstor.org/stable/10.1086/678154

Chakrabarty, Dipesh. "Foreword." *Global Ecologies and the Environmental Humanities: Postcolonial Approaches*, edited by Elizabeth DeLoughrey, Jill Didur and Anthony Carrigan, Routledge, 2015, pp. xiii–xv.

Chakravorty, Mrinalini. *In Stereotype: South Asia in the Global Literary Imaginary*. Columbia UP, 2014.

Chari, Anita. *A Political Economy of the Senses: Neoliberalism, Reification, Critique*. Columbia UP, 2015.

Chaudhuri, Amit. *Afternoon Raag*. 1993. Penguin, 2012.

Chibber, Vivek. *Postcolonial Theory and the Specter of Capital*. Verso, 2013.

124 Works Cited

Chow, Rey. *The Protestant Ethnic and the Spirit of Capitalism*. Columbia UP, 2002.

Darda, Joseph. "Precarious World: Rethinking Global Fiction in Mohsin Hamid's *The Reluctant Fundamentalist*." *Mosaic*, Vol. 47, No. 3, 2014, pp. 107–122, *Project Muse*. DOI: 10.1353/mos.2014.0034.

Dasgupta, Shubhoranjan. *Elegy and Dream: Akhtaruzzaman Elias' Creative Commitment*. 2000. The University Press Limited, 2018.

De, Aparajita. "Introduction." *South Asian Racialization and Belonging after 9/11*, edited by Aparajita De, Lexington Books, 2016, pp. ix–xxv.

Detmers, Ines. "New India? New Metropolis? Reading Aravind Adiga's *The White Tiger* as a "condition-of-India novel."" *Journal of Postcolonial Writing*, Vol. 47, No. 5, December 2011, pp. 535–545.

Duménil, Gérard and Dominique Lévy. *Capital Resurgent: Roots of the Neoliberal Revolution*. Translated by Derek Jeffers, Harvard UP, 2004.

Duménil, Gérard and Dominique Lévy. *The Crisis of Neoliberalism*. Harvard UP, 2011.

Elias, Akhtaruzzaman. "Milir Haate Sten Gun." *Akhtaruzzaman Elias Rachanasamagra Ek* [*Collected Works of Akhtaruzzaman Elias Volume One*], Mowla Brothers, 2007, pp. 163–183.

Elias, Akhtaruzzaman. "Kanna." *Akhtaruzzaman Elias Rachanasamagra Ek*, Mowla Brothers, 2007, pp. 336–391.

Elias, Akhtaruzzaman. "Kanna." *Akhtaruzzaman Elias Rachanasamagra One* [*Collected Works of Akhtaruzzaman Elias Volume One*], Mowla Brothers, 2007, pp. 336–391.

Elias, Akhtaruzzaman. "Shongskritir Vanga Setu" ["Culture's Broken Bridge"]. *Akhtaruzzaman Elias Rachanasamagra Teen* [*Collected Works of Akhtaruzzaman Elias Volume 3*], edited by Khaliquzzaman Elias, Mowla Brothers, 2004, pp. 285–289.

Elias, Akhtaruzzaman. "Ami O' Amar Somoy" ["Me and My Era"]. *Akhtaruzzaman Elias Rachanasamagra Teen* [*Collected Works of Akhtaruzzaman Elias Volume 3*], edited by Khaliquzzaman Elias, Mowla Brothers, 2004, pp. 285–289.

Eng, David L. and David Kazanjian. "Introduction: Mourning Remains." *Loss: The Politics of Mourning*, edited by David L. Eng and David Kazanjian, U California Press, 2003, pp. 1–28.

Engels, Friedrich. *The Condition of the Working Class in England*. Penguin, 1987.

Fanon, Frantz. *The Wretched of the Earth*. Translated by Richard Philcox, Grove Press, 2004.

Fischer, Karin. "The Influence of Neoliberals in Chile before, during, and after Pinochet." *The Road from Mont Pèlerin*, edited by Philip Mirowski and Dieter Plehwe, Harvard UP, 2009, pp. 305–346.

Foster, John Bellamy. *Ecology Against Capitalism*. Monthly Review, 2002.

Foster, John Bellamy. *The Naked Imperialism*. Monthly Review Press, 2006.

Foster, John Bellamy. "The New Imperialism of Globalized Monopoly-Finance Capital." *Monthly Review*, www.mothlyreview.org/2015/07/01/the-new-imperialism-of-globalized-monopoly-finance-capital. Accessed 9 Dec. 2019.

Forster, John Bellamy and Paul Burkett. *Marx and the Earth: An Anti-Critique*. Haymarket Books, 2017.

Foucault, Michel. "Nietzsche, Genealogy, History." *The Foucault Reader*, edited by Paul Rabinow, Vintage, 2010, pp. 76–100.

Foucault, Michel. *The Birth of Biopolitics: Lectures at the Collège de France 1978–1979*. Translated by Graham Burchell, Picador, 2008.

Works Cited 125

Frank, Andre Gunder. *Latin America: Underdevelopment or Revolution: Essays on the Development of Underdevelopment and the Immediate Enemy.* Monthly Review Press, 1970.

Freud, Sigmund. "Mourning and Melancholia." *The Standard Edition of the Complete Works of Sigmund Freud: Volume XIV*, Hogarth Press, 1957, pp. 243–258.

Friedman, Milton. *Capitalism and Freedom.* U Chicago P, 2002.

Frye, Northrop. *Anatomy of Criticism: Four Essays.* 1957. Princeton UP, 2000.

Gallagher, John, and Ronald Robinson. "The Imperialism of Free Trade." *The Economic History Review*, Vol. 6, No. 1, 1953, pp. 1–15. JSTOR, DOI: 10.2307/2591017

Ghosh, Amitav. *Sea of Poppies.* Farrar, Straus and Giroux, 2008.

Ghosh, Amitav. *River of Smoke.* Farrar, Straus and Giroux, 2011.

Ghosh, Amitav. *Flood of Fire.* Hamish Hamilton, 2015.

Ghosh, Amitav. *The Gun Island: A Novel.* Hamish Hamilton, 2019.

Ghosh, Pothik. "Akhtaruzzaman Elias: Beyond the Lived Time of Nationhood." *Radical Notes*, 1 April 2008, radicalnotes.org/2008/04/01/akhtaruzzaman-elias-beyond-the-lived-time-of-nationhood. Accessed 11 December 2019.

Groz, André. *Farewell to the Working Class: An Essay on Post-Industrial Socialism.* Translated by Michael Sonenscher, Pluto Press, 1982.

Gui, Weihsin. "Creative Destruction and Narrative Renovation: Neoliberalism and the Aesthetic Dimension in the Fiction of Aravind Adiga and Mohsin Hamid." *The Global South*, Vol. 7, No. 2, 2014, pp. 173–190. www.jstor.org/stable/10.2979/globalsouth.7.2.173 Accessed 17 Jan 2017.

Gupta, Dipanker. "Formal and Real Subsumption of Labor under Capital: The Instance of Share-Cropping." *Economic and Political Weekly* Vol. 15, No. 39 (Sep 1980) A98-A99+A101-A103+A 105-A106.

Hakutani, Yoshinobu and Robert Butler. "Introduction." *The City in African-American Literature*, Fairleigh Dickinson University Press, 1995, pp. 9–20.

Hamid, Mohsin. *Moth Smoke.* Riverhead Books, 2000.

Hamid, Mohsin. *The Reluctant Fundamentalist.* Harcourt, 2007.

Hamid, Mohsin. *How to Get Filthy Rich in Rising Asia: A Novel.* Penguin, 2013.

Hamid, Mohsin. *Exit West.* Hamish Hamilton, 2017.

Haq, Kaiser. *The Triumph of the Snake Goddess.* Harvard, 2015.

Hardt, Michael, and Antonio Negri. *Empire.* Harvard UP, 2000.

Hardt, Michael. "Foreword: What Affects Are Good For." *The Affective Turn: Theorizing the Social*, edited by Patricia Clough and Jean Halley, Duke University Press, 2007, pp. ix–xiii.

Hart, Matthew and Jim Hansen. "Introduction: Contemporary Literature and the State." *Contemporary Literature*, Vol. 49, No. 4, 2008, pp. 491–513, *Project Muse.* DOI: 10.1353/cli.0.0037

Harvey, David. *Limits to Capital.* 1982. Verso, 1999.

Harvey, David. *Spaces of Hope.* University of California Press, 2000.

Harvey, David. *The New Imperialism.* Oxford, 2003.

Harvey, David. *A Brief History of Neoliberalism.* Oxford, 2005.

Harvey, David. *Spaces of Global Capitalism: Towards a Theory of Uneven Geographical Development.* Verso, 2006.

Harvey, David. "Neoliberalism as Creative Destruction." *The Annals of the American Academy of Political and Social Science*, Vol. 610, March 2007, pp. 22–44, www.jstor.org/stable/25097888, accessed 8 Dec. 2015.

126 Works Cited

Harvey, David. *Cosmopolitanism and Geographies of Freedom*. Columbia UP, 2009.

Harvey, David. *A Companion to Marx's Capital: Volume 2*. Verso, 2013.

Harvey, David. *Seventeen Contradictions and the End of Capitalism*. Oxford UP, 2014.

Hayek, F. A. *The Road to Serfdom: Texts and Documents*. Edited by Bruce Caldwell, U Chicago P, 2007.

Heidemann, Birte. "'We are the glue keeping civilization together': Post-Orientalism and counter-Orientalism in H. M. Naqvi's Home Boy." *Journal of Postcolonial Writing*, Vol 48, No. 3, July 2012, pp. 289–298.

Hogg, Emily J. "Introduction." *Precarity in Contemporary Literature and Culture*, edited by Emily J. Hogg and Peter Simonsen, Bloomsbury, 2021, pp. 1–25.

Huehls, Mitchum. *After Critique: Twenty-First Century Fiction in a Neoliberal Age*. Oxford UP, 2017.

Hussain, Mamun. *Necropolis*. Shuddhashar, 2011.

Iqbal, Shahid. *Akhtaruzzaman Elias: Manush O Kothashilpi [Akhtaruzzaman Elias: The Man and the Writer]*. Dhaka: Annesha Prokashon, 2009.

Jahan, Nasreen. *Urukku*. 1993, Kolkata: Prativash, 2013.

Jameson, Fredric. *The Political Unconscious: Narrative as a Socially Symbolic Act*. Cornell UP, 1982.

Jameson, Fredric. "Third-World Literature in the Era of Multinational Capitalism." *Social Text*, No. 15, Autumn 1986, pp. 65–88.

Jameson, Fredric. *Valances of the Dialectic*. Verso, 2009.

Jameson, Fredric. *Representing Capital: A Reading of Volume One*. Verso, 2011.

Jameson, Fredric. *The Antinomies of Realism*. Verso, 2013.

Jameson, Fredric. "An American Utopia." *An American Utopia: Dual Power and the Universal Army*, edited by Slavoj Žižek, Verso, 2016, pp. 1–96.

Jameson, Fredric. *Allegory and Ideology*. Verso, 2019.

Joseph, Betty. "Neoliberalism and Allegory." *Cultural Critique*, Vol. 82, Fall 2012, pp. 68–94, muse.jhu.edu/journals/cul/summary/v082/82.joseph.html. Accessed 26 May 2015.

Joyce, James. "Ulysses." *The Complete Novels of James Joyce*, Wordsworth, 2012.

Karim, Lamia. "The Production of Silence: The State-NGO Nexus in Bangladesh." *Feminists Rethink the Neoliberal State: Inequality, Exclusion, and Change*, edited by Leela Fernandes, NYU Press, 2018, pp. 106–135.

Klein, Naomi. *The Shock Doctrine: The Rise of Disaster Capitalism*. Picador, 2008.

Kumar, Amitava. "Bad News: Authenticity and South Asian Political Novel." *Boston Review* 2008, http://www.bostonreview.net/archives/BR33.6/kumar.php

Laclau, Ernesto. "Feudalism and Capitalism in Latin America." *New Left Review*, Vol. 1, No. 67, 1971, pp. 19–38.

Lahiri, Jhumpa. *The Namesake*. Mariner, 2004.

Lahiri, Jhumpa. *The Lowland: A Novel*. Vintage, 2013.

Lazarus, Neil. "Fredric Jameson on 'Third-World Literature': A Defence." *The Postcolonial Unconscious*. Cambridge UP, 2011, pp. 89–114.

Lefebvre, Henri. *The Production of Space*. Translated by Donald Nicholson-Smith, Blackwell, 1991.

Lenin, V. I. "Imperialism, the Highest Stage of Capitalism." *Essential Works of Lenin: "What is to be Done?" and Other Writings*, edited by Henry M. Christman, Dover Publication, 1987, pp. 177–270.

Lewis, David. *Bangladesh: Politics, Economy and Civil Society*. Cambridge UP, 2011.

Lukács, György. *The Meaning of Contemporary Realism*. Translated by John and Necke Mander, Merlin Press, 1969.

Luxemburg, Rosa. *The Complete Works of Rosa Luxemburg: Volume I: Economic Writings*. Edited by Peter Hudis, Verso, 2014.

Luxemburg, Rosa. *The Complete Works of Rosa Luxemburg: Volume II*. Edited by Peter Hudis and Paul Le Blanc, Verso, 2016.

Marx, Karl and Friedrich Engels. *The Communist Manifesto and Other Writings*. Barnes & Noble, 2005.

Marx, Karl and Friedrich Engels. *Karl Marx Frederick Engels Collected Works: Volume 30*. International Publications, 1988.

Marx, Karl. *Economic and Philosophic Manuscripts of 1844*. Translated by Martin Milligan, Prometheus Books, 1988.

Marx, Karl. "The Eighteenth Brumaire of Louis Bonaparte." *Surveys from Exile: Political Writings Volume II*, edited by David Fernbach, Random House, 1973, pp. 143–249.

Marx, Karl. *Grundrisse: Foundations of the Critique of Political Economy*. 1973. Translated by Martin Nicolaus, Penguin, 1993.

Marx, Karl. *Capital Volume I: A Critique of Political Economy*. 1976. Translated by Ben Fowkes, Penguin, 1990.

Marx, Karl. *Capital Volume II*. Translated by David Fernbach, Penguin, 1992.

Marx, Karl. *Capital: Volume III*. Translated by David Fernbach, Penguin, 1991.

Marx, Karl. *Capital Volume I*. Translated by Ben Fawkes, Penguin, 1990.

Mendes, Ana C. and Lisa Lau. "The Precarious Lives of India's Others: The Creativity of Precarity in Arundhati Roy's *The Ministry of Utmost Happiness*." *Journal of Postcolonial Writing*, Vol. 56, No. 1, 2020, pp. 70–82, *Project Muse*. DOI: 10.1080/17449855.2019.1683758

Mistry, Rohington. *A Fine Balance*. Vintage, 1995.

Mohapatra, Himanshu S. "Babu Fiction in Disguise Reading Aravind Adiga's *The White Tiger*." *Writing India Anew: Indian English Fiction 2000–2010*, edited by Krishna Sen and Rituparna Roy, Amsterdam UP, 2013, pp. 129–144.

Moore, Jason W. *Capitalism in the Web of Life*. Verso, 2015.

Mondal, Alauddin. *Akhtaruzzaman Elias: Nirmane Binirmane*. Dhaka: Mowla Brothers, 2009.

Mucci, Clara. "Allegory." *A Companion to English Renaissance Literature and Culture*, edited by Michael Hattaway, Blackwell, 2003, pp. 298–306.

Muhammad, Anu. *Development or Destruction? Essays on Global Hegemony, Corporate Grabbing, and Bangladesh*. Shrabon Prokashoni, 2007.

Muhammad, Anu. *Rastro Ace, Rastro Nai* [*The State is there, the State is Not*]. Samhati Prokashan, 2019.

Muhammad, Anu. "*Khobnama*: Khoabe-Chetonay Manush O' Shomoy." *Elias Ebong Proshner Shokti*, Shrabon Prokashoni, 2009, pp. 28–45.

Mukherjee, Neel. *The Lives of Others*. Random House, 2014.

Mukherjee, Neel. *A State of Freedom*. Penguin, 2017.

Nandi, Swaralipi. "Narrative Ambiguity and the Neoliberal Bildungsroman in Aravind Adiga's *The White Tiger*. *Journal of Narrative Theory*, Vol. 47, No.2, Summer 2017, pp. 276–301.

Naqvi, H. M. *Home Boy*. Shaye Areheart Books, 2009.

Naipaul, V. S. *The Mystic Masseur*. 1957. Vintage, 2002.

128 Works Cited

Naipaul, V. S. The *Mimic Men*. 1967. Picador, 2002.

"Non-Standard Employment around the World: Understanding Challenges, Shaping Prospects." *International Labor Organization*, 2016, www.ilo.org/wcmsp5/groups/public/---dgreports/---dcomm/---publ/documents/publication/wcms_534326.pdf, accessed 29 Apr. 2020.

Patnaik, Prabhat. "The State under Neo-Liberalism." *Social Scientist*, Vol. 35, No. 1/2, Jan.-Feb. 2007, pp. 4–15, www.jstor.org/stable/27644193, accessed 28 December 2015.

Patnaik, Prabhat. *The Value of Money*. Columbia University Press, 2009.

Patnaik, Prabhat. "Growth and Poverty in the Indian Economy." *Social Scientist*, Vol. 39, No. 9/10, September-October 2011, pp. 19–34, www.jstor.org/stable/23070102, accessed 28 Jun. 2014.

Patnaik, Prabhat. "Trends of Centre–state Relations in India Under the Neo-liberal Regime." *Studies in People's History*, Vol. 5, No. 1, 2018, pp. 83–91, DOI: 10.1177/2348448918759872

Patnaik, Utsa, and Prabhat Patnaik. "Imperialism in the Era of Globalization." *Monthly Review*, July 1, 2015, monthlyreview.org/2015/07/01/imperialism-in-the-era-of-globalization, accessed 29 Apr. 2020.

Payne, Robert. *Massacre: The Tragedy at Bangla Desh and the Phenomenon of Mass Slaughter Throughout History*. McMillan, 1973.

Perner, Claudia. "Tracing the Fundamentals in Mohsin Hamid's *Moth Smoke* and *The Reluctant Fundamentalist*." *ARIEL: A Review of International English Literature*, Vol. 41, No. 3-4, 2011, pp. 23–31.

Prasad, Madhava. "On the Question of a Theory of (Third World) Literature." *Social Text*, No. 31/32, 1992, pp. 57–83, *JSTOR*, jstor.org/stable/466218, accessed 3 Jan. 2020.

Ragin, Charles C. *American Journal of Sociology*, Vol. 92, No. 2, 1986, pp. 494–496. *JSTOR*, www.jstor.org/stable/2780185

Rashed, Zafar Ahmed. *Akhtaruzzaman Eliaser Chotogolpo* [*The Short Stories of Akhtaruzzaman Elias*]. Dhaka: Ittadi, 2012.

Radice, Hugo. "Neoliberal Globalization: Imperialism without Empires?" *Neoliberalism: A Critical Reader*, edited by Alfredo Saad-Filho and Deborah Johnston, Pluto Press, 2005.

Rahman, Zia Haider. *In the Light of What We Know*. Picador India, 2014.

Reaz, Ali. *Bangladesh: A Political History Since Independence*. I. B. Tauris, 2016.

Rector, John L. *The History of Chile*. McMillan, 2003.

Roy, Arundhati. *Walking with the Comrades*. Penguin, 2011.

Roy, Arundhati. *The Ministry of Utmost Happiness*. Penguin, 2017.

Roy, Binayak. "Exploring the Orient from Within: Amitav Ghosh's River of Smoke." *Postcolonial Text*, Vol 9, No 1, 2014, pp. 1–21.

Said, Edward W. *Orientalism*. 1978. Vintage, 2003.

Said, Edward W. "Secular Criticism." *The World, the Text, and the Critic*. Harvard UP, 1983, pp. 1–30.

Said, Edward W. "Foucault and the Imagination of Power." *Reflections on Exile and Other Essays*, Harvard UP, 2000, pp. 239–245.

Salik, Siddiq. "Operation Searchlight." *The Bangladesh Reader: History, Culture, Politics*, edited by Meghna Guhathakurta and Willem van Schendel, Duke UP, 2013, pp. 231–236.

Santhi, P. "Performing Identities: A Study of H. M. Naqvi's Home Boy." *International Journal of English Language, Literature and Humanities*, Vol. IV, No. VI, June 2016, pp. 59–65.

Sarkar, Sumit. "The Decline of the Subaltern in Subaltern Studies." *Mapping Subaltern Studies and the Postcolonial*, edited by Vinayak Chaturvedi, Verso, 2012, pp. 300–323.

Sawhney, Hirsh. "Home Boy by H M Naqvi-review." *The Guardian*, 17 Nov. 2011, www. theguardian.com/books/2011/nov/17/home-boy-h-m-naqvi-review, accessed 2 Mar, 2020.

Schendel, William Van. *A History of Bangladesh*. Cambridge University Press, 2009.

Schotland, Sara D. "Breaking Out of the Rooster Coop: Violent Crime in Aravind Adiga's White Tiger and Richard Wright's Native Son." *Comparative Literature Studies*, Vol. 48, No. 1, 2011, pp. 1–19. *Project Muse*, DOI: 10.1353/cls.2011.0006

Semmel, Bernard. *The Rise of Free Trade Imperialism: Classical Political Economy, the Empire of Free Trade and Imperialism 1750–1850*. 1970. Cambridge UP, 2004.

Shahriar, Shoeb. *Elias O Khandita Chetonar Nandipath: Collected Essays of Shoeb Shahriar*. Dhaka: Nisharga, 2004.

Shakya, Mallika. *Death of an Industry: The Cultural Politics of Nepal's Garment Manufacturing during the Maoist Revolution in Nepal*. Cambridge UP, 2018.

Shamsie, Kamila. *Home Fire*. Bloomsbury, 2017.

Shingavi, Snehal. "Capitalism, Caste, and Con-Games in Aravind Adiga's *The White Tiger*." *Postcolonial Text*, Vol. 9, No. 3, pp. 2014, pp. 1–16.

Sikand, Yoginder S. "The Tablighi Jama'at." *The Bangladesh Reader: History, Culture, Politics*, edited by Guhathakurta and Schendel, Duke UP, 2013, pp. 336–344.

Singh, Amardeep. "Why I Didn't Like 'The White Tiger.'" Blog. Web. 8 July 2019.

Sipahimalani, Sanjay. "NYC's Metrostani." *The Indian Express*, 9 Jan 2010, www.archive. indianexpress.com/news/nyc-s-metrostani/565109, accessed 15 Mar. 2020.

Smith, Neil. *Uneven Development: Nature, Capital, and the Production of Space*. 3rd Edition, The University of Georgia Press, 2008.

Sobhan, Rehman. "Politics of Food and Famine in Bangladesh." *Economic and Political Weekly*, Vol. 14, No. 48, Dec. 1, 1979, pp. 1973–1980.

Sofa, Ahmed. "Moron Bilash." *Upannashsamagra* [Collected Novels], Mowla Brothers, 2015, pp. 183–236.

Sofa, Ahmed. "Ekjon Ali Kenaner Utthan O Poton." *Upannashsamagra*, Mowla Brothers, 2015, pp. 237–356.

Sofa, Ahmed. "Gavi Bittanto." *Upannashsamagra* [Collected Novels], Mowla Brothers, 2015, pp. 357–466.

Spivak, Gayatri Chakravorty. *A Critique of Postcolonial Reason: Toward a History of the Vanishing Present*. Seagull Books, 2000.

Spivak, Gayatri Chakravorty. *An Aesthetic Education in the Era of Globalization*. Harvard UP, 2012.

Srikanth, Rajini. *Constructing the Enemy: Empathy/Antipathy in U.S. Literature and Law*. Temple University Press, 2012.

Standing, Guy. *The Precariat: The New Dangerous Class*. Bloomsbury, 2011.

Stasi, Paul. "Amitav Ghosh's *Sea of Poppies* and the Question of Postcolonial Modernism." *Novel: A Forum on Fiction*, Vol. 48, No. 3, Nov. 2015, pp. 323–343.

Subrahmanyam, Sanjay. "Diary." *London Review of Books*, Vol. 30, No.31, 2008, pp. 42–43.

Szeman, Imre. "Who's Afraid of National Allegory: Jameson, Literary Criticism, Globalization." *The South Atlantic Quarterly*, Vol. 100, No. 3, Summer 2001, pp. 803–827. *Project MUSE*, https://muse.jhu.edu/article/30727

130 Works Cited

Talbot, Ian. *Pakistan: A Modern History*. McMillan, 2010.

Thangaraj, Stanley. "Managing Race, Class, and Gender: Atlanta's South Asian American Muslims and the Localized Management of the 'Global War on Terror.'" *South Asian Racialization and Belonging after 9/11: Masks of Threat*, edited by Aparajita De, Lexington Books, 2016, pp. 51–66.

Thompson, E. P. "Time, Work-Discipline, and Industrial Capitalism." *Past & Present*, No. 38, 1967, pp. 56–97. *JSTOR*, www.jstor.org/stable/649749

Umar, Badruddin. "The Significance of Victory Day of 16th December." *Badruddin Umar Rachanasangraha 2 [Collected Writings of Bandruddin Umar vol-2]*, edited by Muhammad Saiful Islam, Shrabon Prokashoni, 2012, pp. 680–684.

Upadhyay, Samrat. "The Good Shopkeeper." *Arresting God in Kathmandu*. Houghton Miffin, 2011, pp. 1–19.

Wakabaiyashi, Daisuke. "Google's Shadow Workforce: Temps Who Outnumber Full-Time Employees." *New York Times*, www.nytimes.com/2019/05/28/technology/google-temp-workers.html, accessed 29 Apr. 2020.

Walther, Sundhya. "Fables of the Tiger Economy: Species and Subalternity in Aravind Adiga's *The White Tiger*." *MFS Modern Fiction Studies*, Vol. 60, No. 3, Fall 2014, pp. 579–598. *Project Muse*, doi:10.1353/mfs.2014.0042

Wallerstein, Immanuel. *The Capitalist World-Economy: Essays by Immanuel Wallerstein*. Cambridge UP, 1980.

Wallerstein, Immanuel. *The Essential Wallerstein*. The New Press, 2000.

Want, Lily. "The Poetics and Politics of Cultural Studies in Aravind Adiga's *The White Tiger*." *Asiatic: IIUM Journal of English Language and Literature*, vol. 5, No. 1, 2011, pp. 69–77.

Wickremasinghe, Nira. *Sri Lanka in the Modern Age: A History*. Oxford, 2014.

Williams, Raymond. *Marxism and Literature*. Oxford, 1977.

Williams, Raymond. "Base and Superstructure." *The Raymond Williams Reader*, edited by John Higgins, Blackwell, 2001, pp. 162–178.

Williams, Raymond. "Film and the Dramatic Tradition." *The Raymond Williams Reader*, edited by John Higgins, Blackwell Publishers, 2001, pp. 25–41.

Zahir, Shaidul. "Amader Kutir Shilper Itihash" ["History of Our Cottage Industry"]. *Shahidul Zahir Samagra*, edited by Mohammad Abdur Rashid, Pathak Shamabesh, 2013, pp. 278–294.

Zahir, Shaidul. "Abu Ibrahimer Mrittu" [Abu Ibrahim's Death]. *Shahidul Zahir Samagra*, edited by Mohammad Abdur Rashid, Pathak Shamabesh, 2013, pp. 593–645.

Zahir, Shaidul. "Jibon O' Rajnoitik Bastobota" [Social and Political Reality]. *Shahidul Zahir Samagra*, edited by Mohammad Abdur Rashid, Pathak Shamabesh, 2013, pp. 297–337.

Zamora, Daniel. "When Exclusion Replaces Exploitation: The Condition of the Surplus-Population Under Neoliberalism." *Nonsite*, www.nonsite.org/feature/when-exclusion-replaces-exploitation, accessed 12 March 2015.

Žižek, Slavoj. *Violence: Six Sideways Reflections*. Picador, 2008.

Žižek, Slavoj. *Living in the End Times*. Verso, 2010.

INDEX

Abu Ibrahimer Mrittu (Shahidul Zahir) 18, 33

academic critique of neoliberalism 14

The Accumulation of Capital: A Contribution to the Economic Theory of Imperialism (Rosa Luxemburg) 47

Acocella, Joan 108

Adiga, Aravind 1, 5, 19, 22, 26, 27, 28, 51, 55, 56, 57, 58, 59, 67, 69, 73, 74, 74n1

African American radicalism 13

Ahmad, Aijaz 3, 9, 12, 25, 115, 118, 121n10

Al-Dagamseh, Abdullah 71–72

Ali (protagonist of Naqvi's *Home Boy*) 84–85

Ali, Afaz (protagonist of Elias's "Kanna") 1–2, 17, 30n1, 34–35, 40–51, 52n6, 104

Ali, Monica 75

Ali, Seikh Tobarak 19, 30n2

allegoresis 26, 118

Allegory and Ideology (Fredric Jameson) 5, 6

allegory and the novel 3–8

Amin, Samir 25, 60, 80

Anderson, James 120n6

Anil's Ghost (Michael Ondaatje) 87

Anjum (character of Roy's *The Ministry of Utmost Happiness*) 104, 109–112, 120n8

The Arcades Project (Walter Benjamin) 5

Bakhtin, Mikhail 120n8

Balram Halwai (protagonist of Adiga's *The White Tiger*) 1–2, 22, 55–57, 62, 64–73, 74n4, 100, 101, 104, 118

Banduki Sadagar 106

Bandyopadhyay, Bibhutibhushan 9

Bandyopadhyay, Manik 9

Bangalore 64, 66, 68, 70, 72, 73, 74n4

Bangladesh 2, 13, 14, 27; and bourgeois treason 44; cultural and economic transformation of 43; *moulvi* in 30n1; nationalist politics in 44; neoliberalism in 12; NGO-led aid politics 46, 51; post-burial *monajat* in 52n3; rehabilitation of military leaders in 115

Batra, Kanika 24

Benjamin, Bret 71

Benjamin, Walter 5

Berlant, Lauren 96

Bhutan 13

Bhutto, Zulfikar Ali 12

bildungsroman 57–58, 73, 76, 84

The Birth of Biopolitics (Michel Foucault) 14, 113

Blair, Tony 11

Bloom, Leopold (character of Joyce's *Ulysses*) 8

132 Index

Bonduki Sadagar 105
Bourdieu, Pierre 78
Braz, Albert 93
Brick Lane (Monica Ali) 75
Brouillette, Sarah 58
Brown, Wendy 10, 14, 16–17, 22, 113–116
Buchanan, James 10
Bukharin, Nicolai 79
Burkett, Paul 120n6
Burnham, Benjamin (character of Ghosh's *Sea of Poppies*) 21, 22–23
Butler, Judith 77–78

capitalism 15, 35, 58–61, 63–64, 66, 69, 85, 100, 104; conjoining neoliberalism with 14; corporate 14; crises 23–24, 105; "eternal virginity" 74n5; expansion on global scale 116; global expansion 67; historical emergence of 38, 52n7; imperialism in 98n1; Marxist critiques of 27; metabolic necessity 86; multinational 4; neoliberal 32, 39, 77, 78, 103; predatory 120n5; *raison d'être* 48; and surplus population 81–82, 83; systemic violence of 71; temporality 74n5; temporal progression of 27; violent history of 70–71, 96
Capitalism and Freedom (Milton Friedman) 10–11
capitalist class 4, 13, 31n5, 48, 53n11, 61, 81, 87, 100, 114
capitalist subsumption 62, 64
Capital Volume I (Karl Marx) 27, 36, 37, 38, 52n7, 53nn11–12, 60, 61, 70, 81, 86, 83, 96, 120n6
Capital Volume II (Karl Marx) 24
Carey, Henry 120n6
Chakrabarty, Dipesh 59, 60, 63, 116–117
Chakravorty, Mrinalini 57
Changez (protagonist of Hamid's *The Reluctant Fundamentalist*) 2, 76–78, 91–98, 99n5, 100–101
Chari, Anita 52n2
Chibber, Vivek 25, 99n3
Chile 11, 76, 93, 115
Chilekothar Sepoy (Akhtaruzzaman Elias) 44
Cinta (character of Ghosh's *The Gun Island*) 105

"Climate of History: Four Theses" (Dipesh Chakrabarty) 116
Clinton, Bill 11
Collantai, Alexandra 83
commoditization 24, 32
commodity fetishism 35
The Communist Manifesto (Karl Marx) 60
The Condition of the Working Class in England (Friedrich Engels) 86
consciousness 50, 92, 101; eco-consciousness 13; monetization of 40–45
contemporary theories of neoliberalism 8–17
corporate capitalism 14

Darda, Joseph 77
Dasgupta, Biplab 110, 111
De, Aparajita 89–90
Delhi 55–56, 66, 68–69, 70, 72
de rigueur fetishization of money 45
Devi, Mahasweta 9, 50
"Diary of a Madman" (Lu Xun) 3
Dirlik, Arif 25
Dutta, Dinanath 105
Dutta, Jyotiprakash 18

Economic and Philosophical Manuscripts of 1844 (Karl Marx) 35, 36
Economic Manuscripts of 1861–1863 (Karl Marx) 60
Ekjon Ali Kenaner Utthanpoton (Ahmed Sofa) 18
Elias, Akhtaruzzaman 1, 9, 17, 18, 27, 30n1, 31n2, 34–35, 40, 42–47, 50–51, 52n4
Empire (Michael Hardt and Antonio Negri) 78
Engels, Friedrich 86
Exit West (Mohsin Hamid) 87
expansionist power 80
"Exploring the Orient from Within" (Binayak Roy) 24

Fanon, Frantz 30–31n2, 83
fetishisms 2, 7, 35, 37, 38, 52n2, 97, 104, 105, 118
finance 79–83, 94, 97, 98n1, 102
A Fine Balance (Rohington Mistri) 58
finitude 77
floating surplus population 86

Index **133**

Flood of Fire (Amitav Ghosh) 23, 102, 119n2
Foster, John Bellamy 31n5, 80, 120n6
Foucauldian interpretation of neoliberalism 114
Foucauldians 14, 16, 25, 27, 32, 114
Foucauldian theories 32
Foucault, Michel 14–17, 22, 62, 113
Frames of War (Judith Butler) 77
Frank, Andre Gunder 27, 60, 74n2
Frank, Gunder 80
Freud, Sigmund 89
Friedman, Milton 10, 11
Fukuyama, Francis 96

Gabhi Bittanto (Ahmed Sofa) 18
Gallagher, John 31n3
Geworfenheitins Dasein (Heidegger) 6, 7
Ghosh, Amitav 20–26, 29, 31n3, 102, 104–108
Ghosh, Pothik 52n9
God of Small Things (Arundhati Roy) 58, 108
"The Good Shopkeeper" (Samrat Upadhyay) 19–20
governmentalist approach to neoliberalism 14
"Gram O' Shohor Unnoyoner Golpo" (Jyotiprakash Dutta) 18
Great Bull Run 88
Grundrisse (Karl Marx) 36–37, 38, 60
Gun Island (Amitav Ghosh) 29, 104, 105–112, 119
Gupta, Dipanker 62–63
Gupta, N. Sen 62–63

Hamid, Mohsin 2, 75, 76, 83, 87, 90–91, 93, 97, 99n5
Hansen, Jim 99n5
Hardt, Michael 52n8, 78, 80
Hart, Matthew 99n5
Harvey, David 11, 31n5, 39, 80, 88
Hayat Hosen Khan 40
Hayek, F. A. 113–114
Heidegger, Martin 6
Heidemann, Brite 77
Hilferding, Rudolph 79
Hindutva 115
The History of Sexuality (Michel Foucault) 15
Hogg, Emily J. 78

Home Boy (H. M. Naqvi) 2, 19, 75–77, 79, 83, 84–85, 88–90, 95, 98
Home Fire (Kamila Shamsie) 17, 87
homo oeconomicus 14, 15, 16, 18, 32, 34, 44, 50, 113

Ibis trilogy (Amitav Ghosh) 20, 22–24, 27, 102
Ibrahim, Abu 33
IMF; *see* International Monetary Fund (IMF)
"The Imperialism of Free Trade" (John Gallagher and Ronald Robinson) 31n3
India 2, 5, 12, 13, 64, 115; agriculture sector 62–63; annexation 64; caste-class double bind 58; entrepreneurs in 67; of darkness 55–56, 65, 66, 70, 71; IT elites in 66–67; of light 55–56, 65, 70, 71; market reform 12; neoliberalization in 12, 51; "post-capitalist system" in 69; rural areas of 67, 68; rural economy 62; urban cores 67, 68
industrial reserve army 81–83
In Stereotype: South Asia in the Global Literary Imaginary (Mrinalini Chakravorty) 57
International Monetary Fund (IMF) 11
In the Light of What We Know (Zia Haider Rahman) 75, 102
In the Ruins of Neoliberalism (Wendy Brown) 22, 113–119
Invested Interests: Capital, Culture, and the World Bank (Bret Benjamin) 72
Iraq War 21

Jaal Shopno Shopner Jaal 34, 50, 51
Jahan, Nasrin 18, 33
James, C. L. R. 25, 83
Jameson, Fredric 3–4, 5, 6, 21, 52n8, 74n5, 96, 97, 103, 117–118, 119n3, 119n5
Jamshed (protagonist of Naqvi's *Home Boy*) 76, 84, 87, 88
Jayewardene, J. R. 12
Joseph, Betty 4–5, 56–57, 67
Joyce, James 8
Juan, E. San, Jr. 25, 90
Juan-Bautista 93–94

"Kanna" (Akhtaruzzaman Elias) 1, 17, 27, 32; as a critique of objective condition 45–49; Marx, money, capitalism 35–39; and monetization of consciousness 40–45

Karim, Lamia 12

Khoabnama (Akhtaruzzaman Elias) 43, 44, 50, 52–53n9

Koabnama 51

Kumar, Amitava 57, 74n1

Laclau, Ernesto 52n2, 74n2

Lahiri, Jhumpa 75

Lau, Lisa 109

Lazarus, Neil 3

Lenin, V. I. 79, 80, 98n1

liberalization 115

Lives of Others (Neel Mukherjee) 87

Living in the End Times (Slavoj Žižek) 117, 119n3

The Lowland (Jhumpa Lahiri) 75

Lukács, György 6–7

Luxemburg, Rosa 39, 47–48, 71, 83

Lu Xun 3

The Mahavarata 106

Manasa Devi 105, 106

Marx, Karl 5, 8, 10, 12, 17, 24, 26–28, 52n7, 53nn–12, 60, 61, 62, 70–71, 81–83, 86, 98–99n2, 107, 109, 120n6; on commodity fetishism 35; on expropriation 86; on imperialism 79–80; on money and capitalism 35–39; on "surplus population" 79, 83, 109; on systemicity of the process 83

mawlawi 30n1

The Meaning of Contemporary Realism (György Lukács) 6

Mendes, Ana C. 109

"Milir Haate Sten gun" (Elias) 18

Mimic Men (V. S. Naipaul) 75

The Ministry of Utmost Happiness (Arundhati Roy) 12, 29, 58, 87, 104, 105–112, 119

Mistri, Rohington 58

Modi, Narendra 12, 109, 114

Mohapatra, Himanshu S. 74n1

monajat 30n1, 34, 40–42, 44, 46, 49, 52n1, 52n3

monetization 32, 40–45

money 17, 32–35, 44–49; and affect/emotions 34; *de rigueur* fetishization

of 45; Marx's theory of 35–39; "omnipotence" of 35–36, 39; personhood of 35; power of 39; and reification 45–49; reifying capacity 37

money denominated assets 81

"monologue intérieur" (James Joyce) 8

Moore, Jason 13, 117

Moron Bilash (Ahmed Sofa) 18, 33

Moth Smoke (Mohsin Hamid) 91

moulvi 2, 17, 30n1, 35, 45, 50, 52n3

Muhammad, Anu 12

Mukherjee, Neel 58, 87

Mulligan, Buck (character of Joyce's *Ulysses*) 8

The Mystic Masseur (V. S. Naipaul) 75

Naipaul, V. S. 75

Naked Imperialism (John Bellamy Foster) 80

The Namesake (Jhumpa Lahiri) 75

Nandi, Swaralipi 57, 58, 59, 62, 63, 69, 74n1

Naqvi, H. M. 2, 19, 75, 77, 83, 84, 89, 90

national allegories 3–5, 118

Negri, Antonio 78, 80

neoliberal capitalism 32, 39, 77, 78, 103

"Neoliberalism and Allegory" (essay) (Betty Joseph) 4, 56

Nepal 12–13, 19, 20

Nina (character of Jahan's *Urukku*) 33

"omnipotence" of money 35–36, 39

Ondaatje, Michael 87

Opium War 21

Pakistan 2, 13, 91, 92, 95, 97; labor and land reform programs in 12; neoliberalism in 12; rehabilitation of military leaders in 115

Patnaik, Prabhat 39, 81

Patnaik, Utsa 81

Pinochet, Augusto 11, 115

A Political Economy of the Senses (Anita Chari) 52n2

The Political Unconscious: Interpretation as a Socially Symbolic Act (Fredric Jameson) 6

postcolonialism 25

The Postcolonial Unconscious (Neil Lazarus) 3

Pramod (protagonist of "The Good Shopkeeper") 19–20

Prasad, Madhava 118, 121n10

Index

Precarious Life (Judith Butler) 77
precariousness 28, 77–78, 83, 101
precarity 77, 78, 83
primitive accumulation 21, 68, 71, 86
private labor 27, 36
Provincializing Europe (Dipesh Chakrabarty) 59, 60, 63

racial antipathy 76, 77, 84–90
Racism and Cultural Studies (E. San Juan Jr.) 90
Rahman, Zia Haider 75, 102
Ramsumair, Ganesh (protagonist of Naipaul's *The Mystic Masseur*) 75
redundant working population 81
Reid, Zachary (character of Ghosh's *Sea of Poppies*) 21, 102
reification, money and 45–49
The Reluctant Fundamentalist (Mohsin Hamid) 2, 75, 76, 77, 79, 83, 91–94, 98
Representing Capital (Fredric Jameson) 74n5, 96
River of Smoke (Amitav Ghosh) 22, 23, 24, 25, 102
The Road to Serfdom (Friedrich von Hayek) 10, 11
Robinson, Ronald 31n3
Roy, Arundhati 12, 29, 58, 87, 104–112
Roy, Binayak 24–25
Roy, Debesh 9
Roy, M. N. 83
Rüstow, Alexander 10

Sadagar, Chand 105–106
Said, Edward 25, 99n4
Sarker, Sumit 25
Schiavon, Giacinta/Cinta (character of Ghosh's *The Gun Island*) 105
schizoid constellations 5
Sea of Poppies (Amitav Ghosh) 23, 24–25, 102, 119n2
Sembène, Ousmane 3
Semmel, Bernard 31n3
Seventeen Contradictions and the End of Capitalism (David Harvey) 36, 39
Shamsie, Kamila 17, 87
Shehzad (protagonist of Naqvi's *Home Boy*) 2, 76–77, 84–90, 92–93, 95–98, 100–101, 104, 118
Shingavi, Snehal 57, 58, 74n1

Sing, Ralph (protagonists of Naipaul's *Mimic Men*) 75
Singh, Amardeep 57
Singh, Amrik (character of Roy's *The Ministry of Utmost Happiness*)
Smith, Neil 119n1
Social Text 4
Sofa, Ahmed 18–19, 31n2, 33
spatio-temporality 64–70
Spivak, Gayatri 25
Srikanth, Rajini 91, 93
Sri Lanka 12, 13
Sri Lanka in the Modern Age: A History (Nira Wickremasinge) 12
Standing, Guy 78
A State of Freedom (Neel Mukherjee) 58
subjective insecurity 78
subjective violence 72, 74n6
Subrahmanyam, Sanjay 74n1
surplus population 4, 28, 29, 68, 79, 81–83, 109

The Tevaga Movement 51
"Thesis on History" (Walter Benjamin) 5
"Third-World Literature in the Era of Multinational Capitalism" (essay) (Fredric Jameson) 3–4
Thompson, E. P. 59
Tilottama (character of Roy's *The Ministry of Utmost Happiness*) 104

Undoing the Demos: Neoliberalism's Stealth Revolution (Wendy Brown) 10, 16, 113
uneven spatial relations 59–64
Upadhyay, Samrat 19–20, 25–26
Urukku (Nasrin Jahan) 18, 33
utopian dreams 2, 8, 72, 100–105, 118–119
utopian politics 9, 103, 115

Valences of the Dialectic (Fredric Jameson) 96, 97
The Value of Money (Prabhat Patnaik) 39
variable capital 53n11
ventriloquism 5, 42, 47
von Hayek, Friedrich 10–11
von Liebig, Justus 120n6
vulnerability 77–78, 83

Waliullah, Syed 9
Walking with the Comrades (Arundhati Roy) 12

Wallerstein, Immanuel 27, 60, 80
Want, Lily 62, 69
"War on Drugs" 13
The White Tiger (Aravind Adiga) 1, 5, 19, 27, 40, 51, 55–59, 73, 74n1, 101; and spatio-temporality 64–70; uneven spatial relations 59–64
Wickremasinge, Nira 12
Williams, Raymond 115, 121n9
World Systems theory 27, 60

Xala (Ousmane Sembène) 3
xenophobic fascism 29

Zafar (protagonist of Rahman's *In the Light of What We Know*) 102, 104
Zahir, Shahidul 18, 33
zeitgeist 5, 98
Zia-ul-Haq, Muhammad 12
Žižek, Slavoj 74n6, 117, 119n3
Zunayed, Abu 18–19, 30n2